GODZILLA®

GODZILLA® ON MY MIND

Fifty Years of the King of Monsters

WILLIAM TSUTSUI

palgrave
macmillan

First published 2004 by
PALGRAVE MACMILLAN™
175 Fifth Avenue, New York, N.Y. 10010 and
Houndmills, Basingstoke, Hampshire, England RG21 6XS.
Companies and representatives throughout the world.

PALGRAVE MACMILLAN is the global academic imprint of
the Palgrave Macmillan division of St. Martin's Press, LLC and of
Palgrave Macmillan Ltd. Macmillan® is a registered trademark in
the United States, United Kingdom and other countries. Palgrave
is a registered trademark in the European Union and other
countries.

ISBN 1–4039–6474–2

Library of Congress Cataloging-in-Publication Data
Tsutsui, William
Godzilla on my mind : fifty years of the king of monsters / William
Tsutsui.
    p.   cm.
Includes bibliographical references and index.
ISBN 1–4039–6474–2
1. Godzilla films—History and criticism.   I. Title.

PN1995.9.G63T78   2004
791.43'651—dc22

                                                2004045505

A catalogue record for this book is available from the British
Library.

Design by Letra Libre, Inc.

First edition: October 2004
10 9 8 7 6 5 4 3 2

Printed in the United States of America.

CONTENTS

CREDITS

ILLUSTRATIONS

ACKNOWLEDGMENTS

OVER THE YEARS, MANY PEOPLE HAVE ENDURED, humored, and even encouraged my unnatural affection for the king of the monsters. Special thanks in this regard are due to my friend and associate Michiko Ito, Japanese studies librarian at the University of Kansas. Michiko has been my co-conspirator in several Godzilla-related projects, has kept me supplied with the latest Godzilla toys, books, and collectibles from Japan and has always respected (if not fully understood) my devotion to the saurian giant. Anthony (Toby) Wahl of Palgrave has also earned my undying appreciation, not just for suggesting this book on Godzilla in the first place, but for seeing the project through to conclusion with boundless good humor and patience. I cannot imagine a more agreeable or insightful editor.

My colleagues at the University of Kansas have been generous with their time and assistance. Bill Tuttle was my inspiration and guide in soliciting fan responses to Godzilla through newspapers. Gregory Cushman, Grant Goodman, Paul Lim, Beth Schultz, Janet Sharistanian, and John Simmons furnished me with clippings, pop culture references, and many a good story. George Gibbs of the Music and Dance Library assisted with the hard work of permissions. Nancy Hope, Randi Hacker, Sheree Willis, Elaine Gerbert, and all of the staff at the Center for East

Asian Studies suffered through the writing of this book, putting up with long periods of my absence and feeding my Godzilla habit with yard-sale finds and Internet gleanings. Chancellor Robert Hemenway provided support crucial to the completion of this project.

Over the past decade, it has somehow become the custom that any of my students who travel to Japan bring me back some kind of Godzilla trinket or publication. I have filled up my office with these items—which I, of course, consider research materials, not extorted bribes—and I appreciate the uncoerced generosity of all the folks who have contributed to the collection. Jesse Hodges spent a summer working as my research assistant on the project and John Schneiderwind has been a gold mine of Godzilla references from *South Park* to *Mystery Science Theater 3000.* Jesse and John are responsible for digging up much of the odd, obscure, and wonderful trivia that appears in this book. Former students Gray Ginther (whose M.A. thesis on Godzilla is a tremendous resource) and Paul Dunscomb (who now uses *Gojira* in his own classes at the University of Alaska, Anchorage) tolerated my rantings and helped sharpen my thinking on the king of the monsters. Tracy Burgess and Megan Kettner also helped out in the search for Godzilliana in American popular music, movies, and television.

I owe a particular debt to all the newspapers, editors, and pop culture reporters across the nation who took a chance on an eccentric-sounding professor from Kansas and printed a blurb, column, or full feature article on my quest for fan reactions to Godzilla. And, needless to say, my heartfelt thanks go out to the dozens of people who responded to these newspaper pieces, freely sharing their personal feelings and experiences with a total stranger. Without the tall stack of letters and emails I received from generous fans, this book would not have been possible. Godzilla devotees Richard

Cox and Armand Vaquer responded graciously to my requests for photographs.

No one has been more patient and supportive through the process of writing this book than my wife, Marjorie Swann. Marjorie has gotten used to me singing the Jet Jaguar theme song in the shower, hogging the VCR with monster movies, and holding forth at the dinner table about the relative merits of Gappa and Guilala. She has gone through the manuscript with a fine-toothed comb, rooting out holes in my arguments and grammatical errors, and always challenging me to be more lucid, precise and analytically rigorous. Marjorie has also reconciled herself to the man in my life, the radioactive saurian giant with whom I've had a thirty-five-year-long—and entirely platonic—relationship. I am truly blessed to live in this blissful interspecies ménage.

GODZILLA®
ON MY MIND

GODZILLA MON AMOUR

WHEN I WAS NINE, I WANTED TO BE GODZILLA. I wanted to drag my big reptilian feet through a crowded city. I wanted to swat a helicopter with a scaly hand and crumple a commuter train with my powerful jaws. I wanted to ignite a chemical plant with my radioactive breath.

Lacking the wherewithal to transform myself into a ten-story mutant lizard, I set my heart on the next best thing: becoming Godzilla for Halloween. After a campaign of strategic whining and pouting, my mother was reluctantly enlisted. Never much for sewing, she had acceded to previous years' requests to make me a vampire, pirate, and devil. But Godzilla was pushing the envelope of her costume-making skills. A black cape or a little be-horned jumpsuit, no problem. Dorsal fins, claws, and a prehistoric head were more of a challenge.

The construction of the costume was an epic undertaking, a virtual Manhattan Project of chartreuse rayon, foam rubber, and mild oaths. A pair of white gloves, veterans of many long-ago church socials, were procured from my grandmother and unceremoniously dyed green. Family friends with better handicraft abilities—and more modern sewing machines—were recruited and put to work. I can't remember quite how my feet were disguised: I may have been the only Godzilla in history to have worn Hush Puppies. The pièce de résistance, however, was my snout. To mimic Godzilla's characteristic saurian nose, a tin tea cup (courtesy of Woolworth's on North Main Street) hung from between my eyes underneath the green fabric.

On the big night, I proudly suited up as my hero. Seeing out of the costume wasn't easy, and breathing was a downright chore, but no one ever said being the king of the monsters was a cakewalk. I remember vamping for my father's camera on the front lawn, a plastic model of a fighter plane—complete with Japanese rising sun insignia on the wings—grasped in my gloved claws. The drive to Davy Crockett Elementary School and the annual Halloween Fun Fair was filled with adventure and contortion, as Detroit had not thought to design sedans that could accommodate fins and a sizable tail.

It was at school that my bubble burst. My third-grade classmates and their parents either did not know who Godzilla was or did not recognize what a 4'2" light-green sack with a very odd nose was meant to represent. My mother's artisanal labors received scarcely a compliment. James Box, my erstwhile best friend, had merely donned a rubber werewolf mask and taped some fake fur to the backs of his hands: when he roared, the girls shrieked and ran; when I roared, the kids laughed and the adults looked bemused. The ultimate insult to my pride occurred in the haunted house, somewhere between the bowls of "human eyes" (grapes adrift in reddish Jell-O) and the Mummy rearing up from his cardboard casket. Someone—and to this day

Godzilla in Hush Puppies. Bryan, Texas, 1972.

I think I know just who—had the temerity to step on Godzilla's tail, ripping the stitching and revealing that giant movie monsters prefer briefs to boxers. I stormed outside to my waiting parents and demanded to be taken home immediately, my tail—quite literally—between my legs. I announced gloomily that there would be no trick-or-treating this year, to my father's secret relief but my eternal consternation.

After that ill-fated October 31st in 1972, I never dressed as Godzilla again. The costume hung in my closet for several years, but was quietly disposed of in a later spring cleaning. I learned to be more circumspect in what I wished for, more careful in exploiting the goodwill of my parents, and more private in my fantasies. But I did not stop loving Godzilla.

Indeed, for as long as I can remember, Godzilla has been a part of my life. I can't honestly recall when I saw my first Godzilla movie, but I expect I was on my stomach in front of our family's big Zenith on a Saturday afternoon, tuned to the "Creature Double Feature" from one of the UHF stations in Houston. It seems like just yesterday that I would run expectantly into the neighborhood Piggly Wiggly, looking for the latest issue of *Famous Monsters of Filmland* magazine, hoping that a new article on Godzilla would appear among the stories on Bela Lugosi and the ads for X-ray glasses and Sea Monkeys. And I can vividly remember the thrill of building Aurora's plastic model kit of Godzilla, standing amid the rubble of Tokyo, swinging his glow-in-the-dark hands as if frozen in the middle of a square dance, polymer teeth flashing and eyes glinting. Maybe it was just the plastic cement fumes working on the soft gray matter of a preteen, but that little model—$1.79 plus tax—sent chills up and down my spine.

When I was eleven years old or so, I went to Japan for a summer with my parents. One day we ventured out to Chiba, an unremarkable bedroom community east of Tokyo, to visit one of my father's high school buddies, now the owner of a gleaming local department store. While he and my father reminisced, one of the store's flunkies—sporting rudimentary English and a blue polyester suit—was assigned to take me down to the toy floor and let me pick out whatever item I wanted as a gift. This was, of course, any young consumer's acquisitive wet dream, and images of radio-controlled sports cars and gargantuan model kits—the battleship *Yamato* in 1:32 scale, a Panzer tank as big as a twin bed—danced through my imagination. Arriving in the promised land of the sixth floor, I headed straight for the back counter, behind which—well away from the grubby hands of the average schoolboy—stood the most elaborate, most sought-after, and most obscenely expensive toys. But before I made it back to what I thought I wanted, I saw something else, just out of the corner of my eye. There in a display cabinet was Godzilla, twelve gorgeous inches of richly painted tin with row-upon-row of plastic fins and a cord sprouting from an unmentionable spot at the base of its tail. I was smitten and immediately selected it as my free bounty. A remote-control Godzilla that walked (after a fashion), opened and closed its jaws, and howled in a grating, metallic kind of way: this was better than a puppy, a swimming pool, or a week's excuse from P.E. class. My minder from the department store was dumbstruck. "Are you sure you would like this?" he asked, politely leaving off the words "600-yen piece of crap." I nodded and grinned, and we were done.

When I walked back into the owner's office, Godzilla tucked tightly under my arm, the relief on my parents' faces was obvious. No apologies, no scenes, no discipline were necessary. In latching onto one of the cheapest toys in the whole emporium, I had, it seems, shown great politeness, dignity beyond my years, and restraint betokening a good and proper upbringing. My parents never understood—indeed probably never wanted to understand—that manners had nothing to do with my behavior that day: the tin, growling Godzilla was my deepest desire. The very next morning, my mother took me shopping in the Ginza and, as a reward for my maturity, bought me a stack of expensive plastic models two feet tall. Never, I think, in the history of childhood has such blatant self-interest been rewarded so generously. Thank you, Godzilla.

My regard for Godzilla made the transition to adulthood far more successfully than any of my other childhood obsessions. The GI Joes were donated to Goodwill one summer when I was in high school; the baseball cards were sacrificed when I left for college and my bedroom was redeveloped into a study; my Star Trek collection (with all those autographed stills of James Doohan) simply disappeared in shame. As I grew older and strayed farther from the relatively Godzilla-poor confines of Bryan, Texas, I discovered that Godzilla was not just my personal passion. I was not alone. Lots of people, I came to realize, were closeted fans of Japanese science fiction, some far more lunatic in their devotion than even I was. Almost everyone in America—and certainly the vast majority of those in the long baby boom generation—seemed to know who Godzilla was and have impressions (positive or, more often, negative) of the Godzilla films. Godzilla was not just the perverse delight of one Japanese-American kid from central Texas; Godzilla was—and is—a global pop culture icon.

In 1985, a *New York Times*/CBS News poll asked fifteen hundred Americans to name a famous Japanese person. The top three responses were Hirohito, Bruce Lee, and Godzilla. The American public earned full credit for identifying Japan's emperor, but fell wide of the mark in tapping a Hong Kong martial arts star and a fictional movie monster as prominent Japanese. At the time, media pundits had a field day, excoriating American parochialism and brandishing the survey results as a stinging indictment of America's deficient knowledge of Japan. In an era when U.S. industry was in a funk and every warm-blooded American's dream was a Sony in the rec room and two Toyotas in the garage, such apparent ignorance of Japan led to much public handwringing and lamentation. How could America compete in the world when its knowledge of an economic archrival dead-ended at a giant radioactive lizard?

But the survey results also contained an important—and usually overlooked—lesson: Japanese popular culture exports have had a profound influence in America (and indeed, throughout the world) in the decades since World War II. From Godzilla in the 1950s through Astro Boy in the 1960s, Speed Racer in the 1970s, and the more recent phenomena of the Mighty Morphin Power Rangers, Hello Kitty, Nintendo, and Pokemon, creations of the Japanese imagination have been high profile and big business in the United States. Godzilla, as the pioneering and most prominent character in the globalization of Japanese pop culture, may well have shaped American perceptions of Japan as significantly as quality control circles, just-in-time manufacturing or the once-chilling images of Honda after Honda rolling onto the docks at Long Beach. And though the Japanese industrial machine has stalled in recent years, the Japanese assault on foreign markets continues, though now instead of transistor radios, VCRs, and Walkmen, Super Mario, Yu-Gi-Oh! and the other heirs of Godzilla are in the vanguard of Japan's global reach.

Even today, a full fifty years after the Tokyo premiere of the original film *Gojira* in November 1954, Godzilla remains a pervasive and enduring symbol of Japan around the world. The movies, which now number twenty-seven (not counting the 1998 Hollywood abomination or the new release scheduled for December 2004), have also become cherished icons of camp and cheese, the butt of countless jokes and parodies, cultural touchstones of cheap special effects, bad dubbing and terrible acting. Regarding the Godzilla series as a defining example of the so-bad-it's-good genre of B-moviemaking, fare suitable only for a laugh and a kiddie audience, many Americans have forgotten that the early films were solemn, adult treatments of the costs of war, the dangers of nuclear proliferation, and the folly of humankind's reckless disregard for the natural environment. Many who dismiss Godzilla with a snigger overlook the fact that Godzilla is the longest-running film series in world movie history. And that the Godzilla franchise of DVDs, toys, T-shirts, and collectibles grosses (by some estimates) hundreds of millions of dollars every year. And that Godzilla is ubiquitous in American popular culture today, appearing in Rose Parade floats, Dr. Pepper ads, rap lyrics, episodes of *The Simpsons,* and countless film and television tributes. And, last but not least, the limitless application of the suffix "zilla"—a universally recognized tag for the big, the outrageous, and the ornery—shows just how deeply Godzilla has penetrated into the American collective unconscious.

This book is an attempt to understand why we Americans enjoy, respond to, and, in some cases, love a half-century-old Japanese movie monster. How have so many people, across all the demographic dividing lines of age, sex and race, come to relate to Godzilla? Even the most diehard aficionados will admit that Godzilla is not among the greatest achievements of world cinema or one of the proudest creations of Japan's ancient culture. It is difficult, even for a committed fan, to read too much deep social significance into a stuntman in a bulky rubber suit, lumbering through toy cities or wrestling credulity-stretching adversaries, as crowds of conservatively dressed Japanese extras run screaming through the streets. Good fun, yes. *Citizen Kane* or *The Tale of Genji,* no. Yet in so many ways, Godzilla remains a compelling and dynamic presence in American culture, an icon adored and derided, cheered and jeered, yet never—unlike so much of the elite cultural canon of our society—forgotten, ignored, or benignly neglected. Teasing out the charm of Godzilla is no easy matter, for in our embrace of the beast are entangled strands of nostalgia, the phantoms of nuclear war, the mysteries of childhood, the hard-nosed business of moviemaking, the unresolved tensions of world history, Freudian desires, fantasies of violence, and fundamental questions of humanity, spirituality, and the eternal struggle of good versus evil. Understanding the appeal of Godzilla, when all is said and done, means understanding ourselves.

In writing this book—and putting my real name on the title page—I am "outing" myself as a Godzilla fan. These days, being an active fan of anything in America other than an NFL franchise, a favored NASCAR driver, or Oprah is regarded with a certain suspicion by those who fancy themselves in the cultural mainstream. Being a science fiction fan, in particular, marks one as a potential misfit and guaranteed loser. No matter how "normal" you might look on the surface, friends, relatives and co-workers will inevitably imagine you as an unmarried, overweight forty-something, wearing a T-shirt one size too small and sweat pants one size too large, harboring elaborate fantasies of matching wits with Dr. Who, playing tridimensional chess with Mr. Spock, or laying Princess Leia. Nanu-nanu, beam me up, Will Robinson.

I like to humor myself that although I am a lifelong admirer and student of the Godzilla films, I am resolutely not a geek. I realize that Godzilla, Mothra, and the rest are fictional creations, that there is no Monster Island off the coast of Japan, that Godzilla does not speak to me in dreams or through my neighbor's dog, that I will never be recruited in a quirky twist of fate to don the latex suit and star as Godzilla in a movie. I reassure myself that because I can't name the third assistant director of *Godzilla vs. Megalon* and have never been arrested for stalking, I couldn't possibly qualify for geekdom. Yet such confident pronouncements of self-knowledge are belied by the dozens of Godzilla collectibles—from posters and clocks and snow globes to animatronic figures with glowing dorsal fins—that litter my office. And by the drawers at home overflowing with VHS and DVD Godzillas, grainy Taiwanese bootlegs and old tapes of *Mystery Science Theater 3000*. And by the fact that some people around town, having learned of my once-discreet passion for Japanese sci-fi, greet me in public (and to my wife's considerable distress) with "Hi, Godzilla guy!"

All this is perhaps a somewhat roundabout way of stating that this book is not going to be rigorously and tediously objective, as are most of the volumes penned by professional historians (which I at least claim to be from 9 to 5 on weekdays). As a lifelong fan, not only do I feel a profound affection for Godzilla, but I am—like all such committed admirers—extremely opinionated, passionate, and stubborn when it comes to the relative merits of the Godzilla films, the way Japanese monsters have been embraced (or, quite often, disgraced) by American pop culture, and the cosmic question of "what Godzilla means." Godzilla was not intended to fly on his tail, be a pitchman for burritos or—above all—be portrayed as a hysterical postpartum velociraptor scampering around Madison Square Garden. So even though this book is based on considerable research in Japanese- and English-language sources, the analysis of films, qualitative survey data, and personal interviews—all the makings of a scientific, dry-as-dust academic tome—I won't be checking my opinions at the door or striving for a bloodless, magisterial voice. And if you disagree with my views, all the better. Complaints may be filed with the big radioactive lizard.

Though one should not trivialize the importance of Godzilla to American culture, one should not exaggerate it either. A few years back, an essay appeared in the usually staid and stolid *Bulletin of the Atomic Scientists* on the lessons of the 1964 film *Ghidorah, the Three-Headed Monster* for national security policymakers.[1] Oh, goodness! This book does not pretend for an instant to be an earth-shattering study of profound societal importance. Godzilla cannot cure the common cold, teach the world to sing in perfect harmony, or provide good instruction in nuclear brinksmanship to Pentagon wonks. I've always felt that the joy of the Godzilla movies, when all is said and done, is that they are pure and simple fun. Who can beat 90 minutes of suspended disbelief, moral certainty, and guiltless revels in gratuitous destruction? The Godzilla films were made to be engrossing, exciting, humorous, perhaps a little thought-provoking, and—above all—enjoyable. That's what I would like this book to be as well.

One final stylistic note is in order. Over the years, much debate has swirled around the issue of Godzilla's sex. Whether Godzilla is male or female is by no means apparent. Even if one were skilled in determining the sex of reptiles—a talent I am not ashamed to say I lack—the Godzilla films provide little in the way of physical evidence. Godzilla would seem to be as scrupulously free of genitalia—one way or the other—as your average Ken doll. And although several of the Japanese films posit offspring for Godzilla—the curiously lumpen Minilla of the 1960s, the cartoonish Baby of the 1990s—the precise biological relationship of Godzilla to these annoying young is never made explicit. The Japanese language itself contributes to this ambiguity, since nouns are not classified by gender as in many European languages. Had Godzilla been made in Germany, at least we would have known for sure if the films' creators intended the monster to be masculine, feminine, or neuter.

Many American fans call Godzilla "the Big Guy," a form of address I consider a little too familiar, but one which at least makes clear their assumptions about Godzilla's sex. The fact that the 1998 Hollywood Godzilla was a proud and fertile female really need not distract us too much. Indeed, for me, this fact simply affirms my belief that the real Godzilla, the Japanese Godzilla, the radioactive rebel without a cause, was a pure 50,000 metric tons of foot-stomping, muscle-bound, mad-as-hell-and-I'm-not-going-to-take-it-anymore saurian male. So for the purposes of this book, at least, Godzilla will be referred to as "he."

CHAPTER 1

THE BIRTH OF GOJIRA

EVERY FEW MONTHS, SOMEONE WILL ASK ME, innocently enough, "So what's your favorite Godzilla movie?" And invariably I respond that it's the original 1954 Godzilla film, called *Gojira* in Japanese. "Why that one?" is usually the next question. I always begin to explain that Godzilla's debut was a somber, gripping, and thought-provoking film, though I seldom get to complete my explanation. "What?" my incredulous friend, relative or co-worker will interject, "There was actually a *serious* Godzilla movie?"

Yes, Virginia, there is a Santa Claus, and there was a dead-serious Godzilla movie. Well before the series degenerated into big-time wrestling in seedy latex suits, well before Godzilla had a laughably unlikely son, well before a giant technicolor moth was passed off as a gruesome monster, well before Tokyo was besieged by rapacious aliens or vengeful undersea civilizations (all fluent in Japanese, of course), *Gojira* was a solemn affair, an earnest attempt to grapple with compelling and timely issues, more meditative and elegiac than block busting and spine chilling. Godzilla did not begin his career in the Japan of the 1950s as the tail end of a double bill, a B-list laugher, or a tongue-in-cheek parody. The original *Gojira* was a sincere horror film, intended to frighten rather than amuse, which engaged honestly—indeed, even grimly—with contemporary Japanese unease over a mounting nuclear menace, untrammeled environmental degradation, and the long shadows of World War II. "Classic" is a terribly overused word in the vocabulary of film critics, yet this label undeniably applies to the dark, brooding, and still profoundly compelling 1954 *Gojira*.

The origins of Godzilla, both as a film and as a creature, are a little murky. The time-honored story of Godzilla's genesis begins in the spring of 1954 with Tanaka Tomoyuki, then a young and aspiring producer at Japan's Tōhō Studios.[1] Once dominant in Japan's domestic film industry, Tōhō had fallen on hard times in the wake of World War II and was struggling in the early 1950s to regain its market leadership. The studio was looking to Tanaka to restore some of its sheen and assigned him *In the Shadow of Honor,* a splashy, big-budget Japanese-Indonesian coproduction that would be Tōhō's headlining blockbuster in the competitive fall movie season. But a variety of snags—most notably rising diplomatic tensions between Tokyo and Jakarta well beyond Tōhō's control—compelled Tanaka to shelve the project before filming had even begun. This left a gaping hole in Tōhō's release schedule, and Tanaka was responsible for filling it.

Godzilla, as the legendry has it, was Tanaka's brainchild, the result of a brilliant "lightbulb" moment at a time of intense pressure. Flying home dispirited from Indonesia, Tanaka looked out over the expansive Pacific Ocean and agonized over the box office hit he was expected to deliver in six short months. His mind racing through the headlines of the day, the trends in the film industry, and, just perhaps, a personal nightmare or two, Tanaka hit upon a notion. "The thesis was very simple," Tanaka later recalled. "What if a dinosaur sleeping in the Southern Hemisphere had been awakened and transformed into a giant by the Bomb? What if it attacked Tokyo?"[2]

Many later commentators have been skeptical of Tanaka's dramatic, bolt-from-the-blue account of Godzilla's creation, but even if there is a "true" story of Godzilla's birth out there, we are unlikely ever to discover it. What we can be certain of, however, is that Godzilla did not emerge from a vacuum, even if the monster was originally conceived in the pressurized cabin of a transpacific airliner. Godzilla in all his glory was spawned from a virtual primordial soup of political concerns, cultural influences, cinematic inspirations, genre traditions, economic crassness, simple opportunism, and sheer creativity.

Godzilla was not, as some people may still believe, borrowed wholesale from Japanese folklore. Nonetheless, Godzilla the raging reptile, breathing fire and shattering cities, resonated with legends—both Japanese and Western—stretching back through millennia of civilization. Japanese traditional art and literature, so scholars tell us, boasted bizarre supernatural demons and monsters "in an abundance unequaled in any other culture."[3] Giant serpent deities inhabited remote mountain valleys, and dragons moved across water, land, and sky. In East Asia, according to one folklorist, "the dragon is not the monstrous destroyer found in [Western] tradition, but a majestic and benevolent beast, whose close association with the element of water turns him into a dispenser of fertility in a wet rice growing community. He becomes a potential source of disaster, through flood and storm, only when wrongly treated."[4] In Godzilla one senses the echoes of such legendary beasts, awe-inspiring and ever threatening, associated with the oceans, with longevity and, above all, with ruin and calamity. Godzilla also fits comfortably into the bestiaries of Western mythology, joining a rich heritage of Norse monsters, beasts of Revelation and medieval dragons that ate children, ravaged cities, and heralded apocalypse. As one author plainly put it, Godzilla lies "squarely in the tradition of the fire-breathing dragons of folklore."[5]

The figure of Godzilla played on other long-standing Japanese fears, and particularly on a deeply rooted vulnerability to the awesome and erratic forces of nature. Japan, as geologists, geographers, and meteorologists will attest, lies directly in the crosshairs of almost every destructive power Mother Nature can command. The natives of the Japanese islands have always had to endure the unpredictable assaults of earthquakes and volcanoes, typhoons and tidal waves, floods and landslides. Fire has been another ever-present natural enemy, especially to the dense, wood-built, readily inflammable cities of Japan. The Japanese have an old proverb, *jishin kaminari kaji oyaji,* which lists the four most fearsome things in the world as earthquake, thunder, fire, and father. Given Godzilla's volatility, capriciousness, and propensity for devastation—as well as the monster's fundamental character as a natural phenomenon that brings disaster—that old Japanese saying might well be rewritten as *jishin kaminari kaji Gojira.*

But the original Godzilla film also drew on more immediate and agonizing memories of man-made destruction. Although the Japanese government wishfully announced in 1956 that "the postwar period is now over," the Japan of the

Godzilla's first stroll through Tokyo, 1954.

mid-1950s still bore the scars—both physical and emotional—of total war and defeat. Japan's cities were still rebuilding from wartime fire bombings, families remained broken and grieving, and a complex sense of loss—lost lives, lost dreams, the lost war—tormented many survivors. Long after Japan's surrender in 1945, even long after the departure of General MacArthur and the American occupation forces in 1952, the shadows of war tenaciously haunted the Japanese people. Despite the guarded return of economic prosperity in the 1950s and steady progress on physical rebuilding, the dark memories of war—so compellingly evoked in *Gojira*—remained fresh and traumatic.

The specters of Hiroshima and Nagasaki, though repressed formally and informally by Japanese society, the Japanese government, and the U.S. occupation forces, were particularly vivid, harrowing, and unresolved in 1950s Japan. Worsening Cold War tensions and accelerating nuclear testing contributed to anxiety around the globe, but nowhere more so than in Japan, which alone had suffered the ordeal of atomic warfare. Such issues weighed heavily on the minds of Godzilla's creators. As Tanaka Tomoyuki later observed: "The theme of the film, from the beginning, was the terror of the Bomb. Mankind had created the Bomb, and now nature was going to take revenge on mankind."[6]

The climate of nuclear anxiety in Japan reached new heights in 1954, even well before the film *Gojira* was released. On March 1—only a few weeks prior to Tanaka's storied trip from Indonesia back to Japan—the United States detonated a 15-megaton hydrogen bomb, a weapon almost one thousand times more powerful than that dropped on Hiroshima, on Bikini Atoll in the central Pacific. A small Japanese trawler in search of tuna, named (ironically enough) the *Lucky Dragon No. 5* (*Dai-go Fukuryū Maru*), had strayed perilously close to the testing zone. The twenty-three-man crew reported seeing "the sun rising in the west" and being covered with a powdery white ash as they pulled in their lines and headed for port. The seamen were subsequently found to be suffering from radiation poisoning, tainted tuna entered Japanese markets before the radioactive contamination was discovered, and the news media erupted in a fury of nuclear fear and anti-American hostility. Millions of Japanese (including the emperor) refused to eat fish, the tabloids proclaimed the incident yet another U.S. atomic attack on Japan, and strident antinuclear peace movements sprouted around the country. That *Gojira* emerged from this environment suggests not only the canny opportunism (or, as some at the time complained, bald cynicism) of its creators, but also the extent to which the film and its message engaged with the most profound, contentious, and chilling issues of the day.[7]

But not all of the inspiration for *Gojira* came straight from the current events headlines. Tanaka Tomoyuki and Tōhō Studios were well aware of trends in the international film industry and, perhaps most important, of what sorts of movies were delivering big box-office returns, both in Tokyo and in Hollywood. The year 1952 saw the re-release of the 1933 classic *King Kong,* the prototype of the "giant monster on the loose" genre and a masterpiece of Willis O'Brien's stop-motion special effects. The film earned four times as much in 1952 as it had in its original release and was a hit in Japan as well as in the United States. In the wake of *Kong*'s success, Warner Brothers pushed into distribution the independently produced *The Beast from 20,000 Fathoms,* which proved a worldwide blockbuster in 1953. In this story of a dinosaur thawed from its prehistoric hibernation by American nuclear testing in Baffin Bay, the eponymous beast wreaks havoc on lower Manhattan before expiring in the flaming ruins of Coney Island, a deadly radioactive isotope—launched, of course, by the scientific and military good guys—firmly embedded in its neck. *The Beast* was perceived by many as a mere low-budget rip-off of *King Kong,* but it was based on an original story by sci-fi pioneer Ray Brad-bury and featured the impressive special effects of O'Brien disciple Ray Harryhausen. Although hardly a thoughtful musing on the dangers of nuclear weaponry, *The Beast* was—as Tanaka and Tōhō were well aware—a financial bo-nanza for its creators and distributors.

Many critics have been tempted to see the 1954 *Gojira* as a thinly veiled Japanese remake of *The Beast from 20,000 Fathoms*. And the similarities between the two films are nu-merous: both Godzilla and the Beast result from H-bomb testing, both are amphibious dinosaurs who sink fishing boats and inexplicably attack major cities, both occasion de-bates between scientists intent on studying the monster and army officers preoccupied with exterminating it. The team from Tōhō Studios even quietly admitted that much of their inspiration did indeed come from *King Kong* and *The Beast:* "The basic film is American," the director of *Gojira* once confided to a reporter.[8] Indeed, the Godzilla project al-legedly began under the confidential working title "The Giant Monster from 20,000 Miles Beneath the Sea," a smok-ing gun if ever there was one. But inspiration is far different from imitation, and today no one who has seen *Gojira* would, I suspect, damn it as a simple, slavish copy of earlier American blockbusters. In any case, compared to *The Beast from 20,000 Fathoms* (or even, if I may be sacrilegious, to the great *Kong*), the message of the original Godzilla film is so much more nuanced, the special effects so different, and the emotions stirred so much more profound that any charges of cinematic plagiarism seem all but irrelevant.

Given the personnel, effort, and expense Tōhō invested in *Gojira,* there can be no doubt that the studio intended the film to be an original, polished, serious, honest-to-God blockbuster. The first Godzilla was certainly not a self-consciously cerebral, art-house film like the period drama *Rashōmon,* which had won an Oscar and the 1951 Venice Festival grand prize, bringing unprecedented international attention to the Japanese movie industry. But neither was *Gojira* a cheesy, low-budget exploitation film, just another example of the "plethora of nudity, teenage heroes, science-fiction monsters, animated cartoons and pictures about cute animals" that the esteemed critic Donald Richie once de-cried as the stock-in-trade of Japan's popular cinema.[9] The Godzilla series would, of course, soon descend into the B-movie morass, but the script, acting, special effects, and spir-ited, confident style of *Gojira* would set it apart from the cinematic run of the mill.

The men who made Godzilla were talented, committed professionals who still remain largely unheralded outside fan circles. Tanaka Tomoyuki, the producer, had only over-seen his first film in 1944, but he quickly earned a reputation for delivering quality pictures on time and on budget. Tanaka was also remarkably prolific: he often produced more than ten films in a single year, and *Gojira* was his fifth movie in 1954 alone. Tanaka would later produce critically acclaimed works—including the samurai favorites *Yojimbō* and *Sanjūrō,* both directed by the modern master Kurosawa Akira—as well as twenty-two films in the Godzilla series and a long list of Japanese sci-fi stunners. Honda Ishirō, *Gojira*'s director, studied film at Nihon University and directed dozens of features—including eight starring Godzilla—over a long career. Honda was deeply committed to international cooperation and the cause of world peace, very likely as a re-sult of his experiences in World War II, during which he served three tours of duty in the infantry, was a prisoner of war in China, and passed through the ruins of Hiroshima upon his repatriation to Japan. Honda was a lifelong friend of Kurosawa's and served as associate director on five of Kurosawa's later films, including *Kagemusha, Ran,* and *Rhapsody in August*. Tsuburaya Eiji, who brought Godzilla and his rampages to life, was one of Japan's pioneers in special effects, inspired as a young man by the marvels of *King Kong*. During World War II, Tsuburaya used meticulously detailed miniature models to achieve new standards of realism; his work on naval scenes in one effort, *The War at Sea from Hawaii to Malaya,* was said to be so convincing that occupation authorities initially mistook some sequences for actual newsreel footage. Intense, creative, skilled, and blessed with a childlike joy in making fantasies real, Tsuburaya worked on fifty-six feature films, won numerous professional awards, and went on to create the campy icon Ultraman. As one author acutely observed, Tanaka, Honda, and Tsuburaya were "sophisticated men working in a highly unsophisticated genre."[10]

Making *Gojira* was a substantial financial outlay for Tōhō Studios. The film cost more than ¥62,000,000—about $175,000 at the exchange rate of the day—which was well beyond twice the budget of the average Japanese film. This total was laughable by Hollywood standards, even at the time; *The Beast from 20,000 Fathoms,* for instance, was a low-budget indie production and still came in at $200,000. *Gojira* also took far longer to shoot than was the Japanese industry norm. In the mid-1950s, Tōhō generally aimed to get all of its features in the can within fifty days; for that first Godzilla film, the special-effects crew alone required a whopping seventy-one days to complete its work. The on-screen talent further reflected the importance accorded *Gojira:* while the cast included its fair share of unknowns and fresh faces, its star—at least its *human* star—was the distinguished actor Shimura Takashi. A longtime favorite of Kurosawa, Shimura had major roles in both *Rashōmon* and *The Seven Samurai* (considered by many to be the greatest Japanese film ever made) and was praised by the *New York Times* as "the best actor in the world" for his 1956 lead in *Ikiru*.[11]

The special effects of *Gojira* were not high tech, even for the time, but were painstakingly staged and can still be admired as chillingly convincing. Today's movie audiences, jaded by the latest spectacles of computer-generated animation, may snigger at a few of the effects in the original Godzilla (as, admittedly, do I): a toylike helicopter blown about in a gale, a miniature fire engine with tiny, fake firemen. Yet the overall depiction of the monster taking it to Tokyo remains visually arresting and surprisingly realistic even fifty years—and a technological revolution—later. Tsuburaya was meticulous in creating ½₅ scale miniatures of Japan's capital city: his model buildings were often detailed inside as well as out in order to look most convincing when trampled; he built electric pylons of wax that could be melted with heat lamps to simulate the impact of Godzilla's radioactive ray; hundreds of small pyrotechnic charges were installed and ignited. Tsuburaya's commitment to realism even got him into trouble with the law. One day before filming began, the special effects master and his assistants gathered on the roof garden of one of the tony department stores in the Ginza, looked out over the city, and charted Godzilla's path of destruction. An alert security guard overhead them and, thinking he'd stumbled onto a terrorist plot, informed the authorities.[12] The police eventually let Tsuburaya go, and he went on to create one of the greatest sequences of urban devastation in cinematic history.

The design of the Godzilla suit was drawn from picture books of dinosaurs—as well as some illustrations in an issue of *Life* magazine—and the distinctive physical appearance of the monster was formed from a fossil-record-be-damned fusion of Tyrannosaurus rex, Iguanodon, and Stegosaurus. The costume itself was fabricated from a framework of bamboo stakes and wire, with thick overlays of latex and plentiful padding of urethane foam. The first prototype weighed in at more than two hundred pounds and was too rigid and ponderous to be used as designed. A second, lighter, and more flexible suit was produced, but even it was only slightly more accommodating for the actor chosen to play Godzilla. That honor went to Nakajima Haruo, a bit player and stunt man recruited specifically for the role because of his good physical conditioning, endurance, and dogged determination. To prepare for the role—not that being encased in a cumbersome rubber lizard suit allowed for much in the way of dramatic expression—Nakajima watched prints of *King Kong* and *Mighty Joe Young* and even visited Tokyo's Ueno Zoo to observe the behavior of bears and other large animals. Under hot stage lights, barely able to breathe or see, Nakajima could spend no more than a few minutes at a time sealed within the costume. Technicians would regularly pour a cup of Nakajima's sweat out of the suit between takes and the actor reported losing twenty pounds in weight over the course of the shoot. But from such sacrifice came magic. Although generations of critics may have pooh-poohed Godzilla's special effects—charmingly christened "suitmation" by the folks at Tōhō—no less an authority than Steven Spielberg has declared that *Gojira* "was the most masterful of all the dinosaur movies because it made you believe it was really happening."[13]

Sound complemented image in making the vicarious experience of disaster credible, thrilling, and compelling in *Gojira*. The powerful score to the film—cited by many fans as the element that truly breathed life into Godzilla—was the work of Ifukube Akira, a distinguished classical composer and prolific creator of film music. Born in Hokkaido and influenced by the folk traditions of the indigenous Ainu people, Ifukube composed nationalistic marches during World War II before becoming a workhorse of the postwar Japanese movie industry, completing more than two hundred scores in his

Teatime on the back lot. Nakajima Haruo takes a break during the filming of Godzilla vs. the Thing *(1964).*

forty-year career. Amazingly, Ifukube penned the music for *Gojira* in just one week—having never seen the movie or even any rushes—and directed the recording of the sound-track in only a single day. Ifukube was also responsible for Godzilla's unmistakable roar. After failing to produce any-thing convincing using recordings of wild animals, Ifukube made Godzilla's "melancholy, ear-splitting cry" by drawing a leather glove across the strings of a contrabass and manipu-lating the resulting sound in an echo chamber.[14] Ifukube also created the sonorous, haunting footfalls of the monster, though sources disagree on whether he used a Japanese taiko drum, a scratch-built amplifier, or the electronically altered sound of an explosion to complete the fantasy of Godzilla's resounding, mighty steps.[15]

The origins of the name Gojira and its English-language incarnation Godzilla are mysterious even today. Gojira is a portmanteau word, the creative fusion of *gorira* (Japanese for gorilla) and *kujira* (meaning whale). That Tanaka Tomoyuki's giant radioactive dinosaur bears little re-semblance to an ape, a cetacean, or a biologically inconceiv-able blending of the two was apparently irrelevant; Tanaka liked the sound of the name (as indeed have generations of Japanese fans) and he applied it to his monster. Age-old leg-end has it that Tanaka took his inspiration from an over-weight employee of Tōhō Studios nicknamed "Gojira" by his pesky co-workers. Many observers have cast doubt on this story, however, largely because this supposed burly stage-hand has never been positively identified. As Honda Ishirō's widow once suggested, Gojira was more likely the result of a high-level committee meeting at Tōhō rather than an imagi-native epithet overheard on the back lot.[16] The derivation of the name Godzilla is equally uncertain. Although American fans have longed to believe that the use of the deifying syl-lable "god" was some publicity agent's stroke of genius, it seems that Godzilla was more or less a straight job of transliteration on Gojira: in the 1950s, the Japanese sound "ji" was often rendered "dzi" and "ra" became "la."[17] That Godzilla sounds so appropriate in English, evoking the grandeur, mystery, and saurian nature of the monster, was more the result of dumb luck than shrewd planning. From such fortuitous turns of fate was a cultural icon born.

The 1954 *Gojira* has not—unfortunately—been widely distributed outside Japan. Although bootlegged videotapes and DVDs have circulated among fans the world over and a long-overdue American theatrical release took place in 2004, the original film remains among those in the Godzilla series least seen by international audiences. Thus a brief recounting of *Gojira*'s story—a satisfying blend of conventional movie melodrama, sci-fi tradition, brooding horror tale, Cold War morality play, and sheer innovation—is certainly in order.

The film begins with a thinly veiled reference to the *Lucky Dragon* incident: the crew of a Japanese freighter, the *Glory No. 5,* witness a blinding flash from the sea, the ship bursts into flames, and immediately sinks. One search vessel dispatched from Tokyo disappears, and then another. Survivors recount that "the ocean just blew up." On nearby Ōdo Island, the villagers rescue an all-but-dead local fisherman whose boat was also destroyed and who manages to utter "He did it. . . . A monster . . ." just before expiring. A village elder solemnly intones that Godzilla—a legendary "creature that lives in the sea"—must be responsible. The anxious Ōdo islanders perform a ceremonial dance and traditional exorcism ceremony to appease the monster and preserve their community. But, as it turns out, to no avail: in the teeth of a midnight gale, Godzilla raids the island, crushing houses, killing livestock, and terrifying the populace.

A blue-ribbon fact-finding mission, led by the eminent paleontologist Dr. Yamane (portrayed by Shimura Takashi), is dispatched from Tokyo. The group's geiger counters go crazy on Ōdo Island: the groundwater is found to be tainted by radiation, Yamane inspects a giant footprint, and, in a rivulet of nuclear runoff, a living trilobite is discovered. Godzilla then makes a rare daytime appearance, obligingly rearing up over one of the island's mountains while the natives flee and the scientists take snapshots. Dr. Yamane hastens back to Tokyo and testifies before a committee of the Diet, Japan's parliament. The monster, Yamane pronounces, is an amazing survivor of the Jurassic period who has lingered unnoticed for millions of years in one of the ocean's "deep pockets, abyssal regions that contain secrets we have yet to discover." Disrupted from its habitat and transformed by nuclear testing, the fifty-meter-tall Godzilla, Yamane concludes, "must have absorbed an enormous amount of atomic radiation."

The Japanese authorities prove woefully unprepared to deal with the threat of Godzilla. The nation's political leaders bicker unproductively. The military launches a barrage of depth charges, but with no apparent effect. "International researchers" fly in from around the globe, yet bring with them no silver bullets. The government pleads with Dr. Yamane to find a way of killing the menace, but he refuses, arguing trenchantly that the monster should be investigated, not eradicated. Godzilla, he declares, provides scientists with "a unique opportunity" and, moreover, one that "only those of us in Japan can study."

Amidst the mounting crisis, the story of a rather weepy love triangle is unfolding. Emiko, Dr. Yamane's young daughter, is head over heels in love with the dashing Lieutenant Ogata, an officer in a Japanese shipping firm. But Emiko, it turns out, is betrothed to wed Dr. Serizawa, a former student of her father, in a traditional Japanese arranged marriage. Prepared to reveal her love for Ogata, Emiko pays a visit on Serizawa, who lives in a dark, gloomy castle of a house with a laboratory in the basement and a choice selection of modern electrical appliances. Serizawa, who sports an eye patch (the result of an unelaborated wartime injury) and an unruly mane of hair (befitting an apparent mad scientist), does not seem particularly interested in talking feelings and relationships; instead, he demonstrates for Emiko the amazing and horrible discovery he has made. Serizawa drops a small metallic orb in a tank of fish and Emiko watches in revulsion as the fish are progressively liquefied. Serizawa explains that his "oxygen destroyer" disintegrates the oxygen in water, asphyxiating all living organisms: "Used as a weapon, this would be as powerful as a nuclear bomb. It could totally destroy humankind." Emiko, more than a little frightened by all this, swears to keep her fiancé's awesome discovery a secret.

Godzilla, meanwhile, begins his attacks on Japan proper. Wading ashore from Tokyo Bay one evening, the monster drags his feet through the rail yards at Shinagawa before returning to the sea. The military makes plans to evacuate the city, erect a huge barrier of electric lines and barbed wire around the waterfront, and roll out their best military hardware to confront the next assault. But fifty thousand volts and a few howitzers have little effect on Godzilla. The monster returns the following evening and cuts a swath of destruction across Tokyo, from gritty industrial districts to the chic precincts of the Ginza. Landmarks collapse under Godzilla's feet and from blasts of his radioactive breath: the creature walks through a wing of the Diet; the chiming clock tower on the Hattori Building is silenced by the annoyed monster; in one of the film's only tongue-in-cheek moments, Godzilla crumbles the Nichigeki Theater (Tōhō's flagship property in Tokyo) with a flip of his mighty tail. Looking over a sea of flames engulfing Japan's capital, one reporter asks, "Is the world going to be destroyed by a two-million-year-old monster?"

Godzilla leaves death and devastation in his wake. Vistas of the burned-out city recall images of Hiroshima and Nagasaki, hospitals overflow with the dead and dying, the camera lingers on a little girl, her eyes glazed in shock, whose irradiated body sends a geiger counter gauge off the scale. Emiko, deeply moved by the human suffering, decides that the oxygen destroyer is the only weapon that can stop Godzilla and that she must betray Serizawa's trust. Emiko divulges the secret to Ogata, and the two hurry to Serizawa's laboratory, where they plead with the scientist to allow the use of the device against Godzilla. Serizawa refuses and he scuffles with Ogata—as much, one suspects, over Emiko as over the oxygen destroyer—leaving the seaman bloodied and the doctor contrite. Weighing the horror of Godzilla against the potential misuse of his potent discovery, Serizawa reveals his profound moral torment: "If the oxygen destroyer is used even once, politicians from around the world will see it. Of course, they'll want to use it as a weapon. Bombs versus bombs, missiles versus missiles, and now a new super-weapon to throw upon us all! As a scientist, as a human being, I can't allow that to happen." Burying his head in his hands, Serizawa cries, "What am I going to do?"

A television in the laboratory inexplicably comes on, showing scenes of Godzilla's trail of destruction as a chorus of schoolgirls sings the heart-rending hymn "Oh Peace, Oh Light, Return." Serizawa's will crumbles under the weight of the tragedy, and he relents. But swearing that "this will be the first and last time that I will ever allow the oxygen destroyer to be used," Serizawa methodically burns all his scientific notes. Recognizing his sacrifice, Emiko—once again—breaks into tears.

From a ship in Tokyo Bay, Ogata and Dr. Serizawa descend into the water in deep-sea diving suits, the oxygen destroyer at the ready. They come upon Godzilla casually napping in the depths of the bay. As Serizawa places the device near the monster, Ogata returns to the surface. Seeing that the oxygen destroyer is successful, Serizawa radios Ogata and Emiko on the ship: "It worked! Both of you, be happy. Goodbye . . . goodbye." With a glinting knife, Serizawa cuts his oxygen line, ensuring with his death that the secrets of the oxygen destroyer will never be revealed and that the movie's central love triangle will be resolved.

As the water churns and the ship pitches, Godzilla rises from the bay in agony. His body slowly disintegrates, first to a skeleton and then to nothingness. The crew of the ship is jubilant, but their celebrations are tempered by the self-sacrifice of Serizawa and a nagging cloud of doubt. Dr. Yamane muses aloud: "I can't believe that Godzilla was the only surviving member of its species. But if we keep on conducting nuclear tests, it's possible that another Godzilla might appear somewhere in the world, again." As the film ends, all on the ship come to attention, remove their hats and pay their silent respects. But are they saluting Serizawa or the monster? Are they mourning the dead or lamenting their loss of innocence, humankind's shortsightedness, and the inevitable horrors of the future? Is the final shot, with the sun dancing over the water, a hopeful dawn for Japan or an ominous sunset for the world?

Gojira opened across Japan on November 3, 1954. An elaborate marketing campaign stoked public anticipation of the release: an eleven-installment radio serial told the story of "monster Godzilla" (*kaijū Gojira*), and the creature's image was plastered all over Tokyo. As one observer reported at the time, Godzilla "has glowered from bus and subway posters, has lunged in papier-mache effigy, and at present dangles over Ginza in the form of a rather large balloon."[18] The publicity stunts paid off: *Gojira* recorded the best opening-day ticket sales ever in Tokyo and eventually grossed ¥152 million (well over twice its production costs) on 9.69 million paid admissions. In a memorable year for Japanese cinema—1954 also saw the release of Kurosawa's epic *The Seven Samurai* and Kinoshita Keisuke's sentimental antiwar masterpiece *The Twenty-Four Eyes*—*Gojira* more than held its own at the box office. Tanaka and Honda's offering would end up boasting the eighth-largest gross among Japanese-made films—and the twelfth largest when counting Hollywood imports as well—in 1954.

The critical response was a little less enthusiastic. Some writers had kind words for the much-hyped *Gojira,* although crediting it with "intellectual content usually lacking in foreign pictures of the same genre" may seem like faint praise. Other critics drew less favorable comparisons to American sci-fi imports or damned the film as "grotesque junk" that "looked like something you'd spit up."[19] Donald Richie expressed grudging admiration for *Gojira* and its special effects: "As monsters go, he's quite well done." But even Richie could not see beyond some of the technical lackings of suitmation: "If a film is strong enough, one willingly suspends logic and agreeably refuses to believe that what one sees is false. 'Gojilla' [*sic*], though vastly entertaining, is not that strong. There are so many long talky scenes that the monster's appearance becomes positively welcome. It's fun to watch the man walking on the toy buildings."[20]

Although Richie (and very likely many other viewers) took a childlike delight in Godzilla's rampages, the creators of *Gojira* always intended the film to be an antinuclear fable with a deadly serious message. "When I returned from the war and passed through Hiroshima," Honda Ishirō once recalled, "there was a heavy atmosphere—a fear the earth was already coming to an end. That became the basis for the film." To Honda, Godzilla was a means of "making radiation visible," of giving tangible form to unspoken fears of the Bomb, nuclear testing, and environmental degradation.[21] *Gojira* challenged the morality of the atomic age and rendered terrifyingly real the destructive power of radiation (and did so in ways that contemporary American films seldom, if ever, would). *Gojira,* one critic has written, "was a rare monster movie to go into the nasty details of the catastrophe: hordes of injured refugees, thronging field hospitals, churches full of widows and orphans."[22] Death and suffering are depicted matter-of-factly in Godzilla's attacks; radiation is not something mysterious, antiseptic, or theoretical in *Gojira,* but is an unrelentingly lethal force unleashed against nature and humankind alike. Even Godzilla's skin, thick and furrowed like the keloid scars that afflicted the survivors of Hiroshima and Nagasaki, evoked the agony of irradiation. The moral was clear: nuclear war and the uncontrollable horrors within the atom were to be avoided at all cost. Japanese moviegoers reportedly approached the film and its cautionary message with appropriate solemnity: audiences were said to have watched the destruction of Tokyo—and subsequently of Godzilla—in respectful silence, sometimes leaving the theaters in tears. And the creators of the monster idealistically felt their cinematic statement could have a political impact: "Believe it or not," Honda once confided to an interviewer, "we naively hoped that the end of Godzilla was going to coincide with the end of nuclear testing."[23]

Many critics have looked upon films that exploited Cold War nuclear paranoia—and especially those in the "monster on the loose" genre—with a certain cynicism. Bill Warren, for one, has asserted that the use of radiation in classic science fiction movies "was just a gimmick":

> In the 1930s the equivalent gimmick was electricity; in the 1920s, it was surgery and often gland operations. In the 1950s, it was radiation that got the monster going.

The 1930s didn't suffer from fear of electrical annihilation; although the 1950s did tend to be worried about atomic warfare, radiation in science fiction films wasn't a means of expressing this fear, probably not even unconsciously. It was just a way of originating an unusual or interesting menace. . . . Radiation was used to explain many wonderful things, from giant insects to walking trees to resurrecting the dead. This was not a form of nuclear paranoia, merely cheap and simple plotting.[24]

Other detractors have dismissed allegedly lightweight "creature features" for trivializing the specter of nuclear war. Jonathan Lake Crane ranted:

The characters in most of these efforts are flat caricatures who bathetically spout maudlin clichés, mouth scientific mumbo-jumbo, and scream hysterically for far too long in the direction of monstrously large reptiles. These gross efforts, pathetic claptrap, answer the most significant question of the 20th century with tacky special effects, papier-mâché sets, and idiotic plots. How can lumbering dinosaurs spewing atomic fire, giant carnivorous plants, and implacable mutant insects approach the fiery chaos that engulfed Japan?[25]

Gojira's message may not have been terribly deep or particularly subtle, but the film was not egregiously cynical or disrespectful in its treatment of radiation, nuclear anxiety, or Japan's own atomic-age history. Indeed, there is an appealing ingenuousness and honesty about *Gojira* that makes its antinuclear subtext—what one author has characterized as "easy moral certainties"[26]—seem surprisingly free of didacticism, condescension, and, for want of a better word, preachiness. Perhaps Japan's twentieth-century experience—as the target of atomic attacks and as a mere bit player in the Cold War clash of the superpowers—allowed the nation's filmmakers to reflect with immediacy, authenticity, and passion on the threat of nuclear apocalypse. Even, one might add, when the vehicle for that thoughtful reflection was a huge irradiated dinosaur, mad as hell and headed for Tokyo.

One can also detect in *Gojira* a strong theme of Japanese patriotic bravado and a less explicit, though no less insistent, tone of anti-American resentment. Much of the film's musical score recalls Japan's wartime martial airs, staples of World War II home-front propaganda and today replayed ad nauseam (and at ear-splitting volume) in Japan's *pachinko* pinball arcades. In *Gojira,* heroic scenes of mobilizing troops, crisply efficient naval maneuvers and tanks emblazoned with the rising sun—not images one might expect to see glorified less than a decade after Japan's defeat and supposed demilitarization—are all set to rousing nationalistic marches. Moreover, at one of the emotional high points of the film, just after the oxygen destroyer has been deployed and Ogata begins to ascend to the surface of Tokyo Bay, the soundtrack swells into a few incongruous but majestic bars curiously reminiscent of Japan's funereal national anthem, *Kimigayo.* Just a moment later, after the success of the oxygen destroyer has been confirmed, the assembled mob of reporters, sailors, and military brass aboard the support ship erupt in spontaneous celebration; the cry goes up, "What exhilaration! What jubilation! We have won!" The victory here is clearly Japan's, and not a broader triumph of humankind over the monster. *Gojira* thus closes with a highly charged revision of the outcome of World War II, exemplifying what Joseph Anderson and Donald Richie refer to as "a favorite Japanese science-fiction stance: Japan, saviour of the world."[27]

The manner in which *Gojira* "demonizes American nuclear science"[28]—and by extension the America that invented the atomic bomb and used it on Japan—is revealed in the stark morality play at the heart of the film. Dr. Serizawa is caught in an excruciating ethical quandary: should he reveal the secret of the oxygen destroyer and risk introducing a deadly new superweapon into the volatile Cold War world? Or should he conceal his awesome discovery, keeping humankind safe from a force mightier than the H-bomb but, in the process, forsaking Japan to devastation by Godzilla? Serizawa, of course, chooses the most righteous path of all: the oxygen destroyer is used to liberate Japan from the monster while Serizawa's ultimate self-sacrifice—as noble an act of harakiri as could be performed in a diving suit—ensures that his cataclysmic device will never fall into the wrong hands. The moral here is obvious: "good" Japanese science, which would never be used for aggressive or self-serving ends, triumphs over "bad" American science, which has misused the wonders of technology and bears responsibility, after all, for creating the scourge of Godzilla. Japanese audiences could thus leave *Gojira* confident in the knowledge that the monster was vanquished, that their nation had prevailed single-handedly, and that Japan was superior—technologically as well as morally—to atomic-age America.

Throughout *Gojira*, memories of the past war and fears of a coming war are seamlessly intertwined. Images of chaos, flight, and destruction—families pulling cartloads of possessions, children being relocated in Army trucks, Tokyo consumed by flames—surely evoked in *Gojira*'s viewers all-too-real recollections of World War II. Short vignettes in the film make the connection explicit. Prior to Godzilla's attack, a group of commuters chat in a train. "It's terrible, huh?" one remarks. "Radioactive tuna, atomic fallout, and now this Godzilla to top it all off." "I guess I'll have to find a shelter soon," another chimes in. "The shelters again?" one of their companions exclaims, "That stinks!" Later, when the monster is bringing ruin to the city, the camera falls on a woman cowering beside a Ginza building, holding her young children close as flaming debris rains down upon them. "We'll be joining your father soon," she moans, referring (one must assume) to a husband killed in the war. "Just a little longer, a little longer." Godzilla, as one author has perceptively suggested, takes on the dark character of "war personified."[29]

The association of Godzilla's attacks with the ravages of World War II on the Japanese homeland undoubtedly brought with it substantial ideological baggage. To a Japanese populace that earnestly (and, to a certain extent, justifiably) wished to see itself as the victim—rather than the aggressor—in the recently ended war, *Gojira*'s implications could in some ways have proven very welcome and therapeutic. Godzilla, like the physical and emotional suffering of war, was an uncontrollable, unfathomable curse visited upon a helpless, blameless Japan. The land of the rising sun was culpable for neither the atomic bomb nor Godzilla, yet had borne the unique agonies of them both. But at the same time that Godzilla may have helped naturalize Japanese victimhood, it also brought to the fore a welter of unsettled memories and unresolved issues from Japan's wartime experience. As a number of observers have recognized, Godzilla functioned not simply as a figure of war incarnate or a metaphorical admonition of nuclear annihilation, but also became a reproachful symbol embodying the spirits of Japan's war dead. Ifukube Akira once noted that, for his generation, which came of age in the 1940s, Godzilla was "like the souls of the Japanese soldiers who died in the Pacific Ocean during the war."[30] As the image of a vengeful, violent homecoming of souls in *Gojira* suggests, postwar Japan had not fully come to terms with the human losses of World War II, the unruly memories of wartime trauma, or the guilt of survival, recovery, and forgetfulness. Godzilla thus emerged as something of a conscience for Japanese society in the 1950s, forcefully reminding the reconstructed, prosperous "new" Japan of the sacrifices, losses, and repressed shadows of the recent past.

In the end, belying most preconceptions of the giant monster genre, *Gojira* was a complex film, and Godzilla a multifaceted character. On different levels and in different ways, both movie and monster reassured and unsettled, affirmed and challenged, terrified and amused. *Gojira* explored both an unresolved past and an uncertain future, providing some soothing reassurance but no simple remedies for the fears, phantoms, and profound insecurities of Japanese society. That such meaning, relevance, and intensity of feeling could emerge from an actor in a latex suit, blithely stomping miniature models of Tokyo, is remarkable indeed. Beneath *Gojira*'s "monster on the loose" plot, sci-fi cheapie effects, and radioactive saurian hero lay a thoughtful, sophisticated and timely classic of world cinema.

The domestic success of *Gojira*—along with the international attention accorded Japanese exports like *Rashōmon* and *The Seven Samurai*—convinced Tōhō to seek an American distributor for its first blockbuster monster film. Hollywood dealmakers were very receptive, but their vision of an American *Gojira* was a mass-market, thrill-a-minute horror flick, not a dark and broody, subtitled art-house release. As a result, *Gojira* was cut, edited, shuffled, and augmented to produce a feature that would meet American audiences' action-heavy, substance-lite expectations of a creature film and would cater to the filmgoing masses who demanded to hear their movies rather than read them. Although *Gojira* was not exactly eviscerated in this transition, with the terrifying charm of the monster thankfully surviving the cinematic surgery, much of the emotional power, intellectual depth, social relevance, and visceral impact of *Gojira* was lost in its translation to U.S. movie screens.

The North American rights to *Gojira* were purchased by movie mogul Joseph E. Levine, who along with producers Harold Ross and Richard Kay and writer/director Terry Morse (veterans all of the low-budget B-movie business), created the made-for-America *Godzilla, King of the Monsters*. In order to avoid dubbing the entire film, new footage incorporating a voyeuristic American reporter (who narrates the destruction of Tokyo) and his Japanese sidekick (who conveniently translates and summarizes Japanese dialogue) was added. The use of some neat editing tricks, body doubles, and over-the-shoulder shots allowed for sequences in which the newly inserted characters appeared to talk with Emiko, Dr. Serizawa, and the others. Cheesy, yes, but creative too. *Gojira* was sliced and diced to accommodate the new material, with almost a third of Honda's film left on the cutting room floor. Nevertheless, as one movie critic has acknowledged, "Much has been done to Americanize the Godzilla series over the decades, much of it inane and destructive, but the craft and cleverness of *Godzilla, King of the Monsters* is immediately apparent."[31]

The actor chosen to headline *Godzilla* was Raymond Burr, a hardworking Hollywood leading man but hardly A-list talent. In the mid-1950s—long before he gained fame for his TV roles as Perry Mason and Ironside, his immense physical size, his private South Pacific island, or his alleged coprophilia—Burr could boast some box-office profile, having appeared in Alfred Hitchcock's *Rear Window* as well as a slew of forgettable cheapies from *Bride of the Gorilla* to *Tarzan and the She-Devil*. Not a lot of time or money was invested in shooting the new scenes for *Godzilla:* Burr's contributions were filmed in a small Los Angeles studio in a single day of almost twenty-four hours straight work. All the filming was completed in less than a week and the limited dubbing—including a voice for Dr. Yamane that sounded like a retarded Yogi Bear and stumbled repeatedly on the pronunciation of "phenomenon"—wrapped in only five hours.

Levine's promotional efforts for *Godzilla* were intense and imaginative. The moniker "King of the Monsters" was adopted to connect the newest beast on the block to an established Hollywood property, the great King Kong, in the minds of the ticket-buying public. Needless to say, the American marketing campaign did not focus on the more provocative or compelling aspects of the original *Gojira;* in any case, nuclear anxiety and memories of World War II did not play the same way in 1950s America as they did in Japan. Instead, the movie was promoted as a pure action pulse-pounder that would wow audiences with its realistic, spine-tingling special effects. *Godzilla*'s theatrical trailer was a masterpiece of marketing hyperbole: "It's alive! A gigantic beast, stalking the earth! Crushing all before it in a psychotic cavalcade of electrifying horror! Raging through the streets on a rampage of total destruction!" What red-blooded, flag-loving American moviegoer could ignore the appeal of "Dynamic violence! Savage action! Spectacular thrills! Godzilla, King of the Monsters!"

Donald Richie complained that "all of the good stuff" in *Gojira* was "cut out to accommodate the gesticulations of Raymond Burr" in its American incarnation.[32] This is, at most, only a slight exaggeration. Virtually all sections of the original film that might have reflected negatively on the United States, highlighted Japanese resentments arising from World War II, or explored the nuclear issue in any depth were excised or otherwise neutralized in the Americanization process. The discussion on the commuter train was cropped out, the plaintive cries of the woman crouching on the Ginza are left untranslated, and Serizawa's ethical agonies are abbreviated and trivialized. Many of the meatiest and most stimulating scenes in *Gojira* were unceremoniously cut, sapping the film of its gravity and its message. Most strikingly, the ending of *Godzilla, King of the Monsters* completely ignored the ambiguous and chilling close of the Japanese prototype. Instead of Dr. Yamane's prophetic soliloquy on the threat of future nuclear testing and the possibility of other Godzillas, the American version fades out on a note of contrived closure. "The monster was gone," Raymond Burr's character authoritatively intones. "The whole world could wake up and live again." Americanization thus rendered *Gojira* a standard monster-on-the-loose action film, radiation became a gimmick rather than a moral crisis, and Godzilla was firmly recast in the inoffensive tradition of American atomic-age science fiction cinema. *Godzilla, King of the Monsters* does not challenge its viewers or even pretend to carry a socially relevant moral. In the end, the American Godzilla does nothing to jar the status quo, to question the benevolence of science, the atom, and the good old U.S. of A., or to otherwise mar the average American moviegoer's entertainment experience with unwanted demands of self-reflection or intellectual engagement.

Godzilla, King of the Monsters opened at the palatial Loew's State Theater in New York City on April 27, 1956. As had been the case in Japan, the film garnered mixed reviews but recorded strong box-office receipts. *Variety* praised *Godzilla*'s "startling special effects," though a dyspeptic Bosley Crowther of the *New York Times* rated it "an incredibly awful film," describing Tsuburaya's work as "a miniature of a dinosaur made of gum-shoes and about $20 worth of toy buildings and electric trains."[33] The film grossed more than $2 million, which was a heady figure considering that the rights were purchased from Tōhō for only $25,000 and that the American production costs were minimal. Remarkably, *Godzilla, King of the Monsters* was subsequently subtitled in Japanese and released in Japan in 1957, drawing respectable crowds. And so Godzilla came full circle. Though no one may have realized it at the time, the monster's lasting popularity was assured: for all Hollywood's best efforts to render Godzilla bland and inoffensive to American sensitivities, audiences in the United States and around the world were smitten with the new cinematic creature from Japan. From an unlikely blend of Cold War inspiration, technical proficiency, canny publicity, and industrial-grade latex was a global icon born.

CHAPTER 2

THE GODZILLA FRANCHISE

THE GODZILLA THAT MOST AMERICANS KNOW and love is not the sinister, homicidal, black-and-white, fresh-from-Bikini-Atoll-and-bent-on-revenge monster of the 1954 *Gojira*. Instead, the image rooted in America's pop culture subconscious is that of Godzilla the goofy champion, the saurian defender of the world, the judo-kicking, karate-chopping, bug-eyed, technicolor creature from the films of the 1960s and 1970s. While some fans may prefer the prototype—Godzilla as a sober allegorical figure packing a serious message as well as radioactive halitosis—most seem to identify with the monster of the sequels, Godzilla the benevolent, reptilian superhero, a kind of Japanese Spider-Man *sans* the spandex suit and bulging pectorals.

Despite popular acclaim, critics and scholars have generally not been kind to the entries in the long and ongoing

Godzilla series. "In the West we have tended to situate all Japanese films into 'art films,'" one analyst observed. "Except, of course, Godzilla."[1] Even the most hardcore aficionado would have a tough time arguing that *Ghidorah, the Three-Headed Monster* (1964) or *Godzilla vs. Megalon* (1973) are cinematic landmarks, aesthetic triumphs, or profound statements of social commentary. But the Godzilla sequels never aspired to such heady heights: the now beloved movies of the 1960s and 1970s were made to distract, to entertain and (not insignificantly) to turn a healthy buck or two for Tōhō Studios. With appealing casts of monster characters, charmingly loony plots, endearingly shoestring special effects, enough destruction and choreographed wrestling to keep the kids happy, and even the occasional flashes of brilliance, the Godzilla series was (and is) simple, unadulterated, good clean fun. Ahh . . . the power of cheese.

Beyond the 1954 *Gojira*, looking for much in the way of "deep inner meaning" in the Godzilla films can be a frustrating experience. Although some offerings in the series attempted to moralize—usually in a rather ham-fisted manner—on contemporary problems of global importance like pollution or corporate greed, the vast majority of the movies were devoid of explicit social commentary, allegorical content, or intellectual substance. Nevertheless, simply dismissing the Godzilla films as mindless pap (as so many sniffing, mincing critics have over the years) is going too far. A cinematic series of such length and such global popularity surely reveals something of significance about the time in which it was made, the people and organizations that created it, and the audiences who watched and embraced it. The Godzilla films are not some magical oracle on Japanese culture, late-twentieth-century global society, or the abnormal psychology of prepubescent moviegoers; they are, however, a collection of idiosyncratic—and oddly compelling—

cultural artifacts fully worthy of close scrutiny, sympathetic analysis, and lighthearted celebration.

This chapter will survey the Godzilla franchise, from the first sequel, made hot on the heels of *Gojira*'s box-office triumph, up through the films still being released annually in Japan today. As of early 2004, twenty-seven Godzilla movies have been produced by Tōhō Studios over the course of almost fifty years, making Godzilla the longest running series in world cinema history. The first fifteen of the films, those best known abroad and now referred to by fans as the "Shōwa series," were made between 1954 and 1975, during the reign of Hirohito, Japan's Shōwa emperor. After a long hiatus, Godzilla was revived in 1984 for a string of seven films, known collectively as the "Heisei series" (after the Heisei emperor, who ascended the throne in 1989), which aimed to restore the franchise's glories and make Godzilla relevant to a new generation of movie fans. The current "Shinsei (new generation) series"—in which Tōhō has released a film each December since 1999—has given Godzilla renewed cinematic life after the monster was killed off in *Godzilla vs. Destoroyah* (1995) and badly mangled in Hollywood's 1998 abomination. Over the past five decades, Godzilla and the Godzilla films have undergone a multitude of changes: the series has seen creative ups and downs, at times Godzilla's very cinematic future has seemed doomed, and there have been many films which, for one reason or another, have made even the most dedicated Godzilla fans wince. But the basic character of the Godzilla oeuvre—a man in a rubber suit, pretending to be a mighty, giant lizard, drawn inexorably to the cities of Japan—and the movies' fundamental appeal—broad, unpretentious, and timeless—have always remained the same.

The first sequel, *Godzilla Raids Again* (1955), was premiered just a little more than six months after *Gojira* opened. A bald-faced attempt by Tōhō to cash in on its monster phenom, *Godzilla Raids Again* was successful at the box office (selling an impressive 8.3 million tickets) but was otherwise a pale shadow of the original film. Positing the existence of a new (and slightly more bucktoothed) Godzilla, the sequel traces the creature's destruction of Osaka and its eventual entombment in a Hokkaido glacier. The film featured an embarrassing cameo by Shimura Takashi, reprising (ever so briefly and bloodlessly) his role as Dr. Yamane; a heroic, kamikaze-like suicide all too obviously echoing the sacrifice of Serizawa; and a cast of characters almost unbearably chirpy and optimistic in the face of Godzilla's annihilation of Japan. A slapdash effort overall, *Godzilla Raids Again* revealed tendencies that—for good or for ill (and mainly the latter)—would come to characterize the Shōwa series: a weak script, unimaginative and implausible plotting, and a jarring dissonance of mood, with tragic destruction and lighthearted humor mixed chockablock. The film—which was later released in the United States under the inexplicable (but undeniably cool-sounding) title *Gigantis the Fire Monster*—also set the pattern of trotting out a monstrous adversary for Godzilla to battle. In this case, the opponent was Angilas, a suitably vicious giant ankylosaurus, with whom Godzilla parries before dispatching, in the smoldering ruins of Osaka castle, with a savage vampire bite to the neck.

In the late 1950s and early 1960s, before Tōhō had finally settled upon Godzilla as its monstrous "leading man," the creative team of Tanaka Tomoyuki, Honda Ishirō, and Tsuburaya Eiji developed a string of films starring other giant creatures and sci-fi oddities. The somber and violent *Rodan* (1956) chronicled the attacks of two giant pteranodons who hatch in a coal mine, blow Fukuoka to bits with supersonic gusts from their wings, and eventually perish in a bubbling volcano. Although patterned on the American radioactive ant classic *Them!,* the monsters in *Rodan* are presented simply as prehistoric survivors, not atomic mutants, and the film lacks an overarching message, antinuclear or otherwise. The same could be said of *Varan the Unbelievable* (1958), the story of a huge reptilian flying squirrel which most critics have rightly dismissed as unbelievably bad. Other science fiction and horror pictures, some with giant monsters, some without, also filled out Tōhō's offerings: *The H-Man* (1958) featured radioactive do-gooders who could liquefy their victims; *The Human Vapor* (1960) is the odd story of a librarian able to transform himself into a gas; a trilogy of outer space films, beginning with *The Mysterians* (1957), showcased alien invasions, robots, flying saucers, and a huge intergalactic walrus; *Half Human: The Story of the Abominable Snowman* (1955) is self-explanatory.

A particularly popular and innovative monster film (or *kaijū eiga,* as the genre is known in Japanese) was *Mothra* (1961). The tale of a huge, colorful moth that is the protective god of a small South Seas island, *Mothra* was an imaginative and influential break from the typical "monster on the loose" formula. A sympathetic, intelligent, and even noble monster, Mothra is portrayed (a bit disconcertingly, from a Western standpoint) with Christian imagery, and at the end of the film flies safely back to her native island rather than face the usual military extermination. Mothra thus introduced the unprecedented notion of monster as hero, with crass American commercialism and H-bomb testing standing in as villains in the piece. Moreover, the lighthearted, quirky, and charming *Mothra* demonstrated how a creature feature could be packaged as a "preposterous, beguiling fantasy" rather than a customarily dark, brooding horror film.[2] The success of this novel approach would fundamentally reshape the resuscitated Godzilla series of the 1960s.

In 1962, after an absence of seven years, the king of the monsters returned to the screen in the big-budget blockbuster *King Kong vs. Godzilla.* Taking a page from Mothra's playbook, the film's emphasis was placed squarely on entertainment value rather than weighty allegories or credible scariness: "The main thing I wanted in this picture was enjoyment,"[3] Honda later reflected. With a loopy plot, a clever satirical edge, overtly comic characters and monsters more laughable than terrifying, *King Kong vs. Godzilla* was a runaway box-office hit, bringing more Japanese viewers into the theaters (12.6 million in all) than any other Godzilla movie before or since. Such receipts confirmed Godzilla as Tōhō's marquee monster property and ensured that, up through the mid-1970s, a new Godzilla film—and a fresh slate of curious and horrifying adversaries—would be released in Japan virtually every year.

The creation of an ongoing Godzilla series very much reflected the economic and creative realities of the Japanese film industry in the 1960s. The 1950s—which had given birth to the original *Gojira*—may well have been the greatest decade in the history of Japanese film, both artistically and for the bottom line. Annual movie attendance in Japan peaked in 1958 at more than 1.1 billion; the number of theaters topped out at 7,457 in 1960 and, in the same year, Japanese feature film production hit a postwar high of 547; in the late 1950s, Tokyo had more movie screens than any other city on the globe, and the average Japanese went to a dozen films a year.[4] But during the 1960s, as television and rapidly changing lifestyles took their toll on attendance, the once freewheeling Japanese motion picture industry became less prolific, innovative, and adventuresome. Studios, including Tōhō, became less willing to tackle creative challenges and instead sought mainly to capitalize on proven box office successes. Formulaic movie series and safe genre films became the characteristic product of 1960s Japanese cinema, a fact that may have inspired two prominent critics to damn it as "one of the most conservative, artistically reactionary, inefficient and unprofessional film industries in the world."[5] Godzilla became one of Tōhō's safe and predictable money-makers, joining other series like the comedic "Crazy Cats" films (which totaled fourteen between 1963 and 1970) and the satirical "Company President" (*shachō*) franchise (which logged forty features from the 1950s to the 1970s).

The creative team that developed *Gojira* remained active in the making of the Shōwa series films. Tanaka Tomoyuki produced all of the Godzilla movies from 1954 up through Godzilla's demise in 1995. Eight of the films of the Shōwa series were directed by Honda Ishirō, and five were the work of newcomer Fukuda Jun, a veteran of gangland action pictures who was a reluctant convert to *kaijū eiga*. Fukuda's films, which included the fingernails-on-blackboard groaner *Godzilla vs. Megalon,* are generally regarded as the series' creative nadir, the celluloid apotheosis of rib-splitting cheesiness. Tsuburaya Eiji remained directly responsible for special effects through the mid-1960s. Over time, Tsuburaya became increasingly involved with his independent production company (which made sci-fi programming, including Ultraman, for Japanese television) and following his death in 1970, the special-effects mantle passed to his protégés Arikawa Teisho and Nakano Teruyoshi. Ifukube Akira continued to regularly contribute scores to the Godzilla films, but other—usually less talented and less sought-after—composers were also recruited. And while the human casts of the Godzilla vehicles would change from picture to picture, one constant (at least up through 1972's

Godzilla vs. Gigan) was Nakajima Haruo, the wiry stuntman responsible for bringing the king of the monsters to life.

Honda, Tsuburaya et al. created a veritable pantheon of monster giants—some awesome and memorable, others just downright silly—for Godzilla to taunt, wrestle, or incinerate with his radioactive breath. Some of the creatures, like Rodan and Mothra, joined Godzilla's stable after headlining their own features; others, and specifically King Kong (or at least Tōhō's mangy, out-of-shape and stolid incarnation of the beast), were imported from the golden days of Hollywood. But most of the monsters that washed ashore in Japan, dropped from the skies, or ended up imprisoned on Monster Island with Godzilla were imaginative new creations. Among Godzilla's more impressive and popular enemies was King Ghidorah, a three-headed, two-tailed (but curiously armless) flying dragon from space that appeared in six of the Shōwa films and was reprised for the Heisei series. A particularly worthy opponent was Mechagodzilla, a gleaming robot made of "space titanium" by an evil race of alien invaders, armed with enough flashy weapons systems—a flamethrower mouth, a colorful "space beam" from the eyes, missiles sprouting from every digit, joint, and orifice—to make a Mattel toy designer drool. A few of the monsters were disappointingly pedestrian: Ebirah was an overgrown crustacean who ate mariners like cocktail weenies, but was otherwise no more terrifying than any old 25,000-ton crawdad; King Caesar was an Okinawan lion god whose menace was undermined by fuzzy, floppy ears, a dustmop tail, and abdominal scales that looked just like cedar shingles. Among the craziest creations was Gigan, a reptilian sort of fellow from Nebula M Spacehunter (try finding that in your astronomy textbook!) with a buzz saw protruding from his chest. Megalon was even more peculiar: a 180-foot insect from the undersea Kingdom of Seatopia, the brute had drill bits for hands and a kind of horn affair—described by *Vari-*

ety as "a death-dealing electric daisy"[6]—that surpasseth human understanding. One must marvel that Godzilla never died laughing.

The content and character of the Godzilla films were profoundly affected by the changing audience demographics and ever worsening financial condition of the Japanese movie industry in the 1960s and 1970s. As one commentator has written, "The mighty nuclear monster that once invoked Japan's greatest fears and faced an assembly line of worthy adversaries was powerless against the economic forces that were destroying the once proud Japanese movie business."[7] The ascendance of TV (which soon proved itself more inventive, daring, and technically proficient than much of the film industry) as well as mounting prosperity, suburbanization, and a proliferation of entertainment options all served to drain adult audiences from Japan's movie theaters. In 1963, total theater attendance was only 511 million, less than half what it had been at its 1958 peak; by 1965, the figure had plummeted to 373 million and by the mid-1970s had bottomed out at 170 million annually. The number of theater screens shrank year after year, as did the number of movies produced in Japan. By the 1970s, up to 75 percent of Japanese films were "pink movies, *roman poruno* [pornographic romances], and other marginal sex exploitation pictures"[8]; the rest of Japanese studio production—including Tōhō's Godzilla output—were generally low-budget quickies aimed at the only dependable audience left, children. As the years passed, the target audience of the Godzilla films grew younger and younger, while production budgets (and, by extension, overall quality—special effects, scripts, acting talent) grew leaner and leaner.

Catering to the short attention spans and schoolyard sensibilities of Japan's young moviegoers, the Godzilla films became increasingly action oriented over the course of the Shōwa series. More screen time for the monsters was an important consideration; while Godzilla's appearances were short and intense in the 1954 *Gojira,* creature sequences were long and frequent by the 1970s. Special effects director Nakano Teruyoshi recalled: "Kids complained if there was some slow human drama or a confusing scene, and they started to eat candy bars or run around in the theater. But once a special effects scene came up, they sat quietly and concentrated on the screen. So we had to show Godzilla every few minutes. But we couldn't just throw Godzilla in without any reason, so we had to make the mystery linger throughout the movie to keep the kids at the edge of their seats."[9] Strangely enough, in this emphasis on regular, sustained action, the Godzilla films came to closely resemble the soft-core porn films that were another staple of the Japanese motion picture industry. Skin-flick directors were carefully instructed by the studios that "a stimulating scene should occur every five minutes."[10]

Sex never had much of a role in the Godzilla films, even before they became pure kiddie fare. Both Godzilla's son and Mothra emerged on screen from eggs, but the origins of said monstrous ova were thankfully never discussed. Godzilla's attacks also seemed to scare humans into G-rated asexuality: there is only one kiss portrayed in the entire series, a brief and completely untitillating embrace between Nick Adams (astronaut Glenn) and Mizuno Kumi (the disguised alien from Planet X, Miss Namikawa) in *Godzilla vs. Monster Zero* (1965). It is all too easy to imagine theaters full of Japanese boys sniggering and gagging at this gratuitous "smoochy" scene.

But while the youthful audiences of the Godzilla movies were sheltered from anything approaching graphic depictions of sex, the portrayals of violence in the films were a bit less closely circumscribed. Especially by early twenty-first-century American standards, the Shōwa Godzilla features were hardly violent at all: blood did not often gush, death (either human or monster) was seldom explicitly shown, and even the destruction of cities came to be portrayed as not involving the direct loss of human life. The human story lines of many of the films contained fairly tame and run-of-the-mill violence—fistfights, bullying, a shooting here and there—but nothing was re-created on screen with the gory and voyeuristic verisimilitude so beloved of Hollywood filmmakers. The fighting between Godzilla and his beastly adversaries, which had been depicted as savage and animalistic in *Godzilla Raids Again,* became increasingly stylized and comic. Monsters did not endure the throes of death on film, but fell into the ocean, tripped into volcanoes, or swam off into the sunset. And the hand-to-hand (or claw-to-claw?) combat between monsters—the real signature piece of the Shōwa movies—came to resemble the chorcographed silliness of bigtime wrestling more than the life-or-death struggles of titanic reptiles. Indeed, Godzilla's fight scenes were patterned directly on the routines of professional wrestlers at the time. Wrestling—and especially the antics of Japanese champion extraordinaire Rikidōzan—was extremely popular in postwar Japan, especially among children, and was largely responsible for fueling the early boom in television, since wrestling was shrewdly promoted as televised "spectacle of excess."[11] If two half-naked guys kicking, chopping, and grappling was fun for kids, just imagine the entertainment value of two guys in latex monster suits going at it! The violence of Godzilla thus became safe, humorous, and ritualized.

The very appearance of Godzilla also changed over the years in response to the perceived demand of the films' ever-younger consumers. After the two more serious films of the

1950s, the Godzilla costumes were stripped of their forbidding fangs, and (for reasons known only to the Tōhō designers) the four toes of the original Gojira were reduced to three on each foot. The suit was given a friendly, more mammalian look over the course of time, with the hint of an upturned smile. Godzilla's tail, always a formidable weapon, seemed to become longer, snakier, and more comic. Godzilla's head underwent the most changes in the periodic redesigns: the monster's eyes grew larger, his noggin bigger and rounder, and his features smoothed until he had a virtual pug nose. As one fan has written, by the 1970s Godzilla's makeover had produced a "friendlier, almost Muppetlike, look."[12] In those cheesiest of films at the end of the Shōwa series, the king of the monsters did indeed look like a veritable plush toy, taking on the stereotypical (and most would say cloying) cuteness that is now associated with kiddie characters in Japanese *anime* (animation) and the illustrations on Hallmark cards. Godzilla had gone Hello Kitty and Precious Moments.[13]

Pandering to prepubescent audiences led to some Godzilla sequences that have gone down in *kaijū eiga* history as classic groaners, cinematic moments that can be acutely embarrassing to watch, but which perfectly capture the goofy humor of the Shōwa-series Godzilla that so many American fans adore. In *Godzilla vs. the Sea Monster* (1966), for instance, the king of the monsters is shown scratching his nose (an odd tribute to the lead actor in Tōhō's big-man-on-campus "Young Guy" series) and plays an unlikely game of volleyball with Ebirah, the titular "sea monster," using a giant boulder. In *Monster Zero*, Godzilla does a sprightly little victory jig after knocking around King Ghidorah; the studio crew was against shooting the asinine dance—modeled on the mannerisms of Japanese cartoon favorite Osomatsu-kun—but Tsuburaya Eiji insisted, arguing that "it will make children happy."[14]

Hap-hap-happy feet! The cast members of Monster Zero join Godzilla in his infamous victory dance in this 1965 Tōhō publicity photo. Mizuno Kumi and Nick Adams are pirouetting to the right of the monster.

In two of the Shōwa movies, Godzilla "talks" with other monsters: in *Ghidorah,* a conversation among Godzilla, Mothra, and Rodan is unintelligible, but is conveniently translated by a pair of telepaths; in *Godzilla vs. Gigan,* monsters chat using comic-book balloons over their heads (or, in the dubbed American version, in very broken English). The low point of ridiculous behavior came in *Godzilla vs. the Smog Monster* (1971) when Godzilla flies through the air, jet-propelling himself with his radioactive ray, and breaking all the laws of physics in the process. The kids in Japanese theaters may have loved it, but most fans today can only wince, grin, and bear it.

Audience demographics also led Godzilla's creators to introduce story lines and characters directed squarely at young boys, their concerns, and their fantasies. After the early 1960s, as Godzilla was recrafted as an anthropomorphic, heroic good guy, defeat was no longer a possibility for the king of the monsters. Humor was also a must, and Godzilla (played in a very spirited, upbeat manner by Nakajima Haruo) became the veritable life of the party. The introduction of a supposed son for Godzilla was probably the most obvious concession to the youth audience. Minilla, a shapeless, mid-gray, squeaky voiced, more-fetus-than-infant monster introduced in 1967's *Son of Godzilla,* was an entirely cynical appeal to the kiddie market. Relentlessly and self-consciously cute, particularly in the oft-repeated scene in which Godzilla tries to teach the little tyke to use his radioactive breath, Minilla is hard to stomach for most adult viewers.

The same can be said of *All Monsters Attack* (1969), a film which takes place largely within the daydreams of a downtrodden Japanese schoolboy, who learns important lessons from Godzilla and Minilla on growing up, doing the right thing, and beating the pus out of his tormentors. Who needs an ABC Afterschool Special or a Charles Atlas course if you've got Godzilla in your corner?

"Enough playing horsey. Dad's gotta go pulverize Japan."
Godzilla and Minilla enjoy some quality time on Monster Island.

Plummeting studio budgets—like the demands of a juvenile audience—took their toll on the quality of the Shōwa series. For many critics, the "shoddiness" of Godzilla films became their defining trait and reflected the generally "cheap and nasty" nature of all Japanese exports—carnival novelties, shirts that melted when you washed them, third-rate electronics—in the first decades after World War II. "Japanese monster films," one observer wrote in 1970, "have all the signs of catchpenny productions: faded American stars in featured roles, abysmal dubbing, uneven special effects."[15] But the failings of Japan's *kaijū eiga* productions, especially in the realm of special effects, were not the result of any lack of skills on the part of Japanese technicians, but derived from a dearth of financial resources pure and simple. Tight budgets in an era of falling film revenues—not some sort of congenital preference for cheesiness among Japanese filmmakers—dictated the extensive use of stock footage, the recycling of musical scores, and the thousand and one other cost-cutting, penny-pinching bodges that characterized the later Shōwa series films. Perhaps most obviously, the lack of funds for elaborate sets meant that scenes of monsters destroying tiny models of Japanese cities—one of the great vicarious pleasures of Godzilla fans worldwide—grew increasingly rare as the years went by. The features of the late 1960s and early 1970s were more likely to showcase monster wrestling rather than urban stomping, and the confrontations invariably took place in cheaply and easily modeled unpopulated areas: uninhabited tropical islands, the alleged plains around the base of Mt. Fuji, the barren landscape of Planet X.

Cheapness also meant that the scripts and acting in the Shōwa films suffered, with tight schedules, bare-bones budgets, and low artistic aspirations producing plots and performances either "far fetched, fun and often pleasantly humorous"[16] or just downright awful, depending on your perspective. Some screenplays were the result of public competitions: *Terror of Mechagodzilla* (1975) was originally penned by a female student at a Tokyo film school; the character of Jet Jaguar, a giant robot showcased in *Godzilla vs. Megalon,* was thought up by a Japanese elementary school student in another contest. Endings and story components became formulaic and tired: monsters constantly fall into the sea, Mothra repeatedly appears as a selfless goody-goody, and the Japanese authorities endlessly try to stop Godzilla with barriers of high-tension power lines, though never with the slightest success. Outrageous plots just became the norm. Space aliens were a constant presence, from the impassive but sneaky people from Planet X in *Monster Zero* to the hostile Kilaaks in *Destroy all Monsters* (1968) to the cockroach extraterrestrials of *Godzilla vs. Gigan.* In the last two films of the Shōwa series, the baddies are a race of intelligent space primates (absurdly named "the Simeons"), a none-too-subtle rip-off of the popular *Planet of the Apes* franchise. An interesting, but no more credible, variant on aliens was the Seatopians, an undersea civilization whose watery world has been destroyed by human nuclear testing and who vengefully release their pet monster-god Megalon on Japan.

Although some talented actors did appear in the Godzilla films, most were deserved B-listers and none even approached the stature of Shimura Takashi, who had headlined the two 1950s features. Many of the performances in the Shōwa movies were wooden, uninspired, or exaggerated, though admittedly the casts often had little to work with in the way of convincing or compelling scripts. A few American actors earned roles in the series. Notably, as the result of a coproduction deal with the small-time American impresario

Henry Saperstein, washed-up Hollywood "star" Nick Adams was recruited for *Godzilla vs. Monster Zero*. Adams's work as the endlessly chummy Astronaut Glenn was adequate and amusing; he certainly deserved some kind of award for keeping a straight face while delivering lines like "Double crossing finks!" and "You rats, you stinking rats!" An even more painful performance was turned in by Robert Dunham, an amateur American actor living in Japan, who portrayed Antonio, King of Seatopia in *Godzilla vs. Megalon*. Dressed in a revealing white toga, Dunham's receding hairline, tattoos, foot-long sideburns, and lush growth of body hair—not to mention his overacting—made him an unlikely regal figure.

The Godzilla films of the 1960s and 1970s also became ever less daring and innovative, preferring to copy successful cinematic formulae rather than blaze a pioneering path (as *Gojira* had done years before). Seemingly always willing to cut a corner, the makers of the later Shōwa movies cribbed shamelessly from other popular genres and even other *kaijū eiga* series. The James Bond films, heavy on gadgetry, chases, buff leading men, and predictable suspense scenes, influenced many Godzilla offerings. The Japanese gangster (*yakuza*) genre, a fan favorite in the 1960s, became the model for several Godzilla features, including *All Monsters Attack*. *King Kong vs. Godzilla* was highly derivative of Tōhō's satirical (and very successful) "salaryman" comedy films, a kind of Dilbert for postwar Japan that poked fun at office politics and the petty travails of white-collar life. Not only did *King Kong* satirize corporate greed and incompetence, but it starred many veterans of the "salaryman" series already popular with movie fans. Rival Daiei Studios' Gamera series, which told the story of a violent but child-loving giant turtle (and is discussed in more detail in chapter 6), inspired Tōhō to make Godzilla more of a chum to the kids as well as more of a blood-and-guts fighter. Even TV series became easy inspiration for Godzilla's creators: Ultraman is the unmistakable source for the Jet Jaguar character in *Godzilla vs. Megalon,* and it is said that Mechagodzilla was based on the low-budget superhero Giant Robo (featured on American television in the obscure series *Johnny Sokko and His Flying Robot*).[17]

Although the heavy symbolism and weighty message of the original *Gojira* were quickly and unceremoniously dropped in the later films, a few features in the Shōwa series did attempt to tackle serious and timely issues. Banno Yoshimitsu, the director of *Godzilla vs. the Smog Monster,* was purportedly inspired by Rachel Carson's environmental call-to-action *Silent Spring* and intended his film as a cautionary fable of the effects of unchecked pollution. The result was one of the most peculiar movies in the entire Godzilla opus, in which the king of the monsters battles a living blob of toxic industrial effluvia named Hedorah, a gruesome smokestack-sucking, acid-oozing, smog-exuding advertisement for the Sierra Club and a vegan diet. With graphic scenes of the human costs of environmental degradation, *Godzilla vs. the Smog Monster* engaged with a critical social concern—in this case, Japan's acute pollution problem of the 1960s and early 1970s—like no Godzilla film since the 1950s. Yet this more sober tone was not greeted with great acclaim: fans consider *Godzilla vs. the Smog Monster* one of the weakest Shōwa offerings, and Tanaka Tomoyuki allegedly informed Banno—who would never direct another feature film—"You ruined the Godzilla series."[18] Other Godzilla movies did touch on issues like nuclear proliferation, corporate corruption, rampant commercialism, and schoolyard bullying (a major problem in Japan addressed in a very curious, idiosyncratic way in *All Monsters Attack*). In general, however, reflecting the youth audience of the series and the overriding emphasis on entertainment, the morality of the Godzilla films was simplistic, preachy, didactic, and ultimately insubstantial. In the end, Godzilla's social statements were about as deep as those of *The Brady Bunch* or *Family Ties.*

Indeed, over the two decades following the release of *Gojira,* the Godzilla franchise evolved so far from the model of the original picture that comparisons are virtually impossible. Not only was the dead seriousness of *Gojira*'s message dropped, with almost unseemly haste, in the slew of sequels, but many of the distinctive themes, motifs, and assumptions of the first film were eventually abandoned as dated, depressing, or uncommercial. The death of human beings at the hands (or feet) of monsters was almost entirely stopped from the early 1960s: Godzilla and friends might still obliterate cities, but (except in *Godzilla vs. the Smog Monster*) the human toll of such attacks was left unseen. The emphasis on World War II and its unresolved legacy was also left by the wayside after *Godzilla Raids Again,* as the theme doubtless had little relevance to the legions of little Godzilla fans born after 1945. The nuclear threat, which of course was integral to *Gojira* and the monster's genesis myth, diminished in significance in the films over the years as well. The friendly superhero Godzilla hardly seemed radioactive at all (save perhaps for that melting blue halitosis), reflecting the global politics of détente and the resulting decline of nuclear fear as a hot-button issue.

Virtually across the board, the Godzilla films of the 1960s and 1970s were much more upbeat, optimistic, and vibrant than their 1950s predecessors. Part of this can be ascribed simply to the transition from black-and-white to color, even though Godzilla himself remained a dull slate gray. The increasing focus of the series on a youth audience also played a role, as the action-oriented kiddie crowd doubtless had little patience with the kind of dark broodiness that characterized *Gojira.* One shouldn't forget, however, that the Godzilla films were products of their times, and that the Japan of 1970 was a far, far different place from the

Japan of 1954. The fun-loving, father-figure Godzilla of the later Shōwa films mirrored a nation that was rapidly emerging from the shadow of Hiroshima, shrugging off the baggage of defeat, surging forward economically, and growing increasingly confident and comfortable year after year. In this context, Godzilla became less of a menace—and more of a mascot—for the revitalized, "new" postwar Japan.

By the mid 1970s, the Shōwa series had run out of gas creatively and at the box office. Although *Terror of Mechagodzilla* (1975) featured Honda Ishirō's direction and a fresh Ifukube Akira score, and although the film sought to restore some of the elements of the classic Godzilla features to the series, theater receipts were weak, reviews were damning (as they had been for more than a decade) and studio enthusiasm waned for dusting off the old latex suit and making yet another lackluster sequel. Perhaps not coincidentally, 1975 was the first year that imported films outgrossed domestic products in Japan, with Hollywood's state-of-the-art special effects wizardry—which made suitmation look positively prehistoric technologically—a major contributing factor. Tōhō thus gave Godzilla a pink slip, and for the next nine long years, the king of the monsters languished, presumably in the depths of the Pacific Ocean or in a cave on Monster Island, waiting expectantly for a call from his agent.

But although the Godzilla series was mothballed, Japanese fans of *kaijū eiga* did not forget their hero. Godzilla merchandise continued to sell well through the 1970s. In 1980, Tōhō re-released *Godzilla vs. the Thing,* one of the best of the Shōwa films, and attendance figures were strong. In a 1982 film festival celebrating Tōhō's fiftieth anniversary, the classic Godzilla films attracted larger crowds than critically acclaimed masterpieces like *The Seven Samurai.* By the early 1980s, it was estimated that at least 65 million people had watched a Godzilla film and that worldwide fan club membership exceeded two hundred thousand. One Japanese group, the ten thousand-member-strong Godzilla Resurrection Committee, gathered more than forty thousand signatures on a petition urging Tōhō to revive the Godzilla series. The studio could not ignore the moneymaking potential of a rejuvenated Godzilla franchise and so, in 1984, confident that "the world was ready for another reptilian allegory," Japan's most famous monster roared back to the screen.[19]

Gojira (1984) was an attempt to return Godzilla to his original character and reestablish the quality, relevance, and somber probity of the series. Presented as a direct sequel to the 1954 *Gojira,* the new film simply ignored the intervening decades of the goofy, anthropomorphic, kiddie Godzilla. "It will be a serious film, just like the first movie," vowed Tanaka Tomoyuki, who remained a virtual Energizer Bunny of *kaijū eiga,* orchestrating the cinematic return of Godzilla while in his early seventies. *Gojira* (1984) boasted a huge production budget—reportedly the largest ever for a Tōhō film at the time—and improved special effects, although the trademark man in the rubber suit remained. It also was the first Godzilla offering since the original film to feature the king of the monsters alone, without any giant adversaries to distract from his radioactive, saurian majesty. And the new 1980s Godzilla was majestic indeed: reflecting the growth of the Tokyo skyline, which would have dwarfed the fifty-meter-tall Shōwa monster, the reborn Godzilla was 80 meters in height. Godzilla's angry, frightening looks were restored, as were his hostile attitude, explicit radioactivity, and the extra toe on each foot inexplicably removed in the 1960s and 1970s. Godzilla, to the relief of many fans, was a big, butch, pissed-off badass once again.

Gojira (1984), echoing its predecessor of thirty years before, also aspired to a sober message, this time about the threat of nuclear brinksmanship and the dangers of atomic energy in all its forms. Drawing on public insecurity in the wake of the Three Mile Island accident and global edginess over Reagan-era superpower confrontations, the new Godzilla was intended as a cinematic wake-up call. "We wanted to show how easily a [nuclear] incident could occur today," Tanaka remarked, "but vivid images of nuclear war are taboo. Godzilla, on the other hand, can bring the message to light and still be entertaining."[20] *Gojira* (1984) is not particularly subtle in its sermonizing, depicting the monster gutting a Japanese nuclear power plant and scarfing down a Russian submarine, which leads to tit-for-tat missile attacks from space (evoking Reagan's "Star Wars" fantasy) by both America and the Soviet Union. And as in the original *Gojira,* helpless, peaceful Japan, caught between the two Cold War goliaths, emerges as the innocent, morally superior victim. Confronted by enraged Russian and U.S. diplomats who demand that Japan consent to the use of atomic warheads against Godzilla, the Japanese prime minister in *Gojira* (1984) resolutely (and self-righteously) declares: "We will not make, possess, or allow nuclear weapons. We cannot make an exception, not even in a situation as grave as this."

Gojira (1984) was not a runaway box-office smash, but it was the second-highest grossing Japanese release of the year and sold 3.2 million tickets, well over three times as many as the final Shōwa series offering in 1975. Tōhō made only modest profits off the theatrical release, but the success of Godzilla-related merchandising—some reports stated that the studio raked in more than $30 million in rights and royalties—guaranteed that a new sequence of films would be inaugurated. Although fans had to wait a few years for the second film in the Heisei series, *Godzilla vs. Biollante* (1989), new features were released annually from 1991 to 1995. The

Heisei series would trace a similar trajectory in many respects to the one charted by the Shōwa films: monstrous adversaries—some new creations, some reprised classics—were trotted out to fight Godzilla; the scripts became increasingly fantastic, with time travelers, alien invaders, and bioterrorists entering the mix; and any attempts at social commentary became diluted and shallow, affording only confused and preachy messages about issues like genetic engineering, environmentalism, and corporate hubris. The Heisei Godzilla may never have been dumbed down and defanged to the extent that the lighthearted, Barney-like monster of the 1970s was, but the declining quality and creative vigor of the new series was apparent over time.

In some ways, the Heisei series was a significant departure from Shōwa precedent. Perhaps most noticeably, all of the 1980s and 1990s Godzilla films were big-budget extravaganzas, with plentiful funds for high-ticket special effects (urban sets, trendy computer-generated animation) and splashy promotional campaigns. And the Heisei pictures all delivered financially: each was among Tōhō's top-five money earners in its year of release, and *Godzilla vs. Mothra,* which drew 4.2 million fans into the theaters, ended up being the highest-grossing Japanese-made movie of 1992. There were also many changes in terms of personnel: although some crew made the transition from the Shōwa series, the creative team behind the new films included many fresh faces. Tanaka was listed as executive producer for all the Heisei offerings, but failing health forced him to pass most day-to-day duties over to his protégé Tomiyama Shōgo after *Godzilla vs. Biollante.* Honda Ishirō, who died in 1993, just two years before Godzilla and four before Tanaka, spent most of his later life collaborating with Kurosawa Akira and did not direct any of the Heisei offerings. Ifukube Akira returned to score four of the 1990s films. Nakano Teruyoshi, a veteran of the cheesiest of the Shōwa features, directed the special effects for *Gojira* (1984) but was replaced by the more technologically proficient Kawakita Kōichi for the rest of the Heisei series. Like Kawakita, virtually all of the young men who took over the scriptwriting, directing, editing, and production of the Godzilla films in the 1980s had grown up with the king of the monsters, and consequently approached their work with nostalgia, respect, and affection. This was particularly true of Satsuma Kenpachirō, a former steelworker who earned his scales in *kaijū eiga* by playing Hedorah and Gigan before becoming the actor inside Heisei Godzilla. Dedicated to expressing Godzilla's reptilian nature, Satsuma returned the monster (in the words of one admirer) "to a more predatory, animalistic fury reminiscent of the 1954 original."[21]

For all their flash and polish, the Heisei films were not regarded highly either by critics or by hard-core Godzilla fans. Many have disparaged the movies as repetitive and lacking in a consistent creative vision. Others have criticized them for being overblown and including everything but the proverbial kitchen sink; characters, plot twists, cool weaponry, pop culture references, and convoluted subtexts seem to proliferate ad nauseam. Wistful fans bemoaned the loss of some beloved aspects of the Shōwa series: the unintentional humor, the low-tech accessibility, the fact that monsters would actually wrestle. Kawakita's insistence that half-nelsons and karate chops were too humanoid for Godzilla, and that monsters should fight it out with impersonal, antiseptic rays and beams, rubbed many aficionados the wrong way. Detractors also felt that the special effects director's predilection for sleek robotic devices and readily morphing monsters smacked of neato Transformer toys rather than classic *kaijū eiga*. Many of the films were blasted for being derivative: *Godzilla vs. Mothra* contained *Raiders of the Lost Ark* rip-offs, the monster Destoroyah was obviously modeled on *Alien*, and Baby Godzilla looked just like a refugee from the sappy Japanese *Jurassic Park* wannabe

Rex: Kyōryū Monogatari. Reviewer Mark Shilling concluded that "the lameness of the story lines, with their mix of far-fetched international intrigue, belabored techno-jargon, and predictable finales made the series a critical disaster. Not campy enough to be a hoot, they were simply over-produced bores."[22] Damning the Heisei Godzilla as "just a fire-breathing corporate flack," another critic lamented that "the coldness and cynicism of nearly every Gojira film made since 1984 . . . is a sad thing to behold."[23] And indeed, despite all their bells and whistles, the Heisei films did lack that most important of elements, *heart.*

There's no shortage of parties to blame for the failings of the revived Godzilla series. Some analysts point to the Japanese film industry writ large, whose downward spiral from the glory days of the late 1950s continued steadily into the 1990s. By the time of the Heisei series, Japanese filmmaking was largely starved of talent, inspiration and cinematic ambition; as one critic wrote in 1990, the industry was at its "nadir, starving for good scripts, stifling creativity with miserly production budgets and turning out a lot of trashy movies that rarely make money."[24] The skinny on contemporary Japanese movies, another commentator wrote, was that they were "boring, silly, trite, just plain bad."[25] The quality of Japanese films was reflected on the box-office bottom line: in the early 1990s, more than 60 percent of the films released in Japan were imports, the number of theaters in Japan bottomed out at about seventeen hundred, and the average Japanese attended a movie only once a year. In such a depressing context, the Heisei Godzilla films may not look quite so bad.

Many Godzilla fans, however, have placed responsibility for the gimmicky soullessness of the Heisei series squarely at the feet of the corporate "suits" at Tōhō. Critics charge that conservative, bean-counting, creatively challenged studio execs micromanaged the films into mediocrity, insisting that the king of the monsters pander shamelessly to audience demographics. Making a good science-fiction film in the Godzilla tradition was subordinated to catering to all the various market segments of the moviegoing Japanese public. Thus the films had to have lots of action, plenty of explosions, and cool techy gadgetry for the kids. To satisfy nostalgic adults and the fan community, classic monsters were reprised and the films were peppered liberally with tributes to the Shōwa series. Market research suggested that women liked Mothra and men preferred King Ghidorah, so both returned to the silver screen in the 1990s.[26] Particular attention was paid to attracting female audiences, which did not traditionally flock to Godzilla pictures but which constituted up to 70 percent of Japanese moviegoers in the 1990s. Female characters were consequently given major roles in the films, notably the continuing character Saegusa Miki, a rather whimpery psychic who communicated telepathically with Godzilla. Other roles gave women agency and strength unseen in the Shōwa series: for example, the time traveler Emmy in *Godzilla vs. King Ghidorah* (1991) constructs and pilots the cyborg Mecha-King Ghidorah, vanquishing Godzilla and saving Japan. Such pandering may have been successful financially for Tōhō—witness the record-breaking grosses of the "chick flick" *Godzilla vs. Mothra*—but ultimately, in trying to please everyone, the Heisei series may have ended up satisfying no one.

It is all too easy for misty-eyed, hero-worshiping Godzilla fans (like me) to fault the Heisei films for what they *should* have been. For all the disappointment that the rejuvenated series may have brought the Godzilla faithful, the films of the 1980s and 1990s did deliver some remarkable moments. The detailed sequences of urban destruction, pumped up with new special effects technology, were the best since the early 1960s. Seeing virtually all the major cities of Japan—Tokyo (multiple times), Osaka, Sapporo, Fukuoka, Yokohama,

Chiba, Yokkaichi, Kobe—as well as Hong Kong leveled in the seven Heisei features was a guilty pleasure for monster lovers. The series also showed flashes of imagination: Biollante may have been a tad too *Little Shop of Horrors* for some viewers, but the story of a mutant genetic mix of a rosebush, a young girl, and Godzilla has the makings of good-old-days sci-fi movie brilliance. The 1990s Baby Godzilla, though drippy, exaggeratedly cute, and very rubbery looking, was a far sight better than Minilla, who always seemed like an adenoidal mound of gray mashed potatoes. Moreover, while the Heisei tributes to Godzilla history occasionally became a little gratuitous and cloying, the premise of the series finale *Godzilla vs. Destoroyah* (1995)—that the residues of Serizawa's oxygen destroyer from the original *Gojira* generated a fearsome new monster from the depths of Tokyo Bay—ties together the entire Godzilla oeuvre with a satisfying kind of closure. And however staged and cynical Godzilla's meltdown in 1995 may have been—remember the "death" of Superman, anyone?—only a very hard-hearted fan could have watched the monster's demise without a tinge of real grief or a tear in his eye.

The death of Godzilla may be the most memorable scene in the Heisei series, but there are others of truly haunting brilliance. My personal favorite (indeed, my candidate for the best sequence ever in the *kaijū eiga* genre) is from *Godzilla vs. King Ghidorah,* a tortuously plotted and logic-defying film that nonetheless glimmers with sporadic flashes of genius. Near the end of the saga, Godzilla pounds his way through an evacuated Tokyo. From a penthouse office, magnate Shindō Yasuaki watches the prosperous city he helped build being destroyed. As Godzilla approaches Shindō's skyscraper, he stops dead in his tracks and peers in through a picture window at the businessman. Their eyes meet and both recall a time, almost fifty years earlier, when they, as a young Marine officer and an isolated Jurassic survivor, crossed paths on a distant South Pacific island.

"The vain symbols of these abundant days." Godzilla and Mecha-King Ghidorah battle to the death among Tokyo's shiny new high-rises, 1991.

Shindō nods his greetings. Godzilla's saurian face registers recognition, and he closes his eyes and rolls his head, lost in an apparent reverie. Is this a heartfelt reunion? A tender moment of man-lizard love? One doesn't have to wait long for an answer: releasing an ear-splitting, heartbreaking roar, Godzilla lets loose with his radioactive ray, vaporizing Shindō and shattering his corporate monolith. Now that's entertainment!

No one would accuse the Heisei series of being cerebral films, or of being sincere and idealistic statements like the original *Gojira*. Satsuma Kenpachirō, the man inside the monster of the 1980s and 1990s, summed it up nicely: "The Heisei Godzilla series does not have the emotional spirit, that deep spirit that the works of Mr. Honda and Mr. Tsuburaya did. I think that because Mr. Honda, and many members of the staff, had served during [World War II], when the films depicted scenes of destruction it was a reflection somehow of their experiences in the war. There was a profoundness to those films that I do not think can be re-created."[27] The times had indeed changed. Japan of the 1990s was one of the richest countries in the world, with a growing sense of national pride, global ambitions, and a short collective memory. The poor, shell-shocked and powerless Japan of 1954 and the concerns of that age—nuclear testing, the legacies of war, the challenges of reconstruction—were all but forgotten in affluent, self-confident fin-de-siecle Japan. In such a historical context, the Heisei films and the character of Godzilla took on a new cultural and political valence. No longer compelling as radiation-made-flesh or a cinematic metaphor of wartime suffering, Godzilla was transformed in the Heisei series into a conscience for Japan, an uncontrollable natural force that reminded the nation of its vulnerability and popped the bubble of Japan's inflated national pride. Tanaka Tomoyuki was insistent that Godzilla trample the ostentatious landmarks of Japanese 1990s prosperity: the skyscrapers of Shinjuku, the glittering waterfront developments of Yokohama and Chiba, "the vain symbols of these abundant days." "Japan is rich and people can buy whatever they want," Tanaka explained. "But what is behind that wealth? Nothing very spiritual. Everyone's so concerned with the material, and then Godzilla comes and rips it all apart. I suspect that is good for us to see."[28]

There are many possible reasons for Tōhō's decision to kill off the king of the monsters in 1995, not least among them the box-office rewards of such a publicity stunt and the simple truth that the Heisei series had reached a dead end creatively. But the most important consideration was almost certainly the fact that a Hollywood Godzilla movie, licensed by Tōhō and sure to feature top-notch special effects and a big-name cast, was in the works. In order not to compete with the TriStar picture, which Tōhō would release in Japan, the Heisei series was concluded and Godzilla was mothballed once again. Yet the monster's furlough this time around would prove quite short indeed. The disappointment, financially as well as critically, of the 1998 American *Godzilla* (of which more will be said in chapter 6) induced Tōhō to bring the Japanese Godzilla—the *real* Godzilla—back to the silver screen. A new series of films was launched in 1999; though originally intended to be just a trilogy, five fresh Godzilla features have been produced as of the writing of this book, with a gala fiftieth-anniversary feature scheduled for release in December 2004. This latest revival, which has injected a welcome new vigor into the franchise, is known by some as the Shinsei (new generation) series, by others as the Millennium series, and by many hip Japanese fans as the "x" series (since the new films have all used "x" rather than "vs" in their titles).

Tōhō's goal in the Shinsei films has been to develop new talent and allow for the expression of a revitalized creative energy, improving upon the Heisei offerings (which most observers agreed had become stale and predictable), and reconnecting adult and youth audiences (both of which had been turned off by the TriStar fiasco) to the traditional pleasures of Godzilla. The current string of films, at least according to some critics, does not constitute a formal series, since new offerings generally do not build upon prior films narratively. As part of Tōhō's strategy for allowing more imaginative perspectives into the franchise, the first four Shinsei movies were conceived as freestanding creations, each of which sought to break from the hackneyed patterns of blockbuster sequels by assuming different histories for Godzilla. Thus *Godzilla, Mothra, and King Ghidorah: Giant Monsters All-Out Attack* (2001) posited that Godzilla's only prior attack on Japan had been in 1954, while *Godzilla x Megaguirus* (2000) suggested that the monster had raided in 1954 and 1966, and *Godzilla x Mechagodzilla* (2002) was premised on the near-constant postwar terrorization of Japan by all sorts of giant monsters. Some fans have faulted this annual rewriting of Godzilla's life story as disconcerting, but it has given the Shinsei directors and screenwriters new creative latitude, promoted experimentation—some of it, at least, very successful—and helped the series recapture a bit of the sincere, endearing spirit of the classic Shōwa Godzilla.

Despite its apparently genuine commitment to reinvigorating the Godzilla films, Tōhō retained much of the behind-the-scenes talent from the Heisei series for the new-look Shinsei productions. Okawara Takao, who had directed three of the Heisei movies, including *Godzilla vs. Destoroyah,* took the helm of the inaugural Shinsei feature, *Godzilla 2000: Millennium* (1999). Tezuka Masaaki, who was assistant director for *Godzilla vs. Mechagodzilla II* (1993), emerged as the studio's favored *kaijū eiga* specialist, directing three of the last four films. Similar continuities in personnel were evident in special effects and in screenwriting. The basic format of the Shinsei offerings, with Godzilla battling a giant opponent, or sometimes a herd of them, was also much the same as that of Heisei. As before, the monstrous adversaries were a blend of both old and new, with veterans like Mothra and Baragon returning from the *kaijū eiga* stable and largely forgettable newcomers like Orga (the sluggish, hunchbacked alien in *Godzilla 2000*) and Megaguirus (the prehistoric queen of the dragonflies) joining the mix. The special effects were generally of higher quality than those of the Heisei series, with more in the way of sophisticated computer graphics and some ambitious, well-executed fighting sequences.

In many ways, however, the ills of the Heisei series returned to infect the promising Shinsei films. In particular, Tōhō's ongoing desire to pander to important segments of the moviegoing public ensured that the Shinsei movies remained soggy thematic catchalls, with plenty of made-to-measure characters and clichéd storylines for capturing the desired demographics. Thus, child actors—who had never really shined in earlier Godzilla roles—returned in profusion to the casts of the Shinsei films. Women were a major target audience, and Tōhō sought to cover all its bases in attracting them into the theaters: strong female leads—like Lt. Yashiro Akane in *Godzilla x Mechagodzilla,* a virtual anime superheroine—became the norm, a female prime minister (played woodenly by Mizuno Kumi, who had portrayed the very unprime-ministerial Miss Namikawa in *Godzilla vs. Monster Zero*) was concocted, and weepy sentimental subplots (the motherless child, the isolated orphan, yada, yada, yada) were laid on thick. For men and boys, techy, pseudoscientific hardware and beam weapons were everywhere, and even a completely gratuitous cameo by baseball star (and current New York Yankee) Hideki "Godzilla" Matsui was arranged.

The Shinsei films have also suffered from a jarring unevenness in quality, another legacy from the Heisei days. Odd designs for the Godzilla suit have been one issue: the monster in *Godzilla, Mothra, and King Ghidorah* was heavyset, elephant-skinned and milky-eyed; in most of his other Shinsei appearances, Godzilla has been a vibrant green, with exaggeratedly large, almost crystalline dorsal fins in a designer shade of mauve. Credulity-stretching "science"—like "Dimension Tide," a man-made black hole that could be fired from outer space in *Godzilla x Megaguirus*—left many viewers and critics scoffing. Feeble attempts at profundity in most of the films fell flat: the old "kill the monster" versus "study the monster" debate in *Godzilla 2000;* the peculiar "robots are people too" musings on loneliness and the preciousness of life in *Godzilla x Mechagodzilla*. Predictable themes—personal vengeance, the parentless child—are a continuing drag on the series. And in one film, the weak *Godzilla x Mechagodzilla,* the king of the monsters appears a virtual afterthought, a mere prop in a larger mishmash of melodrama, techy fantasy, and anime-inspired plotting.

Despite all these distractions, fans have found much to love in the Shinsei series. Above all, perhaps, the filmmakers' return to tried-and-true, classic Godzilla formulae has been a thrilling (and long-overdue) creative homecoming. The Shinsei Godzilla wrestles other monsters! He's a murderous, ruthless, radioactive villain again! The Japanese military fights with rockets and high-tech weapons, not a gangly teenage psychic! We can laugh with the movies, rather than at them! And homages, always a geeky pleasure for Godzilla fanatics, are littered through the new movies, with plenty a cinematic tribute to the beloved 1954 *Gojira*. What hardcore fan didn't feel a little quiver of joy at seeing a bioengineered trilobite in *Godzilla x Mechagodzilla?* Or Godzilla's appearance over a hill in *Godzilla, Mothra, and King Ghidorah,* evoking the monster's first-ever grand entrance on Ōdo Island? Or, in the same film, Godzilla wading ashore at Yaizu in Shizuoka prefecture, the home port of the *Lucky Dragon No. 5?*

For all the critical quibbling, the Shinsei films have generally been very exciting and enjoyable, more engaging than the Heisei offerings and less cheesy than the 1960s and 1970s Shōwa favorites. Several special-effects sequences have been standouts, like Godzilla's battle with a swarm of pesky Meganeura, monster-sucking giant gnats from hell (think Minnesota on a summer evening) in *Godzilla x Megaguirus.* A few scenes stick in one's mind as truly classic Godzilla moments. In *Godzilla, Mothra, and King Ghidorah,* for example, a man gets a little messy in a urinal when the monster thunders by. Later on, a woman in traction, unable to flee, becomes hysterical when Godzilla stomps by a hospital; with the creature apparently passed, the patient signs in relief, only to have a belated flick of Godzilla's tail blast the ward into oblivion. In many respects, *Godzilla, Mothra, and King Ghidorah* was the most pleasant surprise of the Shinsei series, and is considered by many aficionados (me among them) one of the finest Godzilla films ever. The handiwork of director Kaneko Shūsuke, a former *roman poruno* director at Nikkatsu studios and the individual responsible for reviving the Gamera franchise in the 1990s, *Godzilla, Mothra, and King Ghidorah* was imaginatively crafted, a treat for the eyes, and intellectually substantive. With memorable fight sequences (who knew Baragon was such a good jumper?), a meticulous attention to detail, and healthy dollops of fantasy and mysticism, the movie drew on the best of Godzilla's history while adding ingenious new twists of its own. *Godzilla, Mothra, and King Ghidorah* was also thought provoking, and, although its message was ultimately rather muddled, the film aspired to substantive reflection on nationalism, the legacies of World War II, and the role of the military in contemporary Japan. Such earnestness may have turned the top brass at Tōhō off: while fans applauded Kaneko's efforts, he has not been invited back to direct any subsequent Shinsei features.

For all the allure of the most recent Godzilla offerings, they have not performed particularly well at the box office in Japan. *Godzilla 2000* sold only half as many tickets as *Godzilla vs. Destoroyah* had only a few years earlier, and *Godzilla x Megaguirus* put fewer moviegoing butts in seats than any film since the series' 1975 nadir. The reasons for this slump are unclear, though some argue that Godzilla has become uncool among kids in an anime-packed pop culture world, others suggest that the American *Godzilla* soured the franchise even in Japan, while a few point to pallid publicity efforts by Tōhō as the prime culprit. Even tie-in merchandising, a major cash cow for Tōhō during the Heisei series, has reportedly cratered in recent years. This balance-sheet crisis has led the studio to more creative—or some would say desperate—measures. Not only have production budgets been trimmed but, in an attempt to reclaim the elusive kiddie market, recent Godzilla films have been released as double bills with cartoons featuring Hamutaro, an adventurous and supposedly cute hamster whose grotesquely large head and eyes make him far more terrifying than the king of the monsters. In this light, the future of the Godzilla franchise, once the obligatory golden anniversary blockbuster is complete, can hardly be considered secure.

It is somewhat sobering to see Godzilla reduced, over the course of a half-century-long career, from a chilling cinematic specter of nuclear holocaust to the double-feature sidekick of an animated rodent. In the intervening years, of course, Godzilla learned how to fly, traveled in space, melted the United Nations headquarters, battled a giant moth on innumerable occasions, and served as Japan's yeoman protector from all enemies real or imagined. In other words, a little creative degradation and showboating for the crowds is nothing new for the king of the monsters. If Godzilla can survive the attacks of the universe's most gruesome creatures, he can certainly weather a few cinematic dogs, a temporary downturn at the box office, and the mind-numbing ministrations of Tōhō suits. After all, when everything is said and done, Godzilla's greatest power is not his radioactive breath, or his slashing tail, or his rows of flesh-ripping teeth; what sets Godzilla apart is his enduring charm, heroic presence, and global resonance. Godzilla is not an immortal pop culture icon because each of his films is a top-grossing, Oscar-winning masterpiece; Godzilla is forever because you and I and millions of fans the world over have a certain unaccountable affection for a man in a latex suit, trashing another tiny Tokyo, roaring with our collective glee and horror and sheer exuberance. Go figure.

CHAPTER 3

UNDERSTANDING THE MONSTER

INEVITABLY, AT SOME POINT, AFTER WATCHING ten or eleven Godzilla movies, it will happen. After suffering though some monster kickboxing or another appearance by Mothra's little twin fairies, after exulting through a come-from-behind Godzilla triumph or a good refinery fire, it will happen. Even the most focused, hard-core, un–self-reflective fan has to ask, at one time or another, a simple but dangerous question. What, in the name of all that is good and clean and proper, are these Godzilla pictures all about? *Really* about? Sure, each one of them is an implausible story featuring a radioactive reptile who either destroys or saves Japan, battles aliens, redevelops cities, shares some parenting tips, etc., etc.; we all know the drill. But they have to be something more than that, they have to have some kind of a subtext, some kind of a deeper meaning, some kind of something that isn't just latex and cheese and bad acting, don't they? Somehow, all those youthful hours spent watching Godzilla movies may not seem quite so squandered if we can convince ourselves that the films were somehow educational, or edifying, or even indoctrinating, and not just empty cinematic calories, imported sci-fi junk food with no nutritional value for mind, character, or soul. Maybe our mothers were right, maybe we should have flicked off the boob tube and gone outside to play. Oh, say it ain't so, Godzilla, say it ain't so.

Trying to elucidate precisely what the Godzilla movies "mean" is, of course, impossible. Some authors have tried, attempting to draw narrative continuity, clear allegorical symbolism, and discrete, coherent messages out of the two dozen-plus films in the Godzilla oeuvre. But that way lies insanity. As one astute observed has noted: "In the first Godzilla film, I think Godzilla himself is used symbolically. He represents death. But in the Godzilla films that were produced in the 1960s and certainly during the 1970s, is there much you can read into that, is there some sort of subtext? No. Not at all."[1] Can one really expect to find a lucid moral or thematic consistency in a series of twenty-seven (going on twenty-eight) films, spanning fifty years, that draw on the talents of hundreds of different directors, screenwriters, actors, composers, special-effects technicians, and other crew members? Even attempting to decipher intelligible meaning in such a heterogeneous lot of pictures, running from the atomic age through the sexual revolution, the green revolution, and the IT revolution, and on now to a globalized, postmodern, wired world, seems like a foolhardy undertaking of dubious value and even more dubious chances of success. But, hey, somebody has to do it.

This chapter will look first at a rather idiosyncratic selection of major themes in the Godzilla movies and will attempt to delineate what kinds of commonalities, trends, and submerged echoes of meaning may have marked this diverse series of films. The spotlight will then turn toward scholarly appraisals of what Godzilla means, what the pictures tell us about our society and ourselves, and why it's significant (if indeed it is at all!) to try to make sense out of suitmation, Minilla, and those pesky invaders from Planet X. And lest you fear that incisive academic analysis will answer all your questions, lay Godzilla bare, and ruin the spontaneous joy of *kaijū eiga* with bloodless cerebral logic, worry not. Even the greatest minds of anthropology, film studies, Japanology, and cultural criticism cannot explain with great accuracy or compelling completeness what the heck the king of the monsters is all about. Godzilla doesn't just break all the rules of modern science, but ultimately, it seems, transcends human understanding.

At first glance, very little seems to connect all the Tōhō Godzilla films, save perhaps the centrality of a man in a rubber costume and the existence of a set of logic-defying and ultimately unfathomable assumptions that most of us fans simply take for granted. Like the fact that giant monsters, no matter what their origin, mission or affliction, seem single-mindedly drawn to Japan. Better to trash a sleepy provincial city in western Honshū than flatten New York, London, or Beijing with the thrashing of giant wings, the fiery stings of an electron beam, and swimming-pool-size footfalls. Or like the fact that Japan must always fight its monstrous invaders alone, with the tens of thousands of American troops stationed in the country permanently on the sidelines and the foreign powers offering just diplomatic lip service, if even that. Or like the fact that all space aliens, time travelers, reclusive races of undersea dwellers and South Pacific islanders seem to speak Japanese, and do so at least as fluently as the many residents of "strange new worlds" spoke English on *Star Trek*. *Dōmo arigatō, Mr. Roboto*.

But any other more profound or culturally significant constants of the Godzilla series are few and far between. Even with regard to what might well be the most basic element in the films, the motivation that drives the monster on—is Godzilla antagonistic to Japan or an unlikely defender of the nation?—there were considerable changes over the decades and occasionally from movie to movie. Godzilla, needless to say, began his career in the 1950s as the ultimate threat to Japan, a bipedal atomic warhead with a score to settle and not an iota of compassion or mercy. Over the next fifty years, however, Godzilla would trace a trajectory from menace to friend and back again, ending up in the Shinsei films as a more ambiguous figure, neither bogeyman nor goody two-shoes.

In the 1960s and 1970s, Godzilla was an unabashed hero and protector of Japan: crowds no longer ran from the king of the monsters, but cheered when he appeared; children saw Godzilla as a wholesome and goofy father figure, a radioactive Fred MacMurray without the two-piece suits. In *Godzilla vs. the Sea Monster*, a thankful group of petty criminals, teenage dead-enders, and saronged Infant Islanders tip Godzilla off so that he avoids an atomic blast (although one really must ask whether a little nuclear fission would have hurt him). In the early 1970s, Tōhō produced a series of 45rpm records for Godzilla's kiddie fandom, including a single of the song "Kaijū no kurisumasu" (The Monsters' Christmas), which told of a Santa-hatted, present-toting, white-bearded Godzilla, all to the tune of "Jingle Bells." Even more indicative of Godzilla's domestication was the unforgettable 1971 offering "Yuke! Yuke! Gojira!" (Go! Go! Godzilla!), sung in the traditional *enka* style (think country-and-western meets Muzak), with lyrics that must have made the king of the monsters blush:

Goggly eyes, a huge tail
Even though my looks are a little bit scary,

I really wanna get along with everybody,
I'm Godzilla, I'm Godzilla . . .
I'm everybody's friend![2]

As Susan Napier has suggested: "The Japanese have to some extent held a love-hate relationship toward monsters in the postwar period, starting with Godzilla himself. Godzilla began as the ultimate alien who, as the series continued, became a friend to Japan, an insider, 'one of us.'"[3] Godzilla may never have carried a maroon Nippon passport, but he could sing *enka* and was undeniably integrated into *wareware Nihonjin,* the body politic of "we Japanese." And one shouldn't forget that Minilla, the putative son of Godzilla, appears to have been a native speaker of Japanese, conversing freely in the mother tongue with little, bullied Ichirō in *Godzilla's Revenge.*

The transformation of Godzilla from horror to fun-loving monster-next-door was not without its detractors. Though Tsuburaya Eiji was always ready to cater to the whims of a preteen audience, other members of the Tōhō team were less sanguine about Godzilla's spiffy new image, which even Tanaka Tomoyuki would eventually acknowledge as a creative misjudgment. Nakano Teruyoshi, special-effects director for some of the most forgettable of the Shōwa films, was pragmatic about it: "I believe that without any changes to Godzilla's character, the series would not have been able to continue. If Godzilla had remained a villain, probably only hardcore Godzilla fans would have watched the movies, and not the general audience. I think it was correct to change Godzilla's character. . . . It was a reaction to the times and the changes in the audience."[4] As historian Yoshikuni Igarashi has persuasively described, Godzilla's defanging reflected larger transitions in Japanese society: "In 1960s Japan, a place overflowing with optimism inspired by economic growth, the monsters could not find a place other than as caricatures. The darkness that prevailed in the first two films of the mid-1950s had vanished from the screen and Japanese society." In a reconstructed, growing, increasingly self-confident postwar Japan, audiences—prepubescent as well as adult—had no interest in seeing a creature knock down Tokyo Tower, new highways, or the budding skyline, the very symbols of Japan's economic revival. Instead, Godzilla was "tamed and transformed" as a hometown superhero, "a guardian of postwar Japan's prosperity."[5]

In the 1980s, when a new and improved Godzilla returned after an almost decade-long layoff, the monster's belligerence was restored and would remain through the Heisei and Shinsei series. But the Godzilla of the past twenty years has not just been the blindly destructive and vengeful creature of the 1950s. At times, Godzilla has rampaged, an insatiable and inscrutable enemy of Japan; yet at others, the monster has shown a gentler, more sympathetic, and more protective side, standing up for Japan in moments of acute need. Thus, in films like *Gojira* (1984) and more recent offerings like *Godzilla, Mothra, and King Ghidorah* and *Godzilla x Mechagodzilla,* Godzilla is wrath incarnate and must be controlled by human cunning, scientific prowess, or other monstrous intervention. In several notable outings, however—*Godzilla vs. SpaceGodzilla* (1994), *Godzilla vs. Destoroyah, Godzilla 2000*—Godzilla is instrumental in saving his adopted country from threats both domestic and intergalactic. Even when relatively friendly, however, Godzilla cannot be completely trusted. In *Godzilla vs. King Ghidorah,* for instance, the monster defeats his rampaging three-headed nemesis, rescuing the land of the rising sun from yet another harebrained plot, but then proceeds to turn upon Japan himself, doing quite a bit of infrastructural damage before being disposed of. Some deep genetic programming keeps even the benevolent Godzilla from taking the shortest, least populated route back to the sea; after a busy day of vanquishing outsize enemies and redeeming Japan's future,

Godzilla always seems to have enough energy, before that long swim home to Monster Island, to drag his big scaly feet through the nearest urban area.

Godzilla since the 1980s has been hard to pigeonhole; neither the vengeful god of the 1950s nor the jovial tutelary deity of the 1970s, the monster of the Heisei and Shinsei films has had an uncertain and unpredictable moral charge. Not quite good, not quite evil, Godzilla in recent years has been an ambiguous presence, reflecting perhaps the uncertainties of Japanese life and national destiny in a time of declining economic expectations and global upheaval. If anything, the new, less anthropomorphic Godzilla has often seemed amoral, more like an animal defending its territory or a wandering, displaced force of nature than a crusader on a conscientious mission. Capturing something of the ambiguity of Godzilla, Tanaka Tomoyuki told one interviewer in the 1980s: "Godzilla is the son of the atomic bomb. He is a nightmare created out of the darkness of the human soul. He is the sacred beast of the apocalypse."[6]

Even in features in which Godzilla played the part of the villain—the early Shōwa films, some of the offerings in the Heisei and Shinsei series—the monster has never been portrayed as such a thoroughgoing horror that the audience loses all empathy for him. "Monsters are tragic beings," Honda Ishirō once observed. "They are not evil by choice; they're born too tall, too strong, too heavy. That is their tragedy. They do not attack humanity intentionally, but because of their size they cause damage and suffering. Therefore, man defends himself against them. After several stories of this type, the public finds sympathy for the monsters; in reality, they *favor* the monsters."[7] And indeed, even in the 1954 *Gojira,* in which the monster is a cold and ruthless shatterer of worlds, one cannot help feeling a tinge of conscience and an odd sympathy for the creature when the oxygen destroyer begins its gruesomely efficient work. Takarada Akira, the actor who played the buff Lieutenant Ogata, reported being moved by the film's closing scene: "I went to the very first screening of Gojira on the Tōhō lot. I shed tears. Godzilla was killed by the oxygen destroyer, but Godzilla himself wasn't evil and he didn't have to be destroyed. Why did they have to punish Godzilla? Why? He was a warning to mankind. I was angry at mankind and felt sympathy for Godzilla, even if he did destroy Tokyo."[8]

Takarada's response is far from unique. Viewers of the Godzilla films, from the 1954 classic to the most recent releases, have felt the same profound ambivalence about the monster, at once fearing and loving, despising and pitying, shunning and embracing the cinematic beast. For although Godzilla remains a man in a rubber suit, a voiceless, inarticulate representation of violence and fury, the monster has assumed—over twenty-seven films and five decades of history—a personality, even a character, far more complex than that of a nuclear phantom or a cartoonish superhero. By recognizing that a giant fictional lizard might contain hidden depth, that a silver-screen monster need not just be a unidimensional, cardboard-cutout baddie, we may just come to see why the ambiguous, ambivalent Godzilla has become such an enduring and engaging icon for fans around the world.

The portrayal of authority and key social institutions in science fiction films has long been a favorite topic for scholars. Like most sci-fi movies—Japanese or American or whatever—the Godzilla series offers much to chew on when it comes to issues of science, expertise, and government power. On the one hand, Godzilla is part of a long line of screen creatures (from the giant ants of *Them!* to the Incredible

Shrinking Man, from the Triffids to Dr. Frankenstein's monster) to be born of science gone wrong, of man's arrogant attempts to master nature, or of a military-industrial complex dangerously out of control. And yet, in many films, Godzilla is neutralized and Japan saved only through the intervention of science and the level-headed actions of authority figures. In fifty years of cinematic monster attacks, the Japanese state apparatus has never fractured, the military has always fought to the bitter end and, even after the most destructive radioactive rampages, there is always a Japan and a hopeful future to cling onto. So in the Godzilla films, the answer to that fundamental concern of science fiction—can one really trust those people with specialist knowledge and with broad institutional responsibility to be competent, honest, humble and cautious?—is a resounding maybe. Go ahead and put your faith in the men in lab coats, business suits, and uniforms, but don't ever turn your back on them.

Those in authority do have a few bright, shining moments in the Godzilla series, a few SportsCenter highlights in an otherwise pretty dismal record. The success of Dr. Serizawa's discovery is a belated and bittersweet triumph for science; the valiant pilots who bury the monster in ice at the end of *Godzilla Raids Again* and the too-cool-to-believe Admiral Tachibana in *Godzilla, Mothra, and King Ghidorah* affirm our faith in the armed services; Interpol agents usually come off pretty well, as does the trenchcoated Detective Shindō in *Ghidorah, the Three-Headed Monster;* the principled prime minister in *Gojira* (1984) makes even politicians look good for a change. But generally speaking, stuffed shirts in positions of power and individuals with technical expertise do not walk away with the heroic roles in the Godzilla films. Politicians and military leaders more often than not appear blustering, ill prepared, and impotent. Government schemes to stop Godzilla are almost always laughable failures, with Japan's elected leaders and military top brass reduced to frustrated spectators in an under-ground bunker or distant tent. Massive government projects to combat Godzilla, a favorite of the Heisei and Shinsei movies and reflecting the pork-barrel excesses of Japanese public-works spending in the 1990s, were usually overblown flops: the inexplicable Super X vehicles (versions 1, 2 and 3), the screw-nosed robot MOGUERA and the ubiquitous Mechagodzilla are neat as all get-out, but are hardly good uses of the Japanese taxpayers' money. And, of course, there are plenty of government officials who are simply incompetent (a label that applies to just about everyone in *Godzilla vs. the Smog Monster*) or, better yet for dramatic effect, are duplicitous, immoral weasels. The slimy bureaucrat Katagiri in *Godzilla 2000* is perhaps the prime example of such characters, but government deceit is a significant theme in *Godzilla x Megaguirus* and several other series installments.

Business leaders are even less trustworthy than politicians and are the butt of scorn and ridicule in numerous Godzilla films. Shindō Yasuaki, the conspiratorial magnate who gets his comeuppance at the receiving end of the monster's atomic breath in *Godzilla vs. King Ghidorah,* has a commercial empire that includes nuclear submarines; the venal entrepreneurs in *Godzilla vs. the Thing* and the evil Biomajor cartel in *Godzilla vs. Biollante* have nothing to recommend them; Mr. Tako, the PR-obsessed pharmaceutical executive in *King Kong vs. Godzilla,* is a gentle caricature of unbridled capitalism. Scientists and reporters are generally portrayed as more honest and honorable figures, out for the truth in one way or another, and the stereotypical mad scientist is relatively rare in the series (although Dr. Mafune in *Terror of Mechagodzilla* and Shiragami in *Biollante* would seem to qualify nicely). To a large extent, however, eggheads and journalists hold onto their reputations because they remain firmly on the sidelines, observing, commenting, and facilitating rather than taking responsibility for decisive action themselves.

On the whole, the vision of Japan's best and brightest as provided by the Godzilla films is not terribly reassuring. And this impression just reinforces one of the strongest continuing themes in the series, a thread running from the 1954 prototype to the latest feature to hit the theaters: the profound vulnerability of Japan. For whether the king of the monsters is friend, foe, or something in between, a constant subliminal drumbeat in each of the movies is that Japan is under imminent threat from outside, either in the form of a hostile Godzilla himself or some alien force that only Japan's saurian protector can possibly repel. Better root for Godzilla, the movies seem to tell us, since we certainly can't count on the Japanese government, the United Nations, the scientific community, big business, the professional class, or even the world's armies to do a very good job of protecting life, limb, and property.

Godzilla himself tends to stay above the political fray (physically as well as figuratively), but there is a moment in the original 1954 *Gojira* when one wonders if the king of the monsters is trying to make a more explicit political statement. Near the beginning of the film, Dr. Yamane testifies to a Diet committee, reporting on Godzilla's Ōdo Island appearance and the theory that the monster is the direct result of nuclear testing. This incendiary revelation leads to a spirited debate among the parliamentarians. On one side are a group of self-satisfied middle-age men, the very picture of establishment power with crisply pressed suits and brilliantined hair, who clearly represent conservative, pro-American interests, the dominant line in Japanese politics in the 1950s. "Professor Yamane's report is of such extreme importance," their leader blusters, "it must not be made public." With the backbenchers nodding and grunting in agreement, the speaker reflects on the delicate balance of world affairs and the potential for internal panic if Godzilla's presence—and his H-bomb origins—are publicly revealed. On the other side of the issue stand a knot of women, young but frumpily dressed, brusque and strident in tone. Clearly intended to represent left-wing opposition politicians—who in 1950s Japan took a firmly antinuclear, anti-American stance—the women repeatedly interrupt the conservative spokesman, banging their handbags on the tables and shouting "The truth is the truth. . . . The truth must be made public!" The debate degenerates into a shouting match and eventually into a virtual brawl, with rival gangs of politicians pushing and shoving on the Diet floor. Yamane and his associates, safely away from the scrum, simply shake their heads in disbelief and exasperation, silently bemoaning the folly of politicians in a time of crisis.

Godzilla adds his two cents' worth a few nights later. In the midst of his second nighttime rampage through Tokyo, Godzilla comes upon the Diet Building. The monster looms over the structure, spotlights dancing across his body, and the dramatic tension mounts. With no further ado, Godzilla proceeds to walk through (rather, of course, than around) the building, his massive feet reducing one wing—very likely the exact spot where the unruly hearing had earlier been held—into a pile of monumental rubble.

But what is Godzilla's message in this deliberate destruction of the seat of Japan's democracy? Is there a message at all? Was the Diet, like the Empire State Building in *King Kong,* just a convenient landmark for the filmmakers to exploit? Or was Godzilla symbolically sticking one to the smarmy conservative politicians who tried—oh so unsuccessfully—to conceal his very existence? Or, most provocatively of all, might Godzilla have been rendering a judgment on democracy writ large, his actions a damning statement on the divisiveness, infighting, and ultimate impotence of democratic politics and, specifically, of Japan's fractured postwar political system?

How one reads the king of the monster's actions at the Diet is, needless to say, a matter of personal interpretation,

Godzilla, political activist. The king of the monsters votes with his feet in the Japanese Diet.

but one fact is certain. Contemporary reports stated that Japanese audiences in the first theatrical run of *Gojira* were generally somber, watching the film with the gravity that Tanaka and Honda had intended, with a number sobbing or leaving the screenings in tears. Only at one point in the original film did crowds erupt into applause, cheering, and laughter: not when the monster was vanquished at the end, not when he trots down the Ginza or puts his tail through the Nichigeki Theater, not even during some of the groaner moments of weak special-effects work, but instead when Godzilla sashays through the Diet Building.[9] Godzilla for prime minister!

One prominent cultural commentator has written: "There is absolutely no social criticism, of even the most implicit kind, in science fiction films. No criticism, for example, of the conditions of our society which create . . . impersonality and dehumanization."[10] This may be true of the genre in Hollywood's hands, but even a short glance at *Gojira* and its sequels will reveal plenty of social criticism to go around. And while the series' political statements may not always be completely consistent or ideologically profound, no segment of the Japanese elites avoids a pointed barb here or there. Indeed, even the monuments of Japanese democracy come in for a little unwelcome attention in the monster's very public appearances. Godzilla, it seems, casts a vote of no confidence in all that is trumped up, self-important, and, ultimately, like the Wizard in the Emerald City, more bluster than substance.

It is inevitable that the military plays a major role in the *kaijū eiga* genre. Whenever a giant monster appears along Japan's coastline, or comes bubbling out of an inland lake, or crawls forth from hibernation in a mountain cave, the armed forces are Johnny-on-the-spot, tanks rolling, howitzers blasting, machine guns rattling, rockets firing, bombers zooming, frigates doing whatever frigates do. Japan's men and women in uniform dutifully undertake the requisite humanitarian and administrative functions—evacuating cities, ministering to the injured, snapping to attention for high muckety-mucks—but it's the pyrotechnic defense of the realm that really catches one's attention. And Japan's front-line troops usually put up at least a creditable fight against unbeatable adversaries, getting their licks in before being blasted to smithereens by Godzilla or falling back in orderly, efficient, and well-advised retreat. For all that fans crave monster-to-monster confrontations, the Godzilla series contains some truly top-notch battle sequences: the rousing aerial attacks in *Godzilla Raids Again;* the assault by land, air, and great whomping electrode in *Godzilla vs. the Thing;* the numerous heart-racing clashes of the Heisei and Shinsei films, from the flight of Super X in *Gojira* (1984) to the sleekly choreographed martial extravaganzas of *Godzilla 2000* and *Godzilla x Mechagodzilla.*

One might understandably be surprised to find this focus on the military—indeed, the glorification of soldiers, weaponry, and the thrill of combat—in postwar Japanese cinema. After the devastating experience of World War II, Japan had sought to redefine itself as a kind of Asian Switzerland, a nation publicly forsaking the scourge of war. To make it official, in 1946 MacArthur and the U.S. occupation wrote for Japan an admirable and thoroughly idealistic constitution that enshrined the theory and practice of pacifism. As the famous Article 9 of the document declared: "Aspiring sincerely to an international peace based on justice and order, the Japanese people forever renounce war as a sovereign right of the nation and the threat or use of force as means of settling international disputes. . . . Land, sea, and air forces, as well as other war potential, will never be maintained." Eventually, under the pressures of the Cold War, Japan did cautiously remilitarize, but only under the banner of "Self Defense Forces" (*Jieitai*), ground, maritime, and air units charged and equipped solely for limited defensive action. Although sentiment in Japan favoring a more substantial military capability has surged from time to time (most

notably in recent decades), the majority of the Japanese populace has strongly embraced pacifism and resisted Japan's
reemergence as a regional military power.

In this historical and political context, the high-profile
depiction of Japan's armed forces in the Godzilla films, especially the earlier offerings in the series, is undeniably
noteworthy. Donald Richie and Joseph Anderson wrote in
1959: "The temper of the Japanese populace in the mid-
1950s was such that no film which in any way favored the
Self Defense Forces and rearmament could have been successful at the box office; hence none was made. The few pictures which used Self Defense Forces for other than minor
characters have shown the new military in an unfavorable
manner."[11] Richie and Anderson must have forgotten about
Gojira and *Godzilla Raids Again,* both of which portray
Japanese soldiers, sailors, and airmen as capable, dedicated,
and honorable, even though their tanks, rifles, and depth
charges all proved useless against the monster. Even the
peppy, syncopated tune that most fans now recognize as
Godzilla's theme was composed by Ifukube Akira for the
1954 *Gojira* as the "Jieitai March," a stirring musical tribute
to the newly formed Self Defense Forces. Through the 1960s
and 1970s, even as popular uneasiness about remilitarization
began to subside, the upbeat—one might almost say gung-
ho—depiction of Japan's military in Godzilla features remained unusual. By the 1990s, many of the taboos against
celebrating Japan's martial achievements in popular culture
had been broken—in some small part because of the
decades of Godzilla films—and the Shinsei series in particular has offered virtually unrestrained tributes to the profes-
sionalism, resolve, and effectiveness of the Self Defense
Forces. That the Japanese armed services are instrumental in
an outright victory over the monster in *Godzilla, Mothra,
and King Ghidorah* and pull off a respectable draw in
Godzilla x Mechagodzilla, shows how far the rehabilitation

of the military's reputation had progressed by the start of the new millennium.

Although it would be all too easy to overestimate the importance of the Godzilla opus in the post–World War II Japanese discourse over militarization, we should not ignore the significance of the movies' battle scenes as forbidden pleasures for filmmakers and audiences alike. Producers and directors, who could not, given the political sensitivities of the day, show the nation's troops engaging Americans, Russians, or Asians of any stripe were able to depict combat, showcase flashy new weapons, and gently stir nationalistic sentiments using Godzilla and other giant monsters as a foil. One of the great spectacles of modern cinema—the heroic battlefield—was thus rehabilitated for use in postwar Japan, with a fictional radioactive reptile installed as a legitimate and ideologically sound target for the nation's military might. One can only imagine, of course, what impact all this had on the viewers of the Godzilla films, and especially the impressionable preteens who have, over the decades, been the series' most devoted audience. We will never know for sure if a steady childhood diet of Godzilla pictures and oh-so-cool battle scenes conditioned today's Japanese adults to favor a more assertive military policy or a less restrictive notion of pacifism. But one has to wonder. Might we even regard the Godzilla films as a kind of military pornography, allowing the guilt-ridden, chastened, and disarmed Japanese public to indulge its illicit (and explicit) martial fantasies on the silver screen? *Banzai!*

Japanese nationalism and the closely intertwined issue of Japan's relationship with the United States have been major themes in the Godzilla films, much discussed by fans, critics and scholars. Expressions of nationalism—and indeed, the very sentiment of patriotism—have been troubling, controversial and often stigmatized in postwar Japan, which has struggled to address its history of expansionist ultranationalism and the complex domestic and international legacies of World War II. Tied up with this has been an acute awareness of Japan's postwar subordination to America, first during the occupation of the nation between 1945 and 1952, and then through the Cold War, when Japan was sheltered under the U.S. nuclear umbrella and remained subservient to Washington's foreign policy. In an even larger sense, America has been an intimidating and ambivalent presence in Japan's collective consciousness over the past sixty years. On the one hand, the United States has been a protector and a model, a generous benefactor and a dependable market; but it has also been a bully and an object lesson, an arrogant autocrat and a threatening nuclear power. Those darned Americans, you can't live with 'em, but you can't live without 'em. Over the past half century, the Godzilla films have reflected Japanese unease and frustration surrounding the issues of nationalism and transpacific politics, and have traced, over time, subtle transitions in the way that Japan has viewed itself, its place in the world, and relations with its most important global ally.

The 1954 *Gojira,* as discussed earlier, was a sophisticated morality play with a therapeutic message for audiences that celebrated the Japanese spirit, reimagined the nation's defeat in 1945, and implicitly demonized the United States and its policies of nuclear testing. At least one commentator didn't think that the film went far enough in underscoring American culpability: Ono Kōsei wrote in 1982 the Godzilla shouldn't have attacked a blameless Tokyo, but should have crossed the Pacific and terrorized the United States, which had, after all, been responsible for the monster's H-bomb–induced mutation.[12] Other critics have noted that American military forces are conspicuously absent from efforts to protect Japan in *Gojira* (and, indeed, throughout virtually the entire Godzilla series), despite the presence of tens of thousands of American troops stationed in the country and the existence of the 1954 Mutual Security Act, which committed the United States to Japan's defense. Kobayashi Toyomasa, for one, argued that the lesson of *Gojira* was that "the Japanese, all by ourselves, had to confront the giant beasts that were trying to destroy our reconstructed nation."[13] On only one occasion in the entire Shōwa series are American units shown attacking Godzilla, a short sequence in *Godzilla vs. the Thing* in which the U.S. Navy futilely bombarded the monster with ultra-new and ultra-deadly "Frontier Missiles." The scene, however, was not included in the Japanese version of the film, but was made specifically at the request of the American distributor, who presumably felt that stateside audiences would want to see some of "our boys" standing up to the king of the monsters.

King Kong vs. Godzilla is often considered to be a straight and very unsubtle allegory, pitting the giant simian representing the United States against Japan's reptilian contender. And there has even been a legend, so oft repeated over the years that some fans still take it to be fact, that two endings for the film were shot by Tōhō, one featuring a Godzilla victory (for the Japanese market), the other showing the ape triumphant (for Kong's hometown American fans). For the record, only one finale was ever made, and it is diplomatic and ambiguous: the two monsters, after flattening the seaside resort of Atami, go rolling off a cliff into the ocean, locked in an angry embrace. King Kong eventually surfaces, presumably walking home to his tropical island (with its solicitous, narcotic-brewing natives) while Godzilla remains submerged, either vanquished or unusually coy.

One might well expect *King Kong vs. Godzilla* to have had a pointed political subtext: in the early 1960s, not only

was Japanese pride on the rise (with the country booming in-
dustrially and Tokyo preparing to host the 1964 Olympics),
but transpacific relations were strained and anti-American
sentiment was running high in Japan. In the imagination of
director Honda Ishirō, at least according to cinematogra-
pher and special-effects assistant Arikawa Teisho, "King
Kong was a symbol of America and Godzilla was a symbol
of Japan. The fighting between the two monsters was to represent conflict between the two countries."[14] Tōhō certainly
used this angle in publicizing the film, and especially in drawing American interest to the production. One studio press
sheet, issued in English in 1962, printed supposed statements
from Godzilla and King Kong on their cinematic contest,
phrased much like the trash talking of prize-fighters or professional wrestlers. Godzilla blustered: "At the thought of my
engagement in a decisive bout with King Kong from America, I feel my blood boil and my flesh dance. I am now ap-
plying myself to vigorous training day and night to capture
the world monster championship from King Kong."[15] If only
the king of the monsters could have danced like a butterfly
and stung like a bee, he might not have ended up paddling
away from Kong in apparent defeat.

However tempting a purely allegorical reading may be,
King Kong vs. Godzilla was more comedic parody or cynical
money-spinner than weighty political rumination. The
matchup of the screen's two greatest monster giants made
for easy marketing and great grosses: the movie did generate
the highest attendance, by far, of any in the Godzilla franchise. Moreover, the ideological message of the film—to the
extent there was one—was muddled at best: rather than pre-
senting Godzilla as the champion of Japan, the picture por-
trays him as a perennial threat, with King Kong being used
instrumentally to defend the nation and drive Godzilla off.
Thus the film actually ends up reflecting, rather than cri-
tiquing, Japan's military and political dependence on the

United States, with America (here personified by a mammoth ape) rescuing an embarrassingly impotent Japan from imminent devastation.[16] The 1962 Tōhō movie is, furthermore, so profoundly derivative of the classic 1933 *King Kong*—from the tribal antics on Skull Island to Kong climbing the Diet tower (a poor stand-in for the Empire State Building) with a screaming beauty in one giant paw—that it is hard to imagine any profound cultural criticism of America creeping in.

Fast forward twenty-nine years, and one discovers a much more provocative—even incendiary—film, the 1991 Heisei offering *Godzilla vs. King Ghidorah*. Made at the peak of Japan's postwar ascent, when it seemed that a tsunami of high-quality Japanese exports was sinking the American economy, when national pride was swelling into bravado, when overseas sniping and "bashing" were stirring Japanese indignation, *Godzilla vs. King Ghidorah* was an uneven movie but an unequivocal pronouncement on the state of U.S.-Japanese relations. The plot centers on a group of renegade time travelers, one leader American, the other Russian, who conspire to destroy Japan using King Ghidorah. Their rationale for such action makes sense only in a don't-think-now-because-you're-watching-a-movie, sci-fi world. As one "Futurian" explains it: "In the twenty-first century, Japan will grow even richer. It will buy up whole continents—South America, Africa. . . . It turns out that, by the twenty-second century, the United States, the Soviet Union, and China aren't even world powers anymore." Thus, uber-Japan has to be stopped before it's too late, with a scaly, golden, triheaded flying dragon if at all possible. As one commentator has explained it, "The implication seems to be that Japan is smarter and richer than everybody else, and political tensions over trade issues are borne out of America's fears of being left behind in the coming century."[17]

The makers of *Godzilla vs. King Ghidorah* didn't stop there. The film also posited a new genesis story for Godzilla, depicting the monster as having begun life on an isolated central Pacific atoll as a lone surviving dinosaur, later rendered huge, radioactive, and irate by American atomic testing. During World War II, the dinosaur's coral home was occupied by a company of Japanese marines and when, in 1944, U.S. troops tried to raid the island, the proto-Godzilla obligingly trotted out of the jungle, stepped on a few G.I.s, and repelled the American assault. Yep, that's right. Believe it or not, the ur-Godzilla actually fought for the imperial Japanese cause. Think how the course of the war might have changed had the prehistoric samurai been there at the Battle of Midway or on the sands of Iwo Jima! Needless to say, this revisionist view of Godzilla's inception did not go down well in the good old U.S. of A.: veterans groups howled, Hollywood was chilly, and the film was not released in America until 1998.

With the turn of the millennium, after Japan's once fearsome economy had fallen and couldn't get up, the spirited rivalry with the United States cooled, and international relations did not figure prominently in the first five Shinsei features. But concerns over Japanese national identity have not faded away. Reflecting trends in the larger society—with persistent recession and political instability driving a marked conservative drift among the Japanese public—the most recent Godzilla films have embraced a nationalism and a celebration of military prowess that would have been unthinkable fifty (or even twenty) years ago. This is particularly true of *Godzilla, Mothra, and King Ghidorah: Giant Monsters All-Out Attack,* Kaneko Shūsuke's ripsnorting 2001 gem that fused cherished *kaijū eiga* traditions with a strong nationalistic subtext and sincere approbation for Japan's armed services.

Godzilla, Mothra, and King Ghidorah (or *GMK*, as fans know it) is based on an interpretation of Godzilla long favored by right-wing critics in Japan. According to scholars like Akasaka Norio, film reviewers like Kawamoto Saburō, and even composer Ifukube Akira, Godzilla represents the unquiet souls of the soldiers and sailors who died in the Pacific during World War II, returning to Japan to wreak vengeance, to demand belated acknowledgment, and to rekindle national spirit. As one ghostly character in *GMK* explains, "The souls of countless people who fell victim in the Pacific War congregated in Godzilla's body." The monster proceeds to attack Japan "because people have forgotten the agony of those killed in the war, forgotten their cries. . . ." This explanation for Godzilla and his blind fury not only links *GMK* to the original *Gojira* and its elegiac invocation of war memories, but also places the king of the monsters squarely in the midst of contentious debates over the public commemoration of World War II and the ongoing renaissance of Japanese nationalism. Strikingly, *GMK* transforms Godzilla from a patchwork of accreted imagery—the monster as a specter of nuclear war, a good-natured defender, a conscience for an arrogant economic superpower— into a powerful symbol of Japan's repressed memories and suppressed patriotism.[18]

As if this were not provocative enough, *Godzilla, Mothra, and King Ghidorah* also seeks to root giant movie monsters in the foundational mythology of the Japanese state. The film posits that three legendary guardian deities—the "Sacred Beasts" of Yamato (an evocative, traditional name for Japan)—rise from the earth to defend the nation from Godzilla's rampages. The folklore is, of course, entirely fictional—what ancient culture could possibly conceive of a fearsome guard-moth?—but the explicit sacralization of monsters as the ultimate protectors of Japan is an intriguing nationalistic twist. Moreover, in the closing moments of the film, as the "Sacred Beasts" fight side-by-side with the valiant Self Defense Forces to subdue Godzilla, the filmmakers' implication is clear: the Japanese military, every bit as much as Mothra, Baragon, or King Ghidorah, is a noble guardian spirit of Japan's past, present, and future. That's pretty heavy stuff for a film aimed at elementary school kids and twin-billed with the vacuous animated adventures of a punkin'-headed hamster.

Despite the enduring popularity and sheer number of Godzilla films, *kaijū eiga* have not received all that much scholarly attention over the years. This is hardly surprising, considering the widespread perception that the Godzilla series is just fatuous kiddie fantasy and that the king of the monsters, in the words of one crabby critic, "is nothing more original than a crude guttapercha dinosaur."[19] But popular culture in its many incarnations has been the darling of the academic establishment for well over a decade now, and serious scholarly tomes on *The Planet of the Apes* jostle with turgid dissertations on Mickey Mouse and Mister Ed on research library shelves everywhere. So it is only appropriate that some anthropologists, historians, and film studies experts should turn their attention to Godzilla, a pop culture icon virtually as omnipresent globally as a certain big-eared, talking mouse. And though scholars have bandied about lots of highfalutin psychoanalytical jargon and constructed plenty of elaborate theories as to why we all enjoy watching big lizards destroying little cities, many of us who really love Godzilla are likely to find such ivory tower perspectives more far-fetched and perplexing than enlightening and compelling.

For a good many commentators, Godzilla can be distilled down to a very simple message or a straight, one-to-one allegory. Scores of aficionados, yearning to find a legible and logical thread running through all the Godzilla films, have fallen into this trap. Thus, Godzilla fan publications may include statements like "Mothra represents the resources of the Pacific used in Japan's defense" and attempt to map Cold War politics onto monster grudge matches (if Godzilla is Japan and King Kong is America, then surely Angilas is the U.S.S.R.!).[20] Scholars are not above such reductive theorizing, either. Film historian Charles Derry, in an early study of the horror genre, pares down the deep inner meaning of the Godzilla films to nuclear fear, arguing that the Shōwa series aims "to explain away the unexplainable atomic holocaust and to build from those fears a creative world with its own rules and moral order."[21] Although Godzilla's intersection with Cold War nuclear paranoia is undoubtedly a major theme, given the extent to which the monster's H-bomb origins and lingering radioactivity are unceremoniously forgotten in later sequels, no analysis that lives or dies on the primacy of nuclear symbolism in the Godzilla series can be terribly convincing.

Film scholar Chon Noriega, whose 1987 essay "Godzilla and the Japanese Nightmare: When *Them!* is U.S." is probably the best-known scholarly treatment of the king of the monsters, pivots his arguments on the nuclear theme, but adds some interpretive subtlety and nuance as well. Citing the Godzilla films between a fairly pedestrian psychoanalytic framework and the broad sweep of Cold War international relations, Noriega asserts that the series reveals "a self-conscious attempt to deal with nuclear history and its effects on Japanese society."[22] In Japan's therapeutic search for closure to the trauma of World War II and Hiroshima, "the films transfer onto Godzilla the role of the United States in order to symbolically re-enact a problematic United States-Japan relationship that includes atomic war, occupation and thermo-nuclear tests."[23] Godzilla, Noriega tells us, eventually comes to represent self (Japan) as well as repressed "other" (Uncle Sam), which makes things very complicated indeed, though profound nuclear anxieties and deep anti-American hostility remain at the root of it all. Although Noriega's analysis recognizes some of the inherent complexity and contradiction within the Godzilla oeuvre, his description of what Godzilla is "all about" becomes somewhat cartoonish in the end. Just because Godzilla seems a simple, straightforward monster doesn't mean he can be reduced to a simple, straightforward theory.

As horror films, at least of a sort, as well as works of science fiction, the Godzilla features are inevitably wrapped up with the fears and anxieties of their makers and audiences. But what specific terrors and dreads do the Godzilla films evoke? "The monster is the symbol of what we have to fear," Brian Murphy wrote in 1972. "It is not fear itself; it is the horror of what we have done, scientifically and militarily, to bring the world to the brink of destruction."[24] *Kaijū eiga,* like their giant monster brethren from Hollywood, reflected fears of technology out of control, of poorly understood science in an age of rapid change, of dehumanization in a managed, top-down society, of a rapidly escalating Cold War, of retribution—perhaps divine, perhaps monstrous—for humankind's tampering with the forces of nature. A touch of guilt may have been mixed in there as well, although one doubts that audiences either Japanese or American felt too much remorse about the atomic bombings and the harnessing of nuclear power. Anxiety, yes; anger, perhaps; personal culpability, no.

Susan Napier, a scholar of Japanese literature and popular culture, has argued convincingly that the terror of the Godzilla films, and particularly the 1954 *Gojira,* is not actually all that terrifying. Napier places Godzilla within the convention of "secure horror," in which the ultimate message of a nominally scary movie is (ironically enough) psychologically reassuring and emotionally comforting. Thus, in watching *Gojira,* a viewer may well be frightened by the monster and all that he signifies (nuclear Armageddon, memories of the past war, etc., etc.) but by the time "The End" flashes on the screen, the monster is surmounted, Japan is saved, and society as we know it endures. "Secure horror" lets us see our worst nightmares and conquer them cinematically, exorcising our deepest demons in the process. Moreover, as film historian Andrew Tudor notes, films like *Gojira* end up buttressing the status quo, making filmgoers feel good about the power structures they inhabit: we can all breathe easily thanks to "secure horror's stress on effective expertise, on clear boundaries between known and unknown, on the desirability of existing order and on the significance of our dependence on socially central paternalistic authorities."[25] In other words, the military and the wonks can handle things, so sit back, relax and don't worry, be happy. While the critiques of Japan's political and economic elites that run through the Godzilla films may subtly undermine this moral, *kaijū eiga* is, as Napier tell us, "a fundamentally optimistic genre."[26]

A very different approach is proposed by Susan Sontag in her seminal 1965 essay "The Imagination of Disaster." In Sontag's view, science fiction films like *Gojira* and *Rodan* are not about science per se, but instead are about disaster. Or to be more precise, they are about the voyeuristic spectacle of disaster. "Monster on the loose" pictures are concerned first and foremost with "the aesthetics of destruction, with the particular beauties to be found in wreaking havoc, making a mess." In "a panorama of melting tanks, flying bodies, crashing walls, awesome craters and fissures in the earth," Sontag argues, we viewers experience "the primitive gratifications of science fiction films . . . the aesthetic enjoyment of suffering and disaster." Yet *kaijū eiga* are not just safe, vicarious and cathartic ecstasies of urban obliteration; as Sontag further claims, films like the Godzilla series address two fundamental dilemmas characteristic of atomic-age life:

> We live under continual threat of two equally fearful,
> but seemingly opposed, destinies: unremitting banality
> and inconceivable terror. It is fantasy, served out in
> large rations by the popular arts, which allows most
> people to cope with these twin specters. For one job
> that fantasy can do is to lift us out of the unbearably
> humdrum and to distract us from terrors—real or an-
> ticipated—by an escape into exotic, dangerous situa-
> tions which have last-minute happy endings. But
> another of the things that fantasy can do is to normal-
> ize what is psychologically unbearable, thereby inuring
> us to it.[27]

Godzilla's orgies of destruction thus relieve us of the tedium
of modern life while simultaneously dulling us to the horrors
of nuclear holocaust, neutralizing our fear of actual annihilation by the recurrent spectacle of cinematic doomsdays.

This brings us, unavoidably, to Freudianism. According
to theorist and critic Noel Carroll, "As a matter of social convention, psychoanalysis is more or less the *lingua franca* of
the horror film and thus the privileged critical tool for dis-
cussing the genre." "We have all learned," he adds, "to treat
the creatures of the night . . . as creatures of the id."[28] That is
to say, in a Freudian universe, monsters like Godzilla are an
externalization of all civilized people's internal conflicts with
their primitive, instinctual, wishful, chaotic id, or unconscious. Monster movies, then, in the words of critic Margaret
Tarratt, "arrive at social comment through a dramatization
of the individual's anxiety about his or her own repressed
sexual desires, which are incompatible with the morals of
civilized life."[29] So far so good. And, as Chon Noriega describes it, such psychoanalytic criticism can even help us understand, in a comprehensible and commonsensical way,
children's fascination with Godzilla:

> The basic framework the films establish may explain
> why these films have been so popular among younger

viewers. The monster can be seen to symbolize the viewer-child's conscious and unconscious antisocial impulses, which are simultaneously acted out in grand spectacle while being redirected toward the good of society by the filmic-child which whom the viewer identifies. The films resolve or alleviate the contradictions inherent in childhood and puberty. Thus Godzilla joins the ranks of the Teenage Werewolf and other archetypal monsters in expressing anxieties about the uncontrollable changes of puberty.[30]

Things only begin to get a little weird when scholars begin to hunt down the hidden sexual symbolism in horror movies and explain—in detail I could really live without—how beasties like Godzilla represent our repressed desires for promiscuity, bisexuality, homosexuality, female and child sexuality, and so on and so forth. Thus the king of the monsters, with that big thrashing tail of his, becomes a phallic symbol, and his devastating rampages become expressions of our unleashed sexual impulses. Giant insects and spiders—which proliferated in classic American sci-fi movies as well as the Godzilla series—arc apparently particularly laden with Freudian meaning. An aversion to monstrous spiders, one analyst tells us, "expresses dread of mother-incest and horror of the female genitals"; to another writer, insects become potent cinematic symbols of desire "not only because of their resemblance to hands—the hairy hands of masturbation—but also because of their cultural association with impurity."[31] Eeewww! I'll never be able to look at Kumonga, a mammoth tarantula that lives on Monster Island and occasionally mixes it up with Godzilla and the gang, in the same way again. And what the heck about Mothra? Especially those larval Mothra: they're as phallic as all get-out, and remember how, in *Godzilla vs. the Thing,* they squirt streams of a sticky white substance out of their "mouths" at Godzilla, gumming him up until he looks like a big marshmallow? Eeewww! Teacher says to wash your mind out with soap and write "I will not listen to Herr Doctor Freud anymore" on the blackboard one hundred times. And stop watching those damned Godzilla movies, they're just *filthy!*

Psychoanalytic criticism can make you cringe and snigger and, if you take it too seriously, can sap the joy out of those beloved old creature features we all grew up with. Thankfully, Freudianism isn't the only theory on the block, and there are plenty more scholarly perspectives on Godzilla that one could pick and choose from, if one had the interest and the time to do so. Some students of environmental studies have begun to reflect on science fiction films from an ecological standpoint, which certainly might be a revealing way of examining the Godzilla series.[32] A new subfield of culture studies, tentatively cohering around the label "monster theory," aspires to investigate how societies and their collective behavior are revealed through the monstrous specters they create. Monsters, it seems, are "a category that is itself a kind of limit case, an extreme version of marginalization, an abjecting epistemological device basic to the mechanics of deviance construction and identity formation."[33] Uh huh. One has to wonder what's really more grotesque, the subject that monster theorists study or the jargon they produce by the ream. Marxist scholars are little better, characterizing monsters as the symbols of entrepreneurial capitalism and "the antihuman power emanating from the predatory bourgeoisie of Leninist demonology."[34] Excellent work has been done on the folklore and history of Japanese ghosts, ghouls, and demons, a context into which Godzilla could fruitfully be placed.[35] And, of course, there will always be those academic purists who refuse to consider Godzilla worthy of serious analysis at all, writing off the denizens of *kaijū eiga* as "a lot of rather stupid monsters" or "bugaboos dressed up in atomic hats."[36]

Where does that leave us, then? What are the Godzilla films all about? Tell us, professor, what does Godzilla *mean?*

One wishes such questions had easy answers. One also wishes, of course, that paper milk cartons opened cleanly, that the Red Sox would win the World Series, and that the government would place a moratorium on reality television and body piercing. But life isn't that simple or kind. Godzilla is not a transparent symbol, a code to be painstakingly deciphered, or a neat building block for the scholarly theory-of-the-month. Godzilla, for those of us who might aspire to analyzing him, is a moving target, a constantly shifting metaphor, an unstable and contradictory icon, a chimera built of as many different interpretations as there are people who've seen a Godzilla film or heard tell of the king of the monsters.

Perhaps this is why so many moviegoers, of such disparate backgrounds, of all ages, sexes, races, creeds and nationalities, can relate to Godzilla and can embrace him as their own monster. The very fact that Godzilla defies easy categorization, that a man in a latex suit can simultaneously critique authority, stoke Japanese nationalism, be a therapeutic balm for tortured adolescents, and signify a wrestling, fire-belching phallus (Eeewww!), may just be the reason we can all love him so much. Godzilla's fundamental character—and charm—may well be his ambiguity, his ambivalence as a symbol, and his frustrating elusiveness as a subject of interpretation. Rooted both in a specific history and in the dispersed imaginations of tens of millions of fans, Godzilla seems at once reassuringly real and magically ephemeral.

So what does Godzilla mean? He means everything and nothing, he means what you want him to and what I want him to, and oh, lest we forget in all this serious cogitating, Godzilla means fun.

CHAPTER 4

THE MAKING OF AN AMERICAN ICON

LATE LAST SUMMER, I HAD THE OCCASION to be marooned for an afternoon at the Kansas State Fair. The "Party on the Prairie," as the marketers called it, was very much what you would expect of such a down-home extravaganza: pig races out by the rodeo arena, rows of threshers, gleaners and other incomprehensible pieces of farm machinery, a faded country music starlet in the amphitheater, the distinctive scent of deep-fried Twinkies and corn dogs wafting over all. To escape the intense heat (and all the perky young people plugging cell phone plans), I ducked into the fine arts pavilion, a very grand name for a utilitarian prefab metal barn. Amidst the countless 4H crocheting projects, photographs of cute cats, hand-carved trolls and creepy, creepy sock monkeys, something caught my eye. It was among the entries in the "sculpture, mixed media (youth division)" category, a group of unintentionally abstract works generally constructed from old egg cartons, pipe cleaners, and Styrofoam packing peanuts. It was Godzilla, no question about it, twelve gleaming inches of reptilian glory fashioned out of cut, torn, and twisted 7-Up cans, with glinting aluminum fangs, spiky dorsal fins and an articulated green tail. The "un-cola" king of the monsters hadn't won a ribbon—darn those snotty State Fair judges and their bias against representational art!—but it made my afternoon. Even here, in the wholesome heart of middle America, Godzilla—or at least a jerry-built, recyclable version thereof—was an unmistakable presence.

Fifty years ago, no one in the United States could have told you what a "Godzilla" was, any more than they could have identified sushi, karaoke, or a Toyota. Today, however, Godzilla is—to the very last scale, sinew, and claw—an inalienable part of American popular culture. A 2002 poll conducted by the American Psychological Association discovered that Godzilla was the third-most-popular movie monster in the United States, just behind Dracula and the uncertainly monstrous Freddy Kreuger, but well ahead of erstwhile competitors King Kong and Frankenstein. Japan's most successful cinematic export is recognized, idolized, and invoked from coast to coast, in newspapers and on television, in Tinseltown movies and Motown hip-hop, in poetry anthologies and the commercial marketplace, and in every imaginable corner of the World Wide Web. Godzilla is a true cultural icon, a celebrity of the first rank, a free-floating symbol with a life of its own, a peer in America's collective imagination of Marilyn Monroe, the Mona Lisa, Barbie, Spam, and the Statue of Liberty.

This chapter will trace the process by which Godzilla came to be imprinted on the American national psyche. How did the Godzilla films come to the United States? In what ways were they altered in the transition across the Pacific? How has the king of the monsters come to infiltrate all the nooks and crannies of American pop culture? Don't expect

an answer here as to why we've embraced Godzilla so en-
thusiastically over the past half century—the next chapter
will take up that topic—but instead, just prepare to revel in
the depth and breadth of our collective obsession with a
cheesy B-movie hero. Teddy Roosevelt once said, "Like all
Americans, I like big things: big prairies, big forests and
mountains, big wheat-fields, railroads, and herds of cattle too,
big factories, steam boats and everything else." There's no
question that the old Rough Rider would have come to love
Godzilla, too; as the biggest media idol ever—forty-eight
meters taller than Elvis, tens of thousands of pounds heavier
than Oprah—how could any of us Americans resist the monster's allure?

Godzilla arrived in the United States at an auspicious time.
The 1950s and 1960s were fat days for imported movies in
America, and—thankfully—not just in the art houses, where
highbrow, subtitled foreign films attracted audiences of
urban sophisticates. No, Godzilla—along with ghouls, mutants, and murderous creatures from studios around the
world—found his stateside home in modest neighborhood
theaters, on Saturday afternoon double bills, on the big
screens of suburban drive-ins, and, eventually, on television
sets across the nation. Godzilla was, from the get-go, a man
of the people and, in particular, of the millions of American
teenagers who flocked to B movies and exploitation pics
through the postwar decades. From saturation bookings,
kooky marketing gimmicks, and endless late-night reruns a
cinematic legend was born.

The trajectory of the American motion picture industry
after World War II very closely paralleled that of Japan. An
incredible postwar boom in movie attendance—with more

than 4.5 billion tickets sold in 1948—quickly soured to a bust in the 1950s, as television and suburbanization sapped audiences away from the downtown movie palaces. The major Hollywood studios were also rocked by sweeping antitrust rulings that prohibited them from operating their own theaters, which in turn forced them to abandon their production of popular (but only marginally profitable) B movies. These developments—described by one scholar as "an apparently irreversible decline in movie attendance and the radical disruption of the industry's integrated and efficient institutional structure"—opened the door for entrepreneurial upstart distributors like the famed American International Pictures (AIP) to claim old markets and develop new ones.[1] AIP, which would eventually handle several of the Godzilla films, prospered in a difficult economic climate by focusing on a key target audience—teenagers—and offering them movies that were timely, sensational, exciting and (above all) profitable. Youth were the most dependable moviegoers of the 1950s and 1960s and distributors like AIP catered to teen tastes shamelessly, supplying low-budget films made by American independent producers or imported from overseas studios.

Japanese *kaijū eiga* fit the bill perfectly for the burgeoning American teenie market. The rights to Godzilla films could be purchased cheaply, and the product met all the expectations of U.S. distributors, exhibitors and audiences: Japanese creature features were visually appealing, packed with special effects, vaguely topical, and, best of all, were not preachy or moralistic, a sure turnoff for independent-minded American teenagers. Moreover, Japan's giant monster output kicked into high gear in the early 1960s, a time when strong demand for science fiction films remained but Hollywood was rapidly abandoning the genre. The uncertain quality of the Shōwa Godzilla offerings was not a barrier to their entry in the U.S. market: Tōhō's pandering to

Japanese youngsters appealed to American audiences as well and, in any case, the films' teenage clientele was not particularly discerning. As the Drifters sang in 1964, "Saturday night at the movies / Who cares what picture you see / When you're hugging with your baby / In last row in the balcony?" The humor of the classic Godzilla films was a plus as well; teen moviegoers expected more "titters than terror" at horror films and, in the industry, Godzilla was recognized as a moneymaking "hoho from Tōhō."[2]

The double feature was the bread and butter of AIP and the other B-movie impresarios. American audiences had, since the first "dual" was introduced in 1932, come to expect the value and variety offered by theatrical double bills. Godzilla performed well in this role and over the years was twinned with some unlikely company: *War of the Gargantuas,* an odd 1966 Tōhō film about shaggy overgrown cavemen; *Island of the Burning Damned,* a British horror cheapie with Christopher Lee; *Agent 8 3/4,* a lamentable James Bond spoof; and, most memorably of all, *Harum Scarum,* a 1965 Elvis laugher set in the Middle East. As Vincent Canby wrote in the *New York Times:* "'Something terrible is about to happen' mutters an inscrutable, English-dubbed Japanese actor early in 'Ghidorah, the Three-Headed Monster,' and during the next three hours his prophecy comes only too true. It is hard to imagine a more perfect blending of witlessness than this double bill of 'Harum Scarum' [and] an all-star Japanese monster film. . . . Elvis is prettier than Ghidorah, and has two fewer heads, but both characters are definitely the products of the special effects departments."[3]

Kaijū eiga also found a welcoming home in drive-in theaters, venues that boomed in number, size, and popularity in the late 1940s and early 1950s. Though there were fewer than a hundred drive-ins in America in 1941, there were more than five thousand by 1956, accounting for a tenth of the nation's moviegoers. The largest of the species—

the twenty-six-hundred-car Timonium in Maryland and the three-thousand-car Troy near Detroit—could accommodate far more people than Radio City Music Hall, the country's largest traditional movie theater. Most of the major Hollywood studios were loath to release first-run blockbusters to the drive-in trade, which made the outdoor theaters natural customers for the independent distributors and their cheap-and-nasty features. The bright colors, big monsters, and clear story lines of the Godzilla films played well at the drive-ins and with their core audiences, working-class families (often with the kids in pajamas in the back seat) and the inevitable teenagers, necking, horsing around, and occasionally watching the movies. Neither the customers nor the exhibitors had very high standards for the features being screened. In fact, many drive-in operators endorsed the booking of third-rate shows: profitability was often dependent on concession income and, as one theater owned testified, "The worse the pictures are, the more stuff we sell."[4] One can only imagine all the popcorn and Milk Duds that must have flown out of the refreshment stands on the nights *Godzilla vs. Gigan* was playing.

Publicity stunts and marketing ploys were a major factor in the success of exploitation pictures and the creation of a campy public persona for Godzilla. One of the secrets of distributors like AIP was that even though their movies might be cheesy, their showmanship and sales campaigns were always aggressive and state of the art. "No gimmick was too farfetched to sell these films," one historian has observed. "Life insurance policies against the unlikely possibility of succumbing to heart attacks brought on by the feeble plot twists and special effects; sections of the cinema fitted with seat belts to prevent you jumping out of your skin; . . . seats wired electronically to give your back a little frisson when the Tingler got loose in the audience."[5] The press books sent out to theater managers invariably contained a

weird and wacky selection of "seat-selling slants" guaranteed to induce teenagers to part with their admission fees.
For *Godzilla vs. the Thing,* for example, AIP advised managers to "spot all places where buildings have been wrecked
or razed . . . and post signs on surrounding fences reading
'Godzilla fought the Thing here.'" Stenciling giant Godzilla
footprints on the sidewalks leading to a theater was an easy
and frequently recommended stunt. To sell *Godzilla vs. the
Smog Monster,* the PR men suggested having "a local bar
owner create a new mixed drink called the Godzilla cocktail—'it clears that five o'clock smog from your brain'"—and
teaming up with local boy scouts to champion "Godzilla as a
fighter against pollution . . . just as Smokey the Bear sym-
bolizes the campaign against forest fires."[6] Silly but true, and
surprisingly effective.

Although double features, drive-ins, and hokey publicity
schemes may have given Godzilla considerable public profile,
especially among America's youth, it was television that
eventually transformed a rubbery movie character into an instantly recognizable national icon. In the early days of TV,
with young stations struggling to fill air time and competing
furiously to wow their audiences, feature films were a highly
desirable commodity. And so for the same reasons that
Godzilla films became staples of atomic-age movie houses—
they were cheap to rent, exciting to watch, popular with the
kids and available for the showing—they also became work-
horses of Saturday afternoon and late-night television. As
early as 1958, only a couple of years after its theatrical release, *Godzilla, King of the Monsters* turned up on WOR-TV,
channel 9, in New York City, where it was shown six times
over the course of a single week. By the 1960s, Godzilla was
making frequent television appearances in the Big Apple, including an occasional Thanksgiving Day slot, and by the
1970s was a real regular, airing monthly and often every few
weeks. A number of Godzilla features bypassed the theaters

altogether and went directly to TV, including the Shōwa groaners *Godzilla vs. the Sea Monster* and *Son of Godzilla,* as well as most of the Heisei and Shinsei offerings, which have migrated straight to video, been released over pay-per-view, or ended up on a cable channel. Henry Saperstein, who was instrumental in bringing many Tōhō films to U.S. screens, reported in 1995 that a Godzilla movie had appeared on some television station somewhere in America every week for the previous thirty-five years.[7] Wow. With national coverage and market penetration like that—not to mention all those footprints painted on sidewalks in the 1960s—it's really no wonder that Godzilla has become such an indelible part of all our lives.

It almost goes without saying that the Godzilla we Americans came to love was quite different from the monster created, screened, and adored in Japan. First of all, and most obviously, was the issue of language. The Godzilla films that you and I grew up with at the drive-in, at the sticky-floored movie palace, or on the "Million Dollar Movie" were invariably dubbed; the original Japanese-language track was, of course, impossible, and who among the teenie moviegoer set or the bleary-eyed late-night TV crowd was prepared to read subtitles, even in the cause of entertainment? The dubbing of the Godzilla films was so memorably and deliciously awful that it has become a running joke and, in many ways, a distinguishing characteristic of the *kaijū eiga* genre in America. Sounds not matching lip motions, fake "Oriental" accents, cartoonish voices, ludicrous translations—either the apotheosis of cheesy goodness or the ultimate degradation of the filmmakers' art, depending on how you look at it. If you can stop laughing, that is.

The crews responsible for dubbing Japanese films like the Godzilla series were an odd and diverse lot of people, running from professionals in New York and Hollywood, to expatriate dilettantes in Tokyo and teams in Hong Kong more used to the grunts and groans of martial arts movies. Many of the operations took the work seriously, laboring assiduously to match dialogue to lip motions on screen, to creating translations that reflected the original Japanese meaning, and to using voices at least similar to those of the Japanese actors in the films. And some respectable talent was used in bringing English to the Godzilla greats: Chinese-American actors James Hong and Keye Luke (who for decades would be the leading Asian men of American movies and TV), George Takei (the inimitable Sulu of *Star Trek*), Hal Linden (who spoke as the bank robber in *Godzilla vs. the Sea Monster* before becoming Barney Miller), Daws Butler (later immortalized as Yogi the Bear), Marvin Miller (the voice of Robby the Robot in *Forbidden Planet*), Peter Fernandez (whose words came out of Speed Racer's disturbing, semianimated lips), and Paul Frees (the "man of a thousand voices," better known as Boris Badenov from the Bullwinkle cartoons and the giggle of the Pillsbury Dough Boy).

The "translated" dialogue of the Godzilla films, often improvised and frequently downright nonsensical, could even be more painful and humorous than the technical deficiencies of the dubbing process. What fan can forget the lines, delivered with perfect seriousness, from *Godzilla Raids Again* (aka *Gigantis the Fire Monster*): "Ah, banana oil!" and "Ha, ha, ha. Trying to please a woman is like swimming the ocean." Or the lines inserted in the English dub of *King Kong vs. Godzilla,* presumably intended to make the American version funnier than the Japanese: "My corns always hurt when they're near a monster" and Mr. Tako's famous exclamation, "King Kong can't make a monkey out of me!"

Or my own favorite, offered by the old seaman in *Godzilla vs. the Smog Monster:* "The fishing in the bay is done now, if all we bring up are monsters."

Love it or hate it, laugh or groan, the dubbing of the classic Godzilla movies has been a much derided but sometimes overlooked part of the series' endearing charm in America. While purists may tisk at the corny, inaccurate translations and technical sloppiness, that certain flavor—of lips and voices doing their own things, of dialogue unaccountably stilted and just plain bad—contributed in both subliminal and laugh-out-loud ways to the fun, fantasy, and refreshing otherworldliness of the Godzilla features. Even if big-time wrestling in rubber suits wasn't your thing, who couldn't manage a smile and a little snigger at a Japanese general—mouth going one way, words another—as he gives the grave order "Contact Space Hunter Universe M. Tell them we need Gigan's help immediately!"[8]

Many of the Godzilla films also underwent heavy editing for American release. Some, like *Gojira* in its transition to *Godzilla, King of the Monsters,* were subjected to major surgery, with whole sections removed and new footage of American actors inserted. *King Kong vs. Godzilla* suffered in this way, with absolutely superfluous scenes of a smug United Nations news anchor inserted; *Gojira* (1984) was repackaged as *Godzilla 1985* with a hefty and grizzled Raymond Burr brought back to reprise his role as Steve Martin in a series of extraneous and uninspired sequences. In other films, the American distributors simply sliced and diced, removing and rearranging scenes to shorten the picture or "improve" upon the Japanese original. As Henry Saperstein explained it: "Every Japanese monster film starts with a conference. Either the press or government officials or scientists, and they lay the foundation for the story and the characters and the threat and a plan of what they're going to do about it. This goes on for five minutes, by which time every American viewer tunes it out, particularly on television. We would edit the films and make such additions or deletions as we felt would make better progression."[9]

In some cases, the search for "better progression" meant a new prologue for the film, as in *Gigantis the Fire Monster,* which began with the condescending voice-over, "This, then, is the story of the price of progress to a little nation of people." Other titles underwent wholesale mangling. In *King Kong vs. Godzilla,* the parodic elements of the Japanese version were excised, and in *Ghidorah, the Three-Headed Monster,* scenes were extensively reshuffled, with no evidence of narrative enhancement. From time to time, even relatively minor tinkering on the American end resulted in head-scratching lapses in continuity, unexplained developments, and sheer nonsense. Violent scenes and the odd mild oath were axed from *Godzilla vs. Gigan* and the later Shōwa films, presumably to protect delicate American sensibilities and ensure a bankable G rating. The musical scores of the Japanese films also received little respect from Saperstein, AIP et al., and Ifukube Akira's magnificent original soundtracks were frequently replaced by chintzy stock music from third-rate old thrillers.

As was the case with less-than-perfect dubbing, the clumsy and obvious American editing often just added to the cheesy, campy appeal of the Godzilla films. Who needs a smooth and logical story line if disbelief has already been so utterly suspended (a giant radioactive lizard, a Christlike moth-savior, etc.)? As later experience would demonstrate, however, while unintentional campiness could be winsome and amusing, trying too hard to make a Godzilla movie deliberately droll and self-consciously cute could be an absolute disaster. For both of the Godzilla features released theatrically in the United States over the past quarter century—*Godzilla 1985* and *Godzilla 2000*—Hollywood distributors attempted to retool the relatively thoughtful, well produced, and serious Japanese films into the cheesy, 1970s-style side-splitters that they believed the American public demanded. *Godzilla 1985* was dragged into very unfunny mediocrity by the inclusion of a wise-cracking, smart-aleck U.S. Army major—who utters idiotic lines like "That's quite an urban renewal program they've got going over there!"—in the scenes added for the American version. The film's marketing campaign also revealed it to be, in the words of one critic, "a half-hearted, half-assed parody": print ads heralded the return of the king of the monsters with slogans like "There goes the neighborhood!" and "The ultimate party animal is dropping by. . . . You're going to get smashed!"[10] In the U.S. release of *Godzilla 2000,* moronic dubbing and ham-fisted cutesiness were the offenders. It might have seemed like a winner of an idea to dub in lines like "Great Caesar's ghost!" and "Gott in himmel!" or close the film with "The End" and a big question mark, but such cynical and artificial yuks just fell flat.

In the final reckoning, that peculiar magic of Godzilla, that odd endearing quality we remember from Saturday matinees, that something special about old, innocent, and authentic creature features, cannot be recaptured with a sneer here and an inside joke there, with a few extra scenes shot on a Burbank soundstage or a tongue-in-cheek publicity blitz. The magic of Godzilla—those fifty years of memories, laughs, groans, roars, wrestling, and stomping—is deeper and more genuine, a quality to be celebrated rather than fabricated, reveled in rather than capitalized on. And, happily, that elusive, contagious magic—Godzilla's mojo, if you will—endures all around us in America today.

We'll probably never know exactly how and why Godzilla—of all the stars of 1960s drive-in howlers, of all the monsters running through our collective imagination—became one of the touchstones of American culture, a symbol rich in meaning, a metaphor for everything from U.S. foreign policy to the behavior of Massachusetts snapping turtles. Godzilla's cultural resonance is clearly of long standing; as early as 1964, a *New York Times* reporter could observe, "A little girl of 7, beautiful as a dream in spite of a temporary absence of front teeth, said to a girl who was walking beside her in a school crocodile supervised by a nun, 'It was like the fight between Godzilla and King Kong.' What was this nightmare battle? The crocodile moved sedately away. We'll never know."[11] This little vignette demonstrates that, even in the mid-1960s, elementary school children, a presumably adult journalist, and much of the readership of the *New York Times* could be reasonably expected to know who Godzilla was and what the epic nature of his fights entailed. Today, of course, the name and image of Godzilla are everywhere, applied to practically everything imaginable, and recognized by virtually every American. Godzilla the movie monster may have started out in Japan, but Godzilla the cultural icon belongs to everybody.

Most Americans would probably first identify Godzilla with something big, mean, and fearsome. Thus, when health activists in 1995 wanted to excoriate movie-theater popcorn as a sodium- and fat-laden diet buster, they billed it as "the Godzilla of junk food." Tiger Woods, when he was the young phenom of the PGA, was often described in the media as the king of the monsters: "He went through championship venues like Godzilla went through Gotham." When soccer star and global heartthrob David Beckham arrived in Tokyo in the summer of 2003 to compete in the World Cup, one newspaper raved that he was "one of the biggest things on two legs to hit this burg since Godzilla waddled up from the murk of the bay."[12] All across America, greasy spoons with mammoth sandwiches call them "Godzilla burgers" while large animals of any genus, species, or order—caddis flies, mussels, raccoons, Florida tarpon, Hawaiian lizards, clams in the soft mud of the Oregon shore—earn the Godzilla sobriquet if they are large, stubborn, or surly enough.

Political commentators are particularly fond of the Godzilla metaphor. Unstoppable front-runners are almost invariably honored with such comparisons, with one pundit christening Arnold Schwarzenegger, in the days just before his run for the California governorship, "Godzilla the Hun." A Green Party presidential candidate, capturing his opinion of the Republican and Democratic alternatives as well as their presumed dominance, described the 2004 election as a choice "between Godzilla and Frankenstein." Linking America's global stance to the actions of the king of the monsters became extremely common after the 2003 invasion of Iraq: the *Village Voice* declared that "Uncle Sam seems to be morphing into Godzilla," and Thomas Friedman wrote in the *New York Times* that "suddenly, Puff the Magic Dragon—a benign U.S. hegemon touching everyone economically and culturally—[has turned] into Godzilla, a wounded, angry, raging beast touching people militarily." Even foreign critics embraced this imagery; as a former Lebanese ambassador to Washington wrote, "The people of the world hate the United States because it touches their lives ... militarily (the so-called Godzilla factor) without giving them a say in the matter."[13]

Godzilla also rears his scaly head in the business pages of the daily newspapers. Aggressive, rapacious firms and monopolies (or at least companies that aspire to such market dominance) are commonly referred to as Godzillas. Not surprisingly, if you had a nickel for every time Microsoft or Wal-Mart has been compared to a certain radioactive reptile from Japan, you'd be very, very wealthy indeed. When it acquired the *International Herald Tribune* in 2002, the *New York Times* was described (by its own editor, among others) as "the Godzilla of U.S. journalism," now taking its predatory ambitions abroad. The merger of three large financial institutions in Japan in 1999 inspired business writers to tag the result—the largest commercial bank in the world— "Godzilla bank." And renowned business strategist Kenichi Ohmae has even included Godzilla in a grand theory of the postindustrial economy that contrasts sluggish old manufacturing titans to the voracious "Godzilla companies" of the new high-tech world:

> The Godzilla companies that have thrived on the new economy have no precedents either for the speed of their ascent or the unconventional methods they used to pursue their goals. They represent a new corporate species, genetically programmed to grow and consume markets and resources at rates that would have seemed unthinkable before. They suck up the world's investment capital; they drain Wall Street and NASDAQ. Money that goes to them is not available elsewhere. Like Godzilla, they hatch fast, grow fast, and consume everything they can.[14]

Maybe the next film from Tōhō should be *Godzilla vs. Sun Microsystems.*

Godzilla is, and apparently long has been, a popular nickname. Way back in 1969, some lighthearted sanitation workers in Scottsdale, Arizona, bestowed the Godzilla moniker on a new (and particularly ungainly looking) garbage truck. In the early 1970s, Rumanian tennis bad-boy Ilie "Nasty" Nastase christened his clean-cut rival Stan Smith "Godzilla," though much of the media felt the name fit the nicknamer far better than the nicknamee. The king of the monsters' most prominent namesake these days is undoubtedly Hideki "Godzilla" Matsui, the New York Yankees slugger, who picked up the tag in his days as the home run–hitting wunderkind of Tokyo's Yomiuri Giants. Numerous American boxers and wrestlers call themselves Godzilla;

pleasure boats across the country bear the name (how appropriate to stalk the Godzilla of bass with Godzilla the bass boat); automobiles, from street rods to rally cars to lowriders, have assumed the monster's menacing, butch identity; pet Godzillas—beloved dogs, cats, guinea pigs, ferrets, goldfish and parakeets—are everywhere. Heck, even the mother of all icebergs, a frozen Antarctic behemoth 180 miles long and known scientifically as B–15, was affectionately nicknamed "Godzilla" by polar researchers.

If Godzilla clearly connotes size, strength, and attitude, the monster also strongly evokes images of Japan, and Asia more generally, among the American public. In the late 1980s and early 1990s, when the Japanese economy seemed to be a clear and present danger to American manufacturing, Godzilla became a powerful metaphor for the Japanese threat, gracing the cover of *Newsweek* and appearing in countless print media stories, wire-service reports and television news segments. When the SARS scare hit in 2002, radio shock-jock Glenn Beck's website included a doctored still from the 1954 *Gojira,* with the monster swinging a commuter train from his mouth, although he now sported a surgical mask as well. The SARS Art Project, a Los Angeles–based online gallery, featured a satirical animated short "Godzilla vs. SARS" that depicted the king of the monsters blasting the renegade virus with an antimicrobial death ray, powered by American cough syrup.[15] The association of Godzilla with Japan is so strong that when Seattle Mariners outfielder Ichirō Suzuki—a Japanese to be sure, but not an acknowledged *kaijū eiga* expert—appeared recently on HBO's "On the Record," Bob Costas felt emboldened to ask him, "Who wins a fair fight, King Kong or Godzilla?" The poised Ichirō responded, none too diplomatically for an American audience, "Hmmm. Godzilla breathes fire, you know. . . . If Godzilla doused King Kong in gasoline and then spat fire on him, he'd be cooked. Godzilla would win the battle." Ouch.

Godzilla, it seems, is just ubiquitous. Sometimes the symbolism is clear, as with Slate.com's parodic website advertising the Godzilla SUV ("When you're driving the Godzilla, they will run for cover. And if they don't? Well, it's not like they weren't warned").[16] But what does it mean that a big flowery Godzilla graced a float (sponsored by Honda nonetheless) in the 1990 Rose Parade? Or that Godzilla won the 1996 MTV Lifetime Achievement Award (following in the hallowed footsteps of Jackie Chan, Shaft, and the Three Stooges)? Or that people the world over, from Yokohama to Racine, Wisconsin, seem to enjoy decorating Christmas trees like Godzilla (an admittedly bottom-heavy, tannenbaum-shaped monster)? Or, in the Shroud of Turin, "Is that Elvis on my pancake?" department, the fact that one Dale Hillyard, an otherwise mild-mannered North Carolinian, spotted a huge mound of kudzu in his suburban Charlotte neighborhood that looked just like . . . you guessed it, Godzilla? The thirty-foot-tall mound of reptilian vine, baptized "Kudzilla" by the awed Mr. Hillyard, may not have been the spitting image of the king of the monsters, but God—and Godzilla—works in mysterious ways.[17]

Godzilla has even become a part of the English language, in the form of the pervasive and ever-popular suffix -zilla. The origins of this distinctive usage are uncertain, although one can easily imagine a young marketing exec, several decades back, in the best traditions of American efficiency (and general laziness), shortening a bulky line like "A milk shake as big as Godzilla!" to a catchy "Shakezilla!" These five little letters, which transform any run-of-the-mill old word into something oversized, mean as heck, and just plain excessive, the king of whatever you want, now pop up virtually everywhere in American culture. Almost a thousand domain names with a -zilla ending have been registered on the Internet, from the humor and blogging site davezilla.com to the open-source software development portal mozilla.org. Bridezilla, a term used to describe a perfectly normal woman who, once she gets an engagement ring, becomes greedy, needy, and obnoxious, has become a commonly used term: a Bridezilla comic strip about "the beast called bride-to-be" appeared in *Modern Bride* in 1999, a book with the title *Bridezilla: True Tales from Etiquette Hell* was published in 2002, and the inevitable Fox reality TV special aired in the summer of 2003. The suffix has been especially well liked by American advertisers, always eager for that little bit of extra hype. Thus Merit cigarettes once billed themselves as "Flavorzilla"; Sears marketed a line of "monstrously strong" garbage bags under the name "Bagzilla"; radio stations and stereo manufacturers have flogged their wares using "Quadzilla." One enterprising restaurant in Panama City, Florida, promoted its lobster and seafood specials with the memorable slogan "Lobzilla vs. Crab Kong."

Even a desultory search on the World Wide Web will reveal that the -zilla suffix has been embraced by Americans of all shapes, sizes, persuasions, and perversions. If you log on to Google and type in the fusion of any noun in the English language and the magical -zilla ending, you are more than likely to get some hits, and often a downright tidal wave of them. "Dogzilla"—which one learns is the title of a popular children's book, the name of a defunct Boston rock band, and the nickname of a prototype guitar amplifier, among other things—gets you more than ten thousand pages to look at. "Spoonzilla" reveals a dishwasher with a silverware basket big enough to accommodate "Count Spatula, Spoonzilla, Forkenstein, and Knife of the Living Dead," as well as 550 other hits. Godzilla seems to be a winner for

XXX sites, as the prominence of "pornzilla" and thumb-zilla.com suggests. "Buttzilla" turns out to be less lurid than one might expect, and brings up yet another rock band (big surprise) and a typographical font (which makes far less sense). "Spongezilla" lives on the web, as do "spudzilla," "deskzilla" and "moldzilla." Tracking all the links for "Je-suszilla" and "Christzilla" could take you most of an after-noon and, in the interests of interfaith evenhandedness, you might want to check out the hits for "Buddhazilla," "Al-lahzilla" and "Yahwehzilla" as well. Don't even get started on perennial favorites "carzilla" and "truckzilla."

What makes the -zilla form so darned popular in Amer-ica is anybody's guess, and even the best lexicographical and sociological tools are unlikely to yield very persuasive ex-planations. Other descriptive suffixes are not uncommon— the compulsive -aholic, the retro -omatic, the superlative -ville—but none seems to have achieved the kind of reso-nance and broad cultural acceptance that -zilla has. The lin-guistic cross-pollination of Godzilla with completely unrelated words is tongue-in-cheek, a bit subversive (as the prevalence of garage bands, porn sites, mass marketers, and bloggers using the term suggests), and is certainly not hoity-toity, high-culture stuff. Like its namesake, -zilla has attitude. And, of course, adding those two reptilian syllables makes just about anything sound cool, as well as a little bit silly and a lot fun. In the creative, fluid linguistic hodgepodge that is American English today, -zilla is, without doubt, the suf-fixzilla of our age.

Next to knocking down cities and battling monstrous adver-saries, Godzilla's most important role over the years has prob-ably been as a commercial shill. In Japan, Tōhō has licensed the use of Godzilla's image to sell almost everything under the sun, from photocopiers to condominiums, from Liquid Paper to Choco-Snack Gojira. A Japanese food processor with an odd sense of humor has marketed "Godzilla Meat" (3.5-ounce tins of corned beef) as well as "Godzilla Eggs" (canned quail eggs) and alleged containers of Rodan (barbecued chicken). If Japanese consumers can stomach whale, why not giant radioactive lizard? There's a Godzilla adventure ride at a theme park outside Tokyo, the king of the monsters has graced Japanese postage stamps, and even Mothra has gotten in on the residuals, hawking the Maiko ski resort to young female urbanites.

Godzilla has also been a popular pitchman in the United States. In a series of television commercials in the 1980s, Godzilla extolled the virtues of Dr. Pepper; under the slogan "Out of the Ordinary," the monster (and a new female creature dubbed "Newzilla") forsake stomping cities for a swig of that sweet, carbonated prune soda. In 1992, in one of his most memorable PR appearances, Godzilla went one-on-one with surly NBA standout Charles Barkley in the smoldering ruins of Tokyo, all for the benefit of Nike. Although the king of the monsters showed some nice moves, Sir Charles—whose ego and massive swooshed shoes would have dwarfed any *kaijū eiga* star—ended up taking it to the hoop and sending Godzilla sprawling. The 1998 TriStar Godzilla was prostituted every which way but loose to turn a marketing buck, most memorably in a couple of clever TV spots featuring the Taco Bell Chihuahua. Hey Tōhō, *yo quiero* royalty income! Just to be fair, Godzilla has done his fair share of public service announcements. He's come out against cigarettes, which makes him the only Japanese male who doesn't smoke. What's more, he recently appeared with Minilla (using stock footage from *Son of Godzilla*) in a disarmingly sweet television ad for the National Fatherhood Institute, the theme song from *The Courtship of Eddie's Father* making it all seem so warm and cuddly.[18]

Before we dismiss Godzilla as a mere pawn of the marketplace, a moneychanger in the temple of monsters, we should recognize that Japan's saurian giant has also appealed to the higher instincts of humankind, stirring the creativity of writers, painters, and musicians the world over. Poets aplenty have been inspired by the king of the monsters, although amateur doggerel in fan publications tends to be the norm. A collection like Jay Snodgrass's *Monster Zero*, which uses the figure of Godzilla to illuminate the painful experiences of an American boy growing up in Japan, shows what more able practitioners can achieve. Not everyone may think a poem entitled "Godzilla Leafs through a Crate & Barrel Catalogue" qualifies as high art, but don't knock it until you've tried it.[19] Dramatists have also been moved by the big reptilian muse. *Godzilla,* a 1987 work by the avant-garde Japanese playwright Ohashi Yasuhiko, won Japan's most prestigious drama prize and has been performed internationally. A satire of the Japanese family system—as well as a heartfelt tribute to the fantasy world of *kaijū eiga*—Ohashi's play is the story of an average Japanese girl who brings her strong-and-silent-type boyfriend, Godzilla, home to meet Mom and Dad. "He was such a late bloomer and our dates were always so platonic," the besotted young woman explains. "But then one day—we'd been talking about family, where we grew up, whatever was on our minds, and then there was a lull in the conversation—he stuck his palm out, urged me to climb up, and brought me right up to his mouth. . . . It was our first kiss. It had a radioactive taste."[20]

Novelists and short story writers have been particularly enterprising in making use of Godzilla. Mark Jacobson's *Gojiro,* a book enigmatically described by its own dust jacket as "a postnuclear, postpunk manifesto of evolution and spiritual redemption" (Huh?), is probably the most ambitious

and critically acclaimed novel to take Godzilla as protago-
nist. A kind of metaphysical autobiography of the monster,
as well as a convoluted musing on nuclear anxiety, fame, and
isolation, *Gojiro* rewrites the Tōhō mythology, imagining
Godzilla as a quick-witted and sharp-tongued—but also sensitive and tortured—radioactive movie star. While Jacobson's novel is probably too self-consciously clever for all but
the hippest readers—would your Godzilla really say something like "Mary Hart! Dixie Whatley! Who are they but
jackboot dupes of the culturato-narco-leptic horde!"?—
other writers have treated the king of the monsters a little
more respectfully.[21] David Zielinski's 1990 novel *A Genuine
Monster* examines a Vietnam vet who cannot distinguish between Godzilla movies and reality; *Monster Makers, Inc.*, a
young adult title by Laurence Yep, considers the travails of
having Godzilla as a pet; distinguished writer Louise Er-
drich's short story "Sister Godzilla" uses the monster as a
metaphor and a cruel nickname. The best read of all, however, might just be Michael Reaves's little gem "Elvis Meets
Godzilla," the hilarious fictional tale of a long-lost Tōhō film
pitting the king of the monsters against The King himself. A
gentle parody of two superstars, each "a creature of excess"
gone to pot, Reaves's story insightfully captures the ways in
which cultural icons permeate, delineate, and haunt our collective imagination.

Visual artists have been inspired by Godzilla as well.
Even here in Lawrence, Kansas, a trip to a local art fair or a
holiday "bizarre bazaar" will unearth an artist or two making a creative nod to the king of the monsters. The Internet
reveals a variety of painters, photographers, and digital
artists, some amateur, some professional, who have created
visual tributes to Godzilla. There are talented illustrators
who specialize in *kaijū eiga* scenes, like the prolific Bob
Eggleton, and drawings, cartoons, and paintings by American Godzilla fans can be exceedingly imaginative, complex,

and skilled. Somewhere out there, hanging in a museum or a private collection, there may be the *ne plus ultra* of Godzilla artworks, that undiscovered Roy Lichtenstein homage to the king of the monsters (Blam! goes Tokyo), but if there is, I'm yet to find it. The noted printmaker James Munce has done a charming etching titled "G is for Giraffes and Godzillas" as part of his "Garage Bestiary" series. And back in the early 1990s, a number of Asian-American artists came together to form a support group—named, needless to say, Godzilla—in response to the lack of Asian representation in the elite Whitney Biennial. Perhaps one of the creative talents in this coalition will be inspired to create an iconic image of the icon that is Godzilla, a radioactive, scaly "Whistler's Mother" or a huge, reptilian "American Gothic."

For some reason, it has been musicians, more than other artists, who have used Godzilla and his symbolism to the fullest. There are the usual parodies and weak efforts: "Waltzing Godzilla" (sung to the tune of "Waltzing Matilda") and the predictably pathetic "Monsta' Rap" by Elvira, Mistress of the Dark, just to name a couple. Bands of all varieties and nationalities have paid their dues to the king of the monsters: Japanese artists (in albums like the 1991 "A Tribute to Godzilla") have long sung the monster's praises in styles from reggae and Celtic to technopop and ska; groups as diverse as Soundgarden, Flaming Lips, and Man or Astro-Man? have sampled Godzilla sound effects and written nostalgic lyrics about monster movies. The Australian band silverchair was one of many top artists (the Wallflowers, Foo Fighters, Puff Daddy, etc.) to contribute to the 1998 TriStar film's soundtrack; the lyrics of their offering—which explore the pain Godzilla suffers, as well as that which he inflicts—are among the most thoughtful musical treatments of the monster. The Brazilian heavy-metal headliners Sepultura, known for dark riffs like "Antichrist" and "Bestial Devastation," used Godzilla as a metaphor for the exploitation of the

Amazon by developed nations in their 1993 song "Biotech is Godzilla." The list goes on and on. But, lest we forget, all true fans must tip their hats to that most celebrated and popular of Godzilla musical memories, the pioneering 1977 rock anthem "Godzilla" by Blue Öyster Cult. The music and lyrics are now so familiar—as much a part of the American pop culture mythos as the monster himself—that it's easy to overlook the song's sober moral on the folly of humankind, so true to the spirit of the king of the monsters. Rock on, Godzilla!

American television is not particularly known for its restrained, respectful, and thought-provoking treatment of celebrities, and Godzilla is no exception. Godzilla, befitting his status as an icon in the pop culture pantheon, has certainly gotten his fair share of TV tributes, ribbings, and send-ups over the decades. Godzilla toys showed up in Murphy Brown's office, Roseanne's living room, and in the opening sequence of the old *Siskel and Ebert* show. The barflies from *Cheers* once attended a *kaijū eiga* marathon, and Godzilla made a cameo on the short-lived 1977 Bill Cosby variety show *Cos*, doing a foot powder commercial. John Belushi made two memorable appearances in a Godzilla suit: first when introducing the network television premiere of *Godzilla vs. Megalon* on NBC in 1977, the other during a mock interview with the king of the monsters on *Saturday Night Live*. Some of the most entertaining, intelligent and biting material on Godzilla—to the extent that some fans considered it almost sacrilegious—was on the now sadly departed *Mystery Science Theater 3000*. The series that made bad movies cool again, *MST3K* gored *Godzilla vs. Megalon* and *Godzilla vs. the Sea Monster*—both admittedly easy targets—with its trademark brand of spoofs, encyclopedic popular culture references, and irreverent commentary ("Monster Island, where they don't take any crap and they don't take American Express"; "You just opened a whole can of whoop-ass!"). Truly classic were two songs dished up by Joel, Tom Servo, and Crow, the "Godzilla Genealogy Bop," which establishes Kermit the Frog, Ernest Borgnine, and Karl Malden's nose as Godzilla's descendants, and a unique rendition of the Jet Jaguar theme song, with singular observations on the robot's eating habits and jockstrap-like outfit. You gotta love it.

Kudos also go to *The Simpsons* for managing to simultaneously mock and pay homage to Godzilla's cheesy goodness. Although academic critics have slammed the animated series for its "quotationalism" (relying on "the device of referring to or quoting other works of popular culture") and "hyper-irony" (a cold humor rooted in "a sense of world-weary cleverer-than-thou-ness"), *The Simpsons* give Godzilla a special place in the crazy universe of America's favorite dysfunctional family.[22] Observant viewers will recall seeing Godzilla signing autographs at a Springfield science fiction convention, Paul Bunyan and Babe the Blue Ox battling Rodan in a tall-tale sequence, and Homer daydreaming that the perfect college homecoming float would feature Godzilla and a knife-wielding Superman. And in the episode where the Simpson clan visits the land of the rising sun, as the family jets away from Tokyo—Bart bidding "Good-bye, Japan! I'll miss your Kentucky Fried Chicken and your sparkling, whale-free seas"—a gaggle of giant monsters assaults the plane. "Uh, everyone, please strap yourselves in, as we are experiencing a little Godzilla-related turbulence," the captain announces while the king of monsters shakes the jetliner in his claws. "It doesn't look too bad, though. He usually lets go at about thirty thousand feet, and, after that, we'll just have to worry about Mothra, Ghidorah, and Rodan."

Hollywood has nodded Godzilla's way more than a few times, not counting that abominable Tinseltown remake, which was more of a spit in the eye than a sincere homage. Gentle parodies of the *kaijū eiga* genre, from screaming Japanese tourists running down a street to poorly executed dubbing, have appeared in many films including Steven Spielberg's *The Lost World, Austin Powers 3: Goldmember,* and *Honey, I Blew Up the Kid* (all of which make one think there's some connection between the imaginative strain of making sequels and poking fun at Godzilla). The king of the monsters has put in cameos, either through the magic of stock footage or using purpose-built costumes, in *Cooley High, Mars Attacks!, Pee Wee's Big Adventure, One Crazy Summer* (imagine Bobcat Goldthwait taking on Godzilla), and *Hollywood Boulevard,* the infamous made-for-nothing spoof of exploitation pictures. A supposedly cute little alien with a Godzilla complex occupies center stage in the supposedly heartwarming Disney 'toon flick *Lilo and Stitch.* And there is always Marv Newland's modest 1969 animated short *Bambi Meets Godzilla,* in which a huge scaly foot descends to crush a doe grazing in a sylvan glade. The end. With low production values, moral ambiguity to spare, and some genuinely gratuitous violence, Newland's two-minute film may well be the greatest cinematic tribute to Godzilla ever.

Cartoons and comics—even those that don't include Bambi—have always been a great medium for Godzilla. Gojira appeared in Japanese comic books (manga) from the 1960s, but only broke into the U.S. market in the late 1970s, when Marvel released a series of twenty-four *Godzilla: King of the Monsters* comics. Godzilla returned to the four-color world in the late 1980s when the upstart publisher Dark Horse Comics acquired the rights and put out a few one-shot issues (like "Godzilla versus Hero Zero") before launching its own *Godzilla: King of the Monsters* series in 1995. Neither the Marvel nor Dark Horse incarnations featured other

Tōhō monsters (for whom licenses had not been purchased), leaving Godzilla to confront recycled adversaries (Spider-Man, The Avengers), uninspiring new creatures (fire the guy who thought "Devil Dinosaur" was a good idea!), and very odd situations (like the Spanish Armada and the sinking of the Titanic).[23] An animated Godzilla series appeared on NBC from 1978 through 1981, marketed variously as *The Godzilla Power Hour, The Godzilla-Dynomutt Hour,* and, most dispiritingly of all, *The Godzilla–Hong Kong Phooey Hour.* Cute and wholesome Saturday morning fare, the Hanna-Barbera offerings made Godzilla into a do-gooding green dinosaur and introduced Godzooky, the spiritual heir of Minilla, an ungainly ten-foot-tall baby Godzilla with wee dragon wings. A second cartoon series, based on the Hollywood version of Godzilla, premiered on Fox in 1998 and proved more of a hit than the TriStar movie had, both with fans and the general public. A kind of Scooby Doo ensemble cartoon, with a robot and a giant velociraptor rather than a dog, the series featured the voice of *Beverly Hills 90210*'s Ian Ziering and cameo voice-overs by the likes of Linda Blair and Roddy McDowell. If camp heaven isn't Steve Sanders, Regan MacNeil and Cornelius rubbing shoulders with the king of the monsters, I don't know what the heck is.

One could keep inventorying the pop culture manifestations of Godzilla forever. *Kaijū eiga* references on *South Park.* Taco Bell fun-meal figurines. The little electronic Godzilla that, activated by high pollution levels, stomps through your urban creation in the computer game Sim City. That *Calvin and Hobbes* sandbox cartoon which at least a dozen of my friends have clipped and sent to me. The fact that Mia Farrow once declared at the Academy Awards that *Godzilla*

was her favorite film ever. The juvenile pleasure of the word "fartzilla."

One could interrogate Godzilla's fame, asking why celebrity has been bestowed on a rubbery B-movie monster without teams of publicists, a troubled personal life of booze, pills and fast cars, or even a secret sex tape floating around the Internet. But trying to get under the skin of an icon can be a dangerous business, especially when you're dealing with a fifty-thousand-ton, radioactive, plenty prickly reptile. It always comes back to one of those unanswerable questions, a veritable Zen *kōan* of pop culture superstardom. Has Godzilla become an American idol because we love him, or do we love him precisely because of his cultural ubiquity? Is Godzilla one of those substanceless media concoctions, a spectral figment of our collective unconscious manipulated by the *National Enquirer,* the Fox Network, and self-proclaimed experts like me into an intangible but enduring monstrosity of hype? I sincerely hope not: Godzilla is more than a sound bite, a knowing wink, a campy inside joke, a hyper-ironic, quotational sneer, an easy giggle for comedians low on material, a superficial shorthand for "big" and "Japanese." I may be a pollyanna, a pie-in-the-sky optimist, or a fool not half jaded enough to live in an age of postmodern artifice, but I do believe that Godzilla is something real, a cherished childhood memory for many, a reassuring touchstone in a world of Britney Spears, spin doctoring, and virtual everything. *In Godzilla veritas!* And don't let the king of the icons fool you: underneath all that glitz and glamour, the *SNL* appearances, rock tributes, and literary accolades, Godzilla is still just a regular guy, a man who steps into a latex monster suit one leg at a time.

CHAPTER 5

A PERSONAL GODZILLA

WHEN I WAS GROWING UP, THE MEMBERS of my family could see eye-to-eye on only a short list of things: none of us ever wanted to mow the lawn or take down the Christmas tree, beef was the only appropriate meat for celebrations and holidays, any exercise more strenuous than bowling was unthinkable. Godzilla was not a subject on which we shared much common ground. For me, of course, the king of the monsters was right up there with snow days, cap guns, and Frito pies as prepubescent superlatives. My father attended a few Godzilla matinees with me, usually under duress, and was never shy about proclaiming them stupid wastes of time: wouldn't I be better off studying a little more pre-algebra and adding the admission fees to my college fund? My mother was relatively sympathetic, but even on those nights when she allowed me to stay up to watch monsters on the late, late show, she could usually take only about ten minutes of dubbing and suitmation before falling off to sleep on the sofa. My school friends were never all that smitten with Godzilla either, despite my best proselytizing efforts: we could find some shared interest in Dracula and the Creature from the Black Lagoon, but the generally tame nature of *kaijū eiga* ("Where's the blood and guts?") made them decidedly uncool for the average preteen Texan. My grandmother probably took the dimmest view of my taste in movies. For Nana, who had never seen a creature feature of any description, Godzilla films were the instruments of the devil, right up there with spicy foods, rock-'n-roll music, and Democrats. The films were, of course, heathen Japanese propaganda (Nana could never let that Pearl Harbor thing go), and all my Godzilla toys were just disfiguring accidents waiting to happen ("You'll put your eye out with that dorsal fin!" "I can't save you if that model cement *melts your brain!*"). If Tōhō had made *Godzilla vs. Nana,* I would have put my money on the Pennsylvania Dutch octogenarian, no question about it.

My point here is not that I was persecuted for my love of Godzilla or that my friends and family were unenlightened louts, although both of these observations, I would hasten to add, may well be true. Instead, I simply want to emphasize that different people invariably see the same thing—in this case, the king of the monsters—in a multiplicity of different ways. And herein lies the rub for anyone foolhardy enough to try analyzing America's ongoing romance with Godzilla, or any screen icon, for that matter. We can easily establish a chronology of giant monster films, retell their plots in excruciating detail, contextualize them in the history of Japan, world cinema, and anything else we choose, and catalogue all the weird and wonderful cultural references generated by them over the years. But—and this is a big but—how do we get at the tricky issue of reception, of comprehending the individual ways in which all the tens of millions of folks who've seen a Godzilla movie understand the experience, view the monster, and relate a fictional

Japanese reptile to their own lives and realities? How, simply put, do we determine who has an affinity for Godzilla, why they find this cinematic creature so appealing, and in what ways they express their affection for the king of the monsters?

My approach in this chapter is not going to be particularly scientific. I have not examined moviegoers as a cognitive psychologist might, attaching electrodes to a statistically balanced sample of "average" Americans and measuring their neural waves as a loop tape of *Destroy All Monsters* plays. I have not wholeheartedly adopted the methodology of the anthropologist either, and have resisted submerging myself as a participant-observer in theater crowds or fan chatrooms. I have also decided not to follow the path of all the media studies scholars who have, over the past decade or so, indulged in the predictably hyperintellectualized theorizing of fan subcultures in contemporary America. Academics have probed fandom with a vicarious gusto, and have treated *Star Trek* devotees in particular like cultural lab rats, dissecting their curious behaviors with the conceptual scalpels of de Certeau and Bourdieu. There will be none of that here; the observations that follow on the nature of Godzilla fans and the reasons for our cultural obsession with the king of the monsters will not be terribly sophisticated theoretically or authoritative scientifically. Loving Godzilla, my grandmother's views aside, is not a neurosis to be monitored, exorcised, or cured. And neither is it a social pathology to be scrutinized with bloodless rigor. Loving Godzilla is, in the end, a personal passion that should be embraced and celebrated every bit as much as it is analyzed and demystified.

Everyone, I think, has a mental picture of the "typical" science fiction fan, the Trekkie, the X-Phile, the Dr. Who aficionado, the anime *otaku,* the *kaijū eiga* groupie. But even if many of us continue to imagine the sci-fi audience as demographically skewed toward pimply teenagers, disaffected misfits, and the undateable geeks nobody wanted to sit with in the cafeteria, fandom today defies ready stereotyping. Who would have guessed that most *Star Trek* fanatics are female or that the average age of *Star Trek Voyager* viewers (a group that apparently included Bill Clinton) was thirty-nine? Or that, according to one recent poll, 53 percent of Americans identify themselves as "*Star Trek* fans"?[1] Not a great deal of sound statistical data on Godzilla devotees exists, but the quantitative and qualitative evidence suggests that they too are a diverse and hard-to-characterize lot. A 1994 survey of more than a thousand readers of *G-Fan,* by far the premier Godzilla fanzine, revealed that the average age of respondents was 27.8 years old, with the majority of fans in their twenties and thirties, and approximately as many over forty as under nineteen. More than 80 percent of those surveyed reported being single—a figure that may confirm many a preconception—and though a sex breakdown was not reported, we can safely assume the fan population was (and is) largely male. Major Godzilla fan conventions have overwhelmingly drawn men and boys—between 66 and 95 percent of all participants, according to fragmentary records from the last few years—but female fans are hardly rare.[2]

Godzilla enthusiasts come from all walks of life and, if their nonsaurian hobbies are any indication, lead rich and varied existences. Respondents to the 1994 survey listed occupations running the gamut from grocery store clerk, elevator inspector, security guard, and dishwasher to medical doctor, financial analyst, lawyer, and psychotherapist. Personal experience suggests that schoolteachers seem to be disproportionately represented in the Godzilla fan community and that the general education level is high. The pastimes of fans, as reported in the survey and in *G-Fan's* annual directory of readers, are as broad and idiosyncratic as those of the general public: muscle cars, camping, Bible study, gun collecting, model railroading, rugby, KISS, art and poetry, "good-looking women," Barbra Streisand, the New England Patriots, gardening, and so on ad infinitum. The occasional outlier admits to less G-rated avocations—"punk rock, piercings, politics, drinking and, of course, *kaijū*"—but the general profile is thoroughly clean and wholesome. Sci-fi beyond Godzilla—Star Wars, Ultraman, anime, Klingons, *Lost in Space*—is a predictably popular hobby, as are activities and subjects that naturally intersect with Godzilla fandom—dinosaurs, wrestling, reptiles, travel to Japan. Godzilla's admirers are distributed all over the United States and Canada as well, it seems, as in Western Europe and throughout Asia. And if the names and photographs in the *G-Fan* directories are any indication, the king of the monsters appeals to all races and ethnicities, with African-Americans, Hispanics, Asian-Americans (and even the physically handicapped) well represented.

For most of the past fifty years, U.S. Godzilla fans have been isolated and poorly served by specialist organizations and publications. As one knowledgeable observer has written, "the lifeline of Godzilla fandom in the West has been the rag-tag world of fanzines, ranging in quality from mere gibberish crudely printed on mimeographed-and-stapled paper to insightfully written, beautifully designed works that rival professional magazines."[3] Through the 1960s and 1970s, *kaijū eiga* aficionados craving fellowship and information had little option other than the sporadic coverage given Japanese sci-fi in general horror and fantasy publications like the legendary *Famous Monsters of Filmland* and the cheesy broadside *The Monster Times*. Magazines and newsletters with more of a focus on Godzilla came and went in the 1970s and 1980s: the intelligent *Japanese Fantasy Film Journal*, the polished (but short-lived) *Markalite*, and the extremely informative *Japanese Giants* were irregularly published and unevenly distributed, but highly sought after. Only in the 1990s did a strong fan organization and a reliable, enduring Godzilla fanzine emerge. (By way of comparison, even in the mid-1970s, every *Star Trek* regular and even actors with bit parts in the series had well-established fan clubs with regular circulars; I myself was a card-carrying member of the James Doohan, Walter Koenig, and Mark Lenard organizations.) In 1992, a high school science teacher in Manitoba, later working with like-minded Godzilla buffs from New York City, established the Godzilla Society of North America under the uncomplicated motto "We love Godzilla!" and the idealistic goal of "International understanding through Godzilla!" *G-Fan,* the organization's publication, has evolved into a well-produced bimonthly of sixty-plus pages that, with more than five thousand subscribers, is now indisputably the leading journal of *kaijū eiga* fandom.

Forging interpersonal connections has always been a challenge for geographically dispersed fans. Prior to the Internet's colonization of every nook and cranny of American society, finding pen pals was one of the few viable options for developing relationships, and early issues of *G-Fan* are filled with subscriber requests for correspondents with similar interests. Today, the World Wide Web, chatrooms, and email have created new opportunities for virtual community building, and, if the proliferation of Godzilla-related sites is any indication (a Google search turns up almost a million hits for "Godzilla"), fans are eagerly taking the opportunity to share information, explore new forms of personal interaction, and blog to their hearts' content. Perhaps the most important means, at least historically speaking, of bringing individual science fiction fans together has been conventions, an institution so firmly rooted in our culture that it has been ruthlessly parodied on *Saturday Night Live* and *The Simpsons* as well as in films like *Galaxy Quest.* But though *Star Trek* and *Star Wars* fans have long enjoyed such meetings, it seems that the first U.S. Godzilla convention was held only a decade ago, in 1994, at a Howard Johnson's in Chicago, with about thirty members of the Godzilla Society of North America in attendance. That small event grew into G-CON and eventually the annual G-FEST, which remains today the premier American Godzilla fan gathering. Other Japanese sci-fi conventions—Kaijū-Con in New York and Philadelphia, G-North in Toronto, the Asian Fantasy Film Expo in New Jersey—have not proven so enduring. A few inventive ideas have been tried and abandoned, such as G2K Virtual Con, an online gathering of five hundred Godzilla fans through chatrooms, message boards, and online contests. Low overhead, yes; a personally satisfying fan experience, probably not.

On a July weekend in 2003, my long-suffering wife and I attended G-FEST X in a nondescript suburban Chicago motel. I didn't know what to expect, having been to my last sci-fi convention at age twelve, at which point (I cringe to confess) I may well have been wearing a homemade phaser and tricorder, as well as (gulp) Vulcan ears. G-FEST was not exactly a star-studded event, but it had enough minor *kaijū eiga* luminaries to satisfy the faithful: the ebullient Yuasa Noriaki, director of the early Gamera films; the rather pathetic Carl Craig, who had played a peppy boy scout in the dreadful 1968 *Gamera vs. Viras;* Robert Scott Field, a professional *gaijin* resident in Japan who was unforgettable as Android M–11 in *Godzilla vs. King Ghidorah;* and a surprise appearance by Kaneko Shūsuke, the creative force behind the new Gamera series and *Godzilla, Mothra and King Ghidorah.* The three days of the convention were tightly packed with events: screenings of classic and recent monster films in a nearby movie palace, talks and panel discussions on subjects ranging from Japanese culture to the latest advances in special-effects technology, activities (storytime, coloring, face painting, supervised chaos) for "G-kids," autograph sessions, game exhibitions, and trivia contests (did I really want to know "From where does Barugon shoot his freezing spray?"). Separate rooms contained model displays (remarkable fan-made dioramas of monsters trashing and wrestling), amateur works of art (if that's the word for crayon drawings of Titanosaurus by eight-year-olds), and displays of Gamera memorabilia.

The highlight of the weekend was the Saturday evening gathering for the "Costume Parade" and video contest. The parade took me back to my third-grade Halloween humiliation, but was lighthearted good fun nonetheless. Little toddler Gameras shyly growled at the standing-room-only audience, more adult Ghidorahs wiggled their multiple necks, tails and wings, a gigantic Godzilla—inventively made by covering a young man with crumpled tin foil and green spray paint—was a big hit.

An impromptu "Kaijū Call Contest" brought aspiring creatures young and old to the microphone to belt out Godzilla's roar or Mothra's squeaky shriek. The amateur videos were real crowd pleasers, from the elaborate stop-action send-up of Minilla's cowardice and some very homemade tapes of toy monsters slugging it out in a sand-box to the polished and hilarious "Beavra," which gently parodied the people and customs of the great white North. The smiling, cheering fans in that motel ballroom were a cross-section of America, albeit one clad almost entirely in T-shirts emblazoned with Godzilla, Gamera and/or Japanese *kanji*. Lots of young families (wives sometimes glazed, sometimes into things) were there, as were knots of teenagers, the odd senior citizen, and countless men in their twenties and thirties. The tone of the weekend was upbeat and wholesome, the assembled fandom was welcoming and good humored, with not a trace of cynicism to

The king has entered the building. A fan transformed into Mechagodzilla at G-Fest. Photograph courtesy of Armand Vaquer.

be found, and all seemed to revel in the accepting comradeship of fellow Godzilla lovers.

By far the busiest place at G-FEST X was the "Dealers and Merchandise Sales Room." Handlers fed fans in small groups—from the long line that always seemed to stretch through the motel lobby—into the consumeristic promised land. Inside a relatively large (but always swarming) meeting room, purveyors of Godzilla "stuff" of all shapes and descriptions—bootleg videos and DVDs, still photographs, books and magazines from Japan, and endless, endless toys and figurines—hawked their wares on tables and in stalls. Fistfuls of cash changed hands; kids doled out allowance money coin by coin; elevators grew crowded with shopping bags full of plastic monsters and animatronic beasts; fans boasted of their deals and showed off their rarities in almost primal rituals of one-upsmanship ("My Megalon's bigger than your Megalon!"). While the Godzilla devotees might lock horns over what the best of the Heisei films was or who would prevail in the fantasy matchup of Gamera and the king of the monsters, everyone at the convention seemed to sense implicitly—to just *know*—that collectibles were a major part of the raison d'être of fandom. In the tribe of Godzilla, you've got to have graven images; just as Roman Catholics have cherished their holy relics and Easter Islanders their huge carved heads, so G-fans rely on little rubbery lizards and *kaijū* snow globes to symbolize their devotion, signify membership in the group, and provide a common currency for interpersonal exchange.

Happily for us, Godzilla collectibles—unlike saints' fingers and giant volcanic rocks—are available in profusion. The first Godzilla toy was apparently a gun and target game marketed in Japan in 1955. American manufacturers got into the act in the early 1960s when an Ideal board game and that famous Aurora plastic model kit were introduced as *King Kong vs. Godzilla* tie-in products. Vinyl figures—by far the favorite among American fans—were pioneered in the 1960s by the Japanese firm Marusan (whose cartoonish toys are big-money collectors items today) and developed in the 1970s by Bullmark and Popy. Bandai, the Microsoft of vinyl monster makers, began production in 1983 when, in tandem with the launch of the Heisei series, Tōhō stepped up licensing of Godzilla goods. Other toy companies—Mattel and Trendmasters in the United States, Marmit and M1 in Japan—have also entered the fray from time to time. The sheer volume and variety of Godzilla collectibles made is truly daunting: one source reported that more than three million Godzilla toys a year were sold in America in the mid-1990s and, at the same time in Japan, more than two dozen licensees were churning out three hundred different Godzilla items.[4] These days, the king of the monsters and virtually all the *kaijū eiga* pantheon are available as plastic toys, in any number of different sizes, colors, and styles (from the supposedly cute "superdeformed" figures to amazingly "realistic" reproductions). Remote- and radio-controlled models that roar, glow, and gyrate in every imaginable way can be found at any convention or with the click of a button on the Internet. Collectors can hoard Godzilla kites, coloring books, piggybanks, slippers, trading cards, Viewmaster reels, tape measures, toilet paper holders, electric shavers, and telephone rests. Godzilla shampoo (odd for a creature that has no apparent hair) has been sold in Japan, as have Godzilla-branded ramen, melon soda, stovetop popcorn, and sausages on a stick. Mothra and Ghidorah beanie babies are current top sellers. One of my favorites was an old plastic Rodan toy made by Mattel. "Giant 'flying' creature!" the colorful box proclaimed. "Wings flap! He squawks! Wingspan 38 inches! Unassembled. Does not fly." Ah, the wonder of being a child . . . and of loving Godzilla.[5]

The significance of all this merchandise to Godzilla fans should not be underestimated. The 1994 *G-Fan* readership

Godzilla fan Richard Cox of Greensboro, North Carolina, poses with some of the 600+ kaijū eiga figures in his collection. Photograph courtesy of Richard Cox.

survey indicated that 90 percent of respondents owned Godzilla-related books and 95 percent vinyl "action figures," with the average fan claiming sixteen books and eighteen of the toys. Interestingly, almost half of the *G-Fan* subscribers reported keeping their Godzilla goods in their bedrooms, though the reasons for this choice (privacy? intimacy? embarrassment at exhibiting them more openly?) were not detailed. A remarkable 8 percent of fans owned up to having a special G-room where they kept and displayed their prized accumulations of Godzilla minivacuums, lapel pins, and whiskey decanters.[6] A special session at G-FEST allowed collectors to show photos or videotapes about their possessions and discuss issues of common interest. The conversation ranged over the best ways of cleaning vinyl (a fan innocently recommended the occasional hot shower with one's figurines), "domestic problems" caused by a proliferation of Godzilla stuff (not to mention those showers), and the strategy of buying two of everything, one to cherish and preserve, the other to use and play with. One devotee explained that "I have Godzillas out on the couch just because I need to bond with them." And while this one individual may have used his plushy monsters and plasticy creatures for human-toy union, more of the fan community appears interested in using collecting as a means of interpersonal connection. Sharing their treasures with others (at conventions, in person, or over the Internet), swapping and trading, comparing collectibles notes, and indulging in some friendly competition are all integral parts of the Godzilla fan experience. They are also important means of establishing relationships and cementing community in a dispersed and disparate group of individuals who, despite the stereotypes, are not all isolated, inveterate loners.

In the most peculiar manifestations of fandom, a Godzilla admirer may not just own an action figure but may actually *become* an action figure. Such is the nature of "Kaiju

Big Battel," a kind of tongue-in-cheek, hypercheesy performance art which, since its origins in the late 1990s in the
nightclubs of Boston and New York, has developed a na-
tionwide cult following. Characterized by one commentator
as "East meets West. It's the WWF in monster costumes,"
Big Battel is an unusual tribute to *kaijū eiga,* Japanese live-
action science fiction television series, and professional
wrestling. Based on a cartoonish internal narrative of four
tribes of giant, angry monsters vying for control of the earth,
Big Battel features performers dressed in ludicrous foam-
rubber costumes (Kung-Fu Chicken Noodle, Dusto Bunny,
the intergalactic space bug Uchu Chu) fighting it out in
wrestling rings liberally sprinkled with models of miniature
skyscrapers and apartment blocks. The kind of silly spectacle—rich in choreographed violence, pop culture parody,
and warped appreciation of Japanese monster traditions—
that could be just side-splitting after four or five beers, Kaiju
Big Battel shows how entrepreneurial and slightly loony individuals can creatively rework sci-fi fandom to create imaginative products, novel economic opportunities, and new
communities of engaged aficionados.[7]

As anyone who has ever opened a fanzine or attended a sci-
fi convention can tell you, creativity is one of the hallmarks
of contemporary American fandom. A small academic cot-
tage industry has even grown up around what some scholars
call "cultural appropriation" and others "textual poaching,"
the use of mass-culture icons in the imaginative writing, art,
cartooning, modeling, costuming, and filmmaking of fans.
According to leading fan watcher Henry Jenkins, American
science fiction devotees have fashioned "a participatory culture which transforms the experience of media consumption

into the production of new texts, indeed of a new culture and a new community."[8] In other words, today's fans are not content to be passive couch potatoes, ready to consume whatever product the media industry generates or engage as mere spectators, empty vessels ready for the filling by Hollywood or Tōhō or whomever. Instead, American fandom is creative and constructive, taking the characters, scenarios, and traditions of popular culture and reimagining them, lifting figures like James T. Kirk and Mothra off the television or theater screen to create personal meaning and affirm communities of like-minded aficionados. And Godzilla admirers, every bit as much as the followers of *Star Trek, Star Wars* and other more established sci-fi properties, have shown great inspiration, ingenuity, and productivity in crafting new ways of appreciating their cinematic idol.

As one speaker at G-FEST described it, writing a poem, building a model, or drawing a cartoon is a fulfilling and meaningful way of showing one's "active love" for Godzilla. If so, love is everywhere and is very energetic indeed in the world of American *kaijū eiga* fans. All fanzines contain fan criticism of the Godzilla films, and most contain fan fiction based on Japanese monster movies. Short stories, serialized works, and even major freestanding novels (like the series of Godzilla volumes published by Random House in the 1990s) are diverse in style and content: many explore ideas for potential sequels and fantasy monster matchups (Could Gabara take Varan, no holds barred?); some allow you to imagine yourself in the minds of Godzilla, Rodan et al.; a few are self-reflective studies of what it means to be a fan and Japanese sci-fi *otaku; G-Fan* even printed an extended account of what reality television would look like in the Tōhō universe—*Survivor, Monster Island.* Fans are also prolific creators of art, from the professionally airbrushed images that appear on the covers of zines (and can sell for top dollar to collectors), to the countless cartoons you can find on sites all over the Internet and the fanciful creations of grammar-school Michelangelos.[9] Modeling, which is no longer limited to sticking pieces of plastic together from a kit, is a highly specialized and skilled form which involves the use of sophisticated materials, expressive sculpting, and artistic paint work. Amateur videos, some of which use suit-mation of a sort, some animation and most stop-motion pho-tography, are a popular form of expression and allow for clever parodies of *kaijū eiga* campiness. Who couldn't love shorts titled "Attack of the Y2K Bug from Outer Space," "Monster Bicentennial" (in which Mothra helps Betsy Ross sew the original stars-and-stripes), and "Destroy All Annoy-ances" (which features a clay Godzilla eating the Teletub-bies, carving up Pikachu, and mashing Barney)?

Some fans imbue their creative tributes to the king of the monsters with an intensity and a kind of technical preci-sion that one can interpret either as the apotheosis of geek-iness or the ultimate in arch humor. This is particularly the case in Japan, where fandom is often pursued with the all-en-compassing gusto and devil-may-care abandon more com-monly associated with kamikaze pilots, sumo wrestlers, and cutthroat businessmen. A number of Japanese profession-als—scientists, economists, engineers—who grew up loving *kaijū eiga* have come to apply their vocational expertise to the study of Godzilla as adults. Thus, relatively serious tomes on the biology of Godzilla have appeared in Japanese, as have fascinating treatises covering topics like the military "lessons learned" from battling giant monsters, the ecologi-cal effects of the oxygen destroyer on Tokyo Bay, and the economic impact of Godzilla's raids on Japanese cities. One such study soberly toted up the property damage from mon-ster mayhem in *Godzilla vs. King Ghidorah* and figured the damage to Tokyo alone in the range of fifteen trillion yen to twenty trillion yen (or $175 billion, give or take a few bucks).[10] A few American fans have indulged in similar flights of scientific fancy. Kenneth Carpenter of the Denver Museum of Natural History, for example, has written an analysis of Godzilla from a paleontological point of view, musing on the monster's role in the Jurassic ecosystem and his evolutionary relationship to fellow theropods, among other things. Dr. Carpenter even named an actual dinosaur after his screen hero, christening the 225-million-year-old ceratosaur he unearthed in New Mexico in 1981 *Gojirasaurus quayi*.[11] One has to wonder, is there a purple, stub-nosed *Barneysaurus* out there somewhere?

Fathoming why fans are drawn to Godzilla is a far less straightforward project than observing their gatherings, surveying their collections, or analyzing their rituals. The $64,000 question—Why in the name of heaven do so many Americans respond so strongly to a latex movie lizard from Japan?—has no easy answers, despite the eagerness of Freudians, Marxists, and culture studies scholars to explain it away with excess repression, excess capital, and excess theory. To establish the contours of a response—and I can claim no more ambitious achievement here—I decided to go back to the fans and to ask them, both directly and indirectly, what they felt were the reasons for Godzilla's particular appeal. I read the writings of committed Godzilla devotees in the letters columns, articles, stories, and want ads of the established fanzines: *The Monster Times, Japanese Giants, Kaiju Fan* and, above all, *G-Fan.* I sampled the web for responses to Godzilla and paid particularly close attention to the unsolicited comments and reviews posted by hundreds of monster movie viewers at Amazon.com and Epinions.com, a kind of electronic bulletin board that bills itself as the web's "most reliable source for valuable consumer insight, unbiased advice, in-depth product evaluations and personalized recommendations." To get at the perspectives of more casual Godzilla fans, the type who might not feel the need to join a club, subscribe to a zine, or disseminate their views all over the Internet, I sent letters to the editors of the 200 largest newspapers in the United States, soliciting responses from their readers on Godzilla and the film series' enduring popularity. At least a dozen of the papers—from Salt Lake City to Tampa to Nashua, New Hampshire—printed my request, inserted a blurb about my project on the pop culture page, or did a full-blown feature article about the eccentric professor from Kansas who wanted to hear why people related to the king of the monsters. In the end, I received almost eighty responses, some a hastily written sentence or two by email, others veritable treatises of several thousand words done in longhand or on a manual typewriter.[12] From this little archive of personal responses, Internet cullings, and fan writings, I began to plumb the depths of Godzilla's mysterious charm.

The first thing I found out about fans is that most of them seem to have very strong memories of their first Godzilla movie. Especially for the many devotees who grew up in the now-distant days before the instant gratification of VCRs, DVDs, laser discs, and downloadable files made the experience of *kaijū eiga* all too easy and "on demand," remembrances of that "first time" are vivid and remarkably immediate. The author of one letter to me precisely identified his introduction to Godzilla as "Friday, November 26, 1976 (8:00 P.M.) *Godzilla vs. the Thing,* WPIX, Age: 7." Another recalled hiding an alarm clock under his bed so he could awaken in time to sneak downstairs to watch Godzilla on the late, late show; yet another reported seeing the king of the monsters as a special treat on "Straight A Wednesday" at his elementary school in Iota, Louisiana; a writer in G-Fan fondly remembered viewing a Tōhō feature on forty TV screens in the electronics section of Macy's as his parents shopped for carpet. Even if they can't dredge up the exact date or time, most fans can recall where they saw their inaugural Godzilla feature, be it a big L.A. drive-in, a neighborhood movie house in Maplewood, New Jersey, the State Theater in Amarillo, the Lyceum in Winnipeg, or the "local flea pit." Television memories are equally intense: who would have thought so many people would remember with such genuine affection *Shock Theater* with Dr. Paul Bearer, the *Plenty Scary Movie* on channel 8 in Tulsa, or WOR's Thanksgiving Godzilla marathons? Indeed, one gets the sense that, in more than a few cases, the circumstances of seeing one's first Godzilla film were at least as significant as the film itself. One correspondent told me of his family's transformation of their modest Alabama den—"all lights off, windows covered with thick blankets, chairs and couches arranged in a semi-circle and both entrance doors locked"— into a suitable venue for watching the Saturday afternoon offerings of *Horror Theater:* "Here inside the dark, locked room is where I first looked into the black-and-white face of Raymond Burr reporting on the destruction of Tokyo by Godzilla." Who could forget that!

For almost everyone, Godzilla began as a childhood experience. Some fans get hooked very young indeed. One mother wrote me about her daughter who "saw her first movie (*Godzilla vs. Mothra*) when she was about two and immediately watched it repeatedly until we said she couldn't watch it more than twice a day. [Now, just before her fourth birthday] she plays Godzilla (stomping, roaring, tipping over, etc.) almost every day and often insists that we call her Godzilla." That little girl may want to think hard about what she's called because Godzilla-related nicknames seem to stick: numerous fans report being tagged "Zilla" or things like "Japan Dan" well into their adult lives, while others eagerly assume *kaijū*-inspired identities like "Gojirathoner" or (in the case of one professional wrestler) "Jet Jaguar." And Godzilla is a lifetime affair for many: one retired physician told me of her thirty-five years of interest in monster movies; another woman wrote me of her educated and cultured mother who had harbored a singular devotion to Godzilla until the day she died. If you think about it, all the baby boomers who discovered the king of the monsters as kids in the late 1950s or early 1960s are now signing up for their AARP cards. And Godzilla, it seems, appeals not just to young and old, but to female fans as well as male ones. As one Indiana woman wrote in *G-Fan,* responding to an article titled "Godzilla Widows," "Just to let you know how much I love Godzilla, let me relate to you about last Valentine's Day. My husband bought what I really wanted. No not flowers, not candy, not jewelry. A Mechagodzilla figure. . . . Who could ask for a better husband?"[13]

Although *G-Fan* once published the photo of a couple at their wedding reception with an ice sculpture of Godzilla, Japanese movie creatures do not seem to be something that brings too many husbands and wives together. However, Godzilla films and fandom do seem to play an important role in establishing and reaffirming intergenerational bonds—especially between children and parents or grandparents—in a surprising number of families. Many adult fans have warm memories of being introduced to *kaijū eiga* by their fathers or mothers. One man wrote me a heartfelt note about his fifth birthday, in 1970, when his father brought home a new color television set and—even more important—spent a rare afternoon together with him, enjoying *Godzilla vs. Monster Zero.* A New England woman reminisced about childhood weekends spent at her father's place, where cable allowed reception of the *Creature Double Feature,* and a fun-filled summer night, many years later, with her mother, a six-pack, and *Godzilla vs. Megalon* at a local drive-in. Psychologists have written sober essays about the Godzilla series as a parenting tool, and many a Godzilla-loving parent told me proudly of their success in passing the obsession along to their young children, creating countless two- or three-generation clans of fans.[14] Perfectly capturing the monster's uncanny ability to span all divides of age, sex, and taste, one devotee wrote in a fanzine tribute:

> My grandmother and I had an agreement: I watched *Lawrence Welk* and *Hee Haw* with her, and she watched Godzilla films with mc. Her favorite was the original *Mothra*. . . . I write this on April 18th, my grandmother's birthday (she passed away in 1982). I'm reminiscing of myself at the age of five, watching *Ghidorah the Three-Headed Monster* with my seventy-year-old grandma in front of an old RCA TV, logs burning in the fireplace, and sipping hot cocoa. . . . Pure sentimental cheese? Sure. But I'm sure every G-fan has had similar experiences, when giant Japanese monsters brought their family closer together.[15]

Not every fan, needless to say, gets all warm and fuzzy when thinking about Godzilla. Many—perhaps even a majority—practice their *kaijū eiga* avocation without a touching history of familial support or, indeed, even the slightest understanding from friends, co-workers, siblings, spouses, or other relatives. Fandom can be a solitary experience: "My friends think I'm nuts . . . and my family remains in the dark," one Coloradan reported. "My husband and children do not understand me," a young woman emailed. "They all run to another TV when his movies come on." "They all look at me like I have two heads (or three, like Ghidorah)," another aficionado confessed. "I am alone in my devotion," a lifelong New York fan claimed. "I've never even met anyone in person that shared my interest." To some, the isolation can be challenging. One high-schooler lamented in G-Fan: "At fifteen, I am in the G-fan minority. I had my own copy of

Godzilla 2000 defaced by a fellow student during biology. I have been mocked for my passion during geometry, and I almost had an issue of *G-Fan* confiscated during English. If I could only find others [sympathetic souls? fanzines? English classes?]. Ah well."[16] Most Godzilla admirers—at least those beyond the peer pressures of puberty—accept the burdens of fandom with resignation, good humor, and a kind of plucky independence. And for some, being a little different, embracing a screen hero a little outside the American mass-culture mainstream, can even be a positive attribute. "I get laughed at for watching Godzilla," one of my correspondents blithely observed, "but I don't care."

When fans are put on the spot and asked why Godzilla has enjoyed such overwhelming popularity in America—and why they in particular relate so strongly to the king of the monsters—an incredible array of answers comes flooding forth. Some are thoughtful and sophisticated, some simple and spontaneous; many responses are divergent or even downright contradictory; more than a few fans will plainly admit that they have no idea. For a good many of the Godzilla faithful, understanding the secret of *kaijū eiga*'s success requires little in the way of analysis, soul searching, or social criticism: we love Godzilla because his movies are so fun. When push comes to shove, many a fan will testify, we keep slipping those tapes into the VCR, buying the vinyl action figures, and enduring the raised eyebrows of friends because Godzilla is a good-time guy, with an infectious roar and an incomparable joie de vivre (which is, simultaneously and a little ironically, a *joie de destruction*). Needless to say, the monster that such fans respond to is the comic, anthropomorphic Japanese Barney of the 1960s and 1970s Shōwa laughers, the very films that have had the widest exposure in the United States, and not the more somber, predatory creature of the 1954 *Gojira* and Tōhō's most recent offerings. The majority of the letters I received ended with a familiar refrain: "It's good entertainment"; "It's just good-old fashioned fun, pure and simple"; "They're fun. They're silly"; "Godzilla is just plain cool." Some female fans even make Godzilla seem like the kind of fellow you'd like to take home to meet mom and dad: "I find Zill to be a good-looking guy with a monstrous sense of humor," one confided; "Godzilla has all the charisma in the world, hasn't he?" another gushed.[17] Sure, he might be a lot of fun, but just watch out for the radioactive morning breath, ladies.

Kids, of course, love the color and action of Godzilla films and their parents often praise *kaijū eiga* as a safe and wholesome viewing option. A 1970 review in the *New York Times* captured these feelings beautifully, noting how Japanese creature features "clip along briskly, without squirting blood in the viewer's eye for the heck of it. . . . There wasn't a smidgin of sex, as usual in these Japanese bundles. And who needs it. . . . The ensuing battle royal, with the Japanese puppeteers working overtime, is a grunting, crushing, squealing and fire-breathing sight—and as amusing as it is clever. The children at the uptown Riverside Theater ate it up happily, as the big boys slugged it out."[18] One father wrote to *G-Fan* expressing relief that his nine-year-old daughter enjoyed watching Godzilla movies: "The fantasy genre in America of late is violent, obscene, and in some cases indecent. . . . Godzilla will hopefully continue to be a clean, clear-cut fantasy genre enjoyed by all ages. Minor cussing aside . . . , parents can let their kids enjoy the films without fear."[19] Many fans find Godzilla features appealing for their good-natured innocence—stylized rather than graphic violence, obviously fake special effects, simple and unambiguous story lines—a quality that seems desperately lacking in recent Hollywood offerings. Some even see Godzilla as a healthy family role model for his obviously affectionate parenting of Minilla. "It's nice to see that Godzilla is active in his child's life," one aficionado wrote me. "But who's the kid's mom?"

The youth perspective on Godzilla yields another significant insight, one that is all too easily overlooked by longtime fans, on the monster's seemingly timeless allure. Those of us who are used to chuckling at Godzilla flicks with a knowing adult worldliness often forget that *kaijū eiga* can actually accomplish what all horror films are meant to do: that is, they can actually scare their audiences. For a veteran and somewhat jaded Godzilla viewer like myself, it was astonishing to be reminded that the classic films actually had (and continue to have) the power to frighten and spook, and even stir the occasional nightmare. One New Jersey fan wrote me of her experiences of watching the king of the monsters back in the 1960s, when she was eight or nine years old. "Godzilla seemed very real and very frightening," she said. "I always felt, as they say, 'butterflies' in my stomach when I heard his unmistakable roar. As so many of us children were, afraid and squirming in our seats, yet compelled to watch." A patient and loving father told me a gem of a story about taking his four-year-old to a showing of *King Kong vs. Godzilla:*

> Suddenly, Godzilla emerged from one side of the screen and flame and smoke shot from this nostrils while, on the other side of the screen, King Kong beat his chest and roared and it was obvious that a battle to the death was about to begin. I felt a small hand tug my left sleeve, and a little voice whispered, "Hey dad, can I sit on your wap?" (My son had trouble pronouncing the letter "l.") "Sure," I said, without thinking, and hoisted him up. Just then the battle began, and the sound was deafening and I suddenly noticed that my lap felt warm. First warm, then wet. The poor kid had wet his pants . . . and mine.

That's family bonding . . . and a truly scary movie.

For a sizable number of Godzilla fanatics, what makes Japanese monster films winners are their reassuring, positive, and unambiguous messages. As U.S. distributor Henry Saperstein understood the Godzilla formula, "It's a morality play. It's the classic story of good vs. evil, white hat vs. black hat. Godzilla is knocked all around until the tenth round, then comes out swinging."[20] Such uncomplicated narratives, which almost inevitably affirmed the triumph of the good guys (in radioactive saurian form) over whatever monstrous baddies might be dreamt up, clearly resonated with American fans. The majority of them see Godzilla as a taller, reptilian Matt Dillon, responsible for keeping Japan as free of riffraff as Dodge City: "He is indestructible and does the right thing and in the end is a hero," one admirer wrote me. Many enjoy rooting for Godzilla much as they would a favorite prize-fighter or a comic-book superhero: "It was very fun to cheer Godzilla on as he fought the 'bad' monsters like Rodan, Monster Zero and the others." But Godzilla is not just a schoolyard goody-goody; fans recognize that Godzilla is a complex and even tragic champion, a character with both the strengths and weaknesses of a human hero. One devotee from New Mexico explained that "the special appeal that Godzilla movies have for me is that Godzilla seems to epitomize so many good human characteristics—courage, intelligence—and he always seemed to do the best with what he had. He'd fling boulders even if his arms were a bit stubby and he had no control of his digits." Indeed. Let's see George Foreman, Flash Gordon, or a cowtown marshal try that!

Another common explanation for Godzilla's celebrity in America is, to borrow a phrase from the marketing folks at TriStar, that "size does matter." A number of fans believe that children respond to Japanese movie monsters because, quite simply, "they're bigger than grown ups!" As one committed enthusiast wrote in a fanzine, "When I was a kid, I liked Godzilla because Godzilla was really, really big. Children feel powerless most of the time, they're subject to constant parental direction and supervision, they are dependent, they are small and weak by human standards. Godzilla was none of these things."[21] The apparent correlation of a childhood interest in dinosaurs and Godzilla fandom (a link explicitly made in many of the letters I received) only affirms the significance of an apparently widespread juvenile attachment to huge, fantastical creatures.[22] In the eyes of other observers, however, Godzilla's grandeur has appealed to a more generalized American love for the colossal, the exaggerated and the brash, those same core values that make us embrace supersize fries, Dollywood, and Donald Trump. "Why is Godzilla so popular?" one correspondent wondered, "Well he is big, powerful and never stays down for long." And more than one fan informed me that they could personally relate to Godzilla because they, like the monster, happened to be "big and tall": "Godzilla may be big and clumsy but, hey, for those of us who are not perfect, we have an idol to look up to who is just like us."

But if Americans have an affinity for large things, they seem to have an even stronger response to destructive ones. Unknowingly echoing Susan Sontag's time-honored observations on giant monster pictures, fans of all ages, sexes, and walks of life have proclaimed the spectacle of Godzilla's rampages a major attraction of *kaijū eiga*. Aficionados simply revel in Godzilla's power and his willingness to use it. "Godzilla as I most prefer him," one New Yorker wrote, "is as an unstoppable, implacable force destroying anything that gets in his way." "Gojira don't take no guff," as another lifelong follower put it. The author of one email told me of a friend who rated the Godzilla films based on the amount of urban demolition accomplished by the king of the monsters. A number of fans tried to rationalize their destruction-happy response: several put it down to a universal childish desire to break things, others wrote it off as human nature ("sometimes you just want to stomp around and crush things"), and one ascribed it to the "American dream" of instant gratification ("the idea of stomping around damaging anything that displeases you appeals to males especially"). For the vast majority of Godzilla lovers, however, no elaborate explanations were necessary. Thanks but no thanks to random acts of kindness, Kumbaya, and the Golden Rule; Godzilla is about mashing things, and don't forget it. As one young devotee frankly declared, "To me, the fun of Godzilla was always watching two monsters (and sometimes way more than that) beat the living crap out of each other and wreak havoc to Japan."

Not all fans, by any means, celebrated the "aesthetics of destruction" as the be-all and end-all of their fondness for the king of the monsters. Some of the individuals who wrote me candidly described Godzilla as their escape from reality, a welcome fantasy haven they used to deal with broken homes, unhappy childhoods, or lonely adult lives. Others looked upon Godzilla as a kind of reassuring cultural touchstone, a cinematic security blanket in uncertain times. "People are tired of so much complexity," one woman emailed, "so many problems that seem to have no solution. Even in the dark days, one knows that Godzilla will always roar, he will always breathe fire, he will always teach a lesson, and he will always return." To several of my correspondents, however, Godzilla is most valuable as an implicit warning, a kind of conscience for a species prone to arrogance, a reminder of our very human frailties: one fan professed an odd kind of comfort in "Godzilla crushing the hubris of humanity and showing us we aren't the most powerful beings on Earth"; another acknowledged soberly that "Godzilla shows me just how insignificant I am." A small minority located their affection for Godzilla in the unique, far-from-Hollywood sensibilities of the *kaijū eiga* genre, praising Japanese monster pics for their stylized aesthetics, delightfully unrealistic special effects, and more soulful take on monsters and horror. And while many fans will tell you that their interest in Godzilla turned into a broader fascination with things Japanese (anime, sci-fi TV, culture, and language), even to the extent of shaping their career choices, very few suggest that a preexisting affinity for Japan is what motivated their initial embrace of Godzilla.[23] Perhaps most lyrically, one insightful writer, reflecting on why her spouse could not relate to the Japanese movie creatures, just surrendered to the mystery, magic, and poetry of Godzilla: "My husband of twenty-three years could care less. He . . . doesn't believe in make-believe heroes. I often wonder where he thinks the thunder and lightning comes from. Doesn't he know that it's Godzilla out there saving the world?"

If all the letters I received, the fanzines I read, and the websites I scoured left me with one abiding impression, it is this: the emotion that Godzilla stirs most powerfully in the hearts of his admirers is, without question, a bittersweet sense of nostalgia. For almost all adult Godzilla fans, the experience of seeing a classic monster movie transports them back to their youth, to a time of innocence and discovery, of endless possibilities and memories heavy with meaning. For many a person, this reverie can be pleasant, soothing, and even therapeutic, as private memories of childhood in a simpler, gentler age come flowing back. "Whenever I watch a Godzilla film," one devotee wrote, "I turn back into [a] small child and a little comfort sneaks into my life."[24] Godzilla is woven tightly into the package of sights, smells, sounds, and tastes that define "when I was little" in the minds of countless Americans. "The thing for me," one middle-age man related, "is that Godzilla is combined with Captain Crunch cereal, candy bars, White Lightning soda pop, bowls of ice cream, dark snakes of licorice, Hostess Twinkies, Cracker Jacks and a hundred more memories." But nostalgia is a tricky thing, and into all the warm remembrances of days gone by—the idyll seen through Godzilla-colored glasses—inevitably creeps a sense of loss, a feeling of regret, and a certain air of sadness. For if Godzilla reminds us of the joys of youth, it also reminds us of how much things have changed since our youth, of innocence lost and hopes unfulfilled, of a world forever altered and a childhood forever gone. "Godzilla is an icon," one woman concluded, "because he came at a more innocent time when movie making was not as sophisticated and we, as children, were also not so hardened and sophisticated. We let him scare us and we accepted him as almost being real." But those un-cynical, uncomplicated days, if they ever actually existed, now survive only in the memories evoked by a B-movie monster with a Japanese accent. As another misty-eyed fan reminisced of his first Godzilla film, at the old Balboa Theater on a 1963 Saturday in a very different Los Angeles:

> That trip to the movies during my childhood was at a much simpler time than now. JFK was at the height of his presidential career, and Monica Lewinsky was not even a gleam in her father's eye. We didn't have to worry about illegal drugs, wars, Watergate, Whitewater (except at the beach), sexual harassment, or career pressures. We were able to walk to the neighborhood corner store without fear of kidnapping, molestation or gangs. Candy bars sold for a nickel, and comic books cost twelve cents. It was a good time to be a kid. It was a great time to go see *King Kong vs. Godzilla* on the big screen. Wouldn't it be nice to have those days again?[25]

Amen, amen.

In the end, establishing the contours of *kaijū eiga* fandom and pinning down what makes Godzilla such a beloved icon in America are tall orders indeed. This is the case not least because of the sprawling dynamism of the fan universe, which intersects and overlaps with so many other subcultures in so many unexpected ways. Godzilla, as a free-floating symbol available to all, has been invested with meanings that few G-FEST conventioneers and few of the fans who wrote me letters would likely recognize or endorse. And, of course, times change. Although Godzilla has been a member of America's pop-culture pantheon for the better part of fifty years, shifting historical circumstances and the vicissitudes of taste inevitably affect how we look at suitmation, cinematic destruction, and even the king of the monsters himself. Appropriately perhaps for an amphibious creature, Godzilla is a fluid presence in the American collective imagination, ever adapting to the restless currents of time and social temperament.

For example, in recent years, Godzilla has been embraced by African-American entertainers and musicians as an evocative symbol of sheer size, intimidation, rage and the transgression of cultural norms. The comedian Dave Chappelle has assumed the identity of Blackzilla and, in one now-infamous skit from his Comedy Central series, terrorized Tokyo in a cream-colored track suit. The giant Chappelle, in a raunchy send-up of suitmation, dragged his feet through a model city, smoked a tree like a joint, urinated on an assembled crowd ("He has a one-eyed brown snake!" "That's no snake, honey"), and battled an ill-costumed Godzilla, sodomizing the monster with his own tail while taunting "I'm from the streets, bitch!" Chappelle proceeded to have sex with a nearby volcano ("Brown snake turns into brown stick") and cooled off with a post-coital smoke. Rap and hip-hop artists have also identified with Godzilla in ways that belie the movie creature's otherwise wholesome, good-for-the-little-ones image. Magic's "Ghetto Godzilla" evokes the figures of inner-city gangbangers, bigger and meaner than

the king of the monsters; D12 and Swifty McVay use similarly vivid imagery in "Rap Game"; Bone Crusher's "New
Scared" video features the rapper stomping through miniature buildings in a clear *kaijū eiga* tribute. And then there's
Yukmouth, whose "Godzilla" is just slightly different from
Blue Öyster Cult's song of the same title: "I'm a straight
killa . . . fuck y'all niggas / I come stompin' to eat 'em up like
Godzilla," Yukmouth raps, ending with the warning "Call the
president! Tell the president to call the Navy Seals! / He's
here, he's steppin' on shit! / He's crushing! Oh my god! /
Godzilla's alive! Oh you got to see this shit!" This may not
be my king of the monsters, but it's an intense, provocative,
and vivid take on Godzilla the outsider, the renegade, and
the threat to "polite" society.

Japanese movie monsters have not become important
icons to the gay community, yet fans and other commentators have shown an ongoing fascination with seeking out
hidden homosexual messages in the Godzilla films. One fan
website proclaims—perhaps tongue-in-cheek, perhaps not—
"Godzilla: Out and Proud." Another seeks to argue for positive portrayals of homosexuality in *Godzilla vs. Megalon,*
"the flaming gay Godzilla movie." Even film critic Vincent
Canby (never a big admirer of *kaijū eiga*) got in on the act,
musing in a 1972 article that Ken-chan, the creature-crazy
grade-schooler in *Godzilla vs. the Smog Monster,* harbored a
"homosexual crush" on the king of the monsters (Canby obviously felt the same-sex nature of this relationship more
noteworthy than the interspecies, boy-and-beast element,
which certainly seems more curious to me).[26] The Gay Asian
Pacific Alliance, an established group in the San Francisco
Bay Area, calls its newsletter "Lavender Godzilla." And although Godzilla's tangles with other cinematic monsters do
not yet seem to be the subject of any fan "slash fiction"—
what Constance Penley describes as the "homoerotic, porno-
graphic, utopian romances" written by female devotees of

Star Trek and other science fiction favorites—Jay Snodgrass does include a poem in his *Monster Zero* collection that features Godzilla, in drag, attempting to seduce King Ghidorah.[27] Tame stuff compared to what Trekkies can dish up about Kirk and Spock, but bizarre enough for me, thank you.

And since this is America, after all, Godzilla has become fully implicated in every imaginable form of religious observance, theological debate, and sectarian differentiation. On the web, one can find Christian message boards dedicated to the king of the monsters, with plentiful discussion along the lines of "if my memory is correct, Godzilla breathed fire, had a nearly impervious skin and when he came out of the water made it 'boil'—these all describe the Biblical creature Leviathan as described in Job chapter 41." Radio evangelist Ken Ham has addressed the pressing issue of "Dragons and Godzilla—What's the Connection?" (hint: look in Genesis), a Lutheran minister promotes Godzilla as a fun and effective means of teaching the catechism and a Seventh Day Adventist pastor in California has used *Bambi Meets Godzilla* to bring life to the story of Hezekiah and the Assyrians.[28] Meanwhile, up in the Yakima Valley town of Zillah, Washington, the uninspiringly named Christian Worship Center rechristened itself the Church of God-Zillah a few years back in a shameless attempt to lure more youngsters in for services. One member of the congregation even made a ten-foot-tall, welded-pipe statue of the church's namesake to stand in the parking lot, decked out with three thousand Christmas lights, a cross, and a sign proclaiming "Jesus Saves." The pastor maintains that Godzilla has seen the light: "We got him saved. He's been reformed. He's not quite the monster of the movies."[29] The creature himself may beg to differ. In a fictional 1998 interview in *Cineaste* magazine, Godzilla was asked "Does having 'God' as part of your name mean you're religious?" "I'm from the animal kingdom," the monster replied. "You basically wake up, find something to kill, eat it, then take a nap. It's you humans that insist on finding religion through that."[30] Thus spake the cultural icon, recognized by all, symbol of all, exclusive property of none. Hallelujah!

Back in 1976, when *Godzilla vs. Megalon* was released in the United States, the distributor produced a poster featuring the two monsters of the title. Under the slogans "Giant against giant . . . the ultimate battle" and "All new, never before seen," the hulking adversaries faced off, each standing atop one of the towers of the World Trade Center, jet fighters soaring and helicopters whirling overhead. The movie, needless to say, was not set in New York City, and one wonders how Godzilla would have climbed a 110-story skyscraper. But the poster made sense to an American audience as an updated tribute to King Kong, reflecting a new age in which Minoru Yamazaki's twin towers had claimed high-rise dominance in Manhattan from the Empire State Building. But what might have seemed desperately cool in the mid-1970s became downright chilling a quarter-century later on the morning of September 11, 2001.

For many fans, the attack on the World Trade Center would forever change the way in which they viewed their favorite monster movies. As the editor of *G-Fan* wrote, "As I watched the World Trade towers collapse on September 11, I felt guilty. The scene looked similar to those that had entertained me in many Godzilla . . . films. But it wasn't a fantasy, the people were real, and their fear and suffering were heartbreaking."[31] "For the first time in my life," another fan reflected, "Godzilla was the last thing I wanted to see. . . . It's no longer cool when the kaiju topple those skyscrapers, and I can now appreciate the absolute terror of the screaming, fleeing crowds."[32] The AMC cable network pulled Godzilla films from its schedule, and one commentator wondered, "Is Godzilla finished?" Much hand-wringing in the fan community ensued: hard questions—"Is there something inherently wrong in being entertained by the wholesale destruction of cities and armies?"—were aired; one *kaijū eiga* devotee who lost two relatives in the attack declared, "I still will like Godzilla movies, but I don't feel the same about them at all."[33] To some fans, such lamentations were a sign of capitulation, of the terrorists' victory in diminishing our way of life: "Godzilla and Spider-Man have nothing to do with terrorism. They are fantasy, and fantasy is a good escape in a world filled with all sorts of concerns. So let's be aware, but let's continue to enjoy life."[34] But before we clutch at the reassuring notion that movies are just empty escapism, we should remember that, according to some reports, one of Godzilla's many Middle Eastern fans was a certain Osama bin Laden, who is said to have watched the 1998 TriStar offering. As a captured al Qaeda operative told interrogators, bin Laden harbored the dream of destroying the Brooklyn Bridge, "the bridge in the Godzilla movie."[35] Though both the Brooklyn Bridge and our love of Godzilla endure, sometimes fact and fiction do draw too close for comfort.

Once in a while it is useful to remind oneself that, in the whole big cosmic scheme of things, Godzilla may indeed be little more than a dancing image on a movie screen, a man in a latex suit, a cheesy bit of Japanese cinema for ankle-biters around the globe. But in fifty years of coexistence with the king of the monsters—the endless television late shows, the burgeoning fan cultures, the icon permeating our collective consciousness—we have come to invest the reptilian giant with a range of meanings, and embrace him with a range of emotions, that can astound even the most diehard devotee or the most cynical skeptic. Godzilla has come to take on a life of his own, a life far removed from a Tokyo soundstage or a somber 1950s feature about nuclear testing gone terribly wrong. In the hearts and minds of fans the world over, Godzilla is constantly being reborn, redefined, and reinvented to meet a seemingly infinite variety of needs, from the most intensely personal to the most crassly commercial. When all is said and done, the Godzilla that is eternal is not the one on the DVDs and VHS tapes, but is the one we've imagined and keep reimagining every day.

GODZILLA'S SPAWN

GODZILLA IS, OF COURSE, QUINTESSENTIALLY Japanese. "Over the years," film critic Mark Shilling writes, "Godzilla has become an instantly recognizable symbol of Japan to the world at large. Folks in the American heartland who wouldn't know Akira Kurosawa from an Achilles tendon know Godzilla as the giant mutant lizard that stomps Tokyo."[1] Along with raw fish, samurai swords, cherry blossoms, and high-tech gadgetry, Godzilla and the images he evokes—crowds running through streets, toppling miniature cities, special effects of exquisite cheesiness—are tightly woven into our collective imagination of what constitutes Japan. As one commentator put it, "Godzilla and his original stomping ground, Japan, are wedded together like Punch and Judy, Cain and Abel, Sid and Nancy. Japan is the point about Godzilla."[2]

And yet, in the five decades since the king of the monsters waded ashore from Tokyo Bay, Godzilla has become a truly global property. Godzilla movies have been screened in every corner of the world, dubbed, subtitled, and edited for audiences from Warsaw to Macao, Karachi to Monterey. Godzilla merchandise—little vinyl Mothras, colorful posters, T-shirts adorned with flashing teeth, glowing dorsal fins, and massive saurian feet—have found their way into the hands of fans and children on every continent. Godzilla also opened the floodgates for other Japanese pop culture exports: just as the first Toyotas to hit the streets of America were followed by an ever-growing procession of Datsuns, Hondas, Subarus, Mitsubishis, Suzukis, and Mazdas, so a radioactive movie monster paved the way for the global advance of Ultraman and Kikaida, manga and anime, Super Mario and Yu-Gi-Oh!, Iron Chef, Shonen Knife and Hello Kitty.

But Godzilla has been even more than a worldwide icon and a market-making pathbreaker for the imaginative creations of the Japanese media industry. Over the past half century, the Godzilla series has become the model and inspiration for films produced all over the globe. Trying to draw on the enduring popularity and box-office power of the king of the monsters, studios from Denmark to North Korea to Tinseltown have fabricated ersatz Godzillas, thoughtful reinterpretations, earnest tributes, shameless rip-offs, and licensed remakes of the Tōhō classic. Although the 1933 *King Kong* may be the prototypical "monster on the loose" creature feature, stop-motion giant ape films are few and far between in the annals of world cinema; the heirs of Godzilla—movies with bipedal giant reptiles, usually breathing fire and portrayed by stuntmen in latex costumes—are plentiful, however, and not only in Japan. One analyst, in examining the international appropriation of the Godzilla formula, noted that *Gojira* "established the blueprint for a classic three-part ritual that was to be re-enacted so many times: the awakening, rampage and, finally, taming or suppression of the beast. The man in the rubber monster suit, stomping on scale models of urban sprawl, became the earthly representative of demon, god and scapegoat, like the priest of some arcane religion."[3] Arcane, perhaps, but undeniably global in appeal.

This chapter will survey the weird and wonderful selection of reptilian suitmation features made in Godzilla's creative slipstream. In monstrous manifestations as varied as Gamera, Reptilicus, Yonggary, and a certain TriStar abomination, Godzilla has been the subject of homages, exploitation, and cinematic plagiarism good, bad, and sometimes just downright ugly. If, as they always say, imitation is the highest form of flattery, then Godzilla has almost been flattered to death by generations of American, European, and Asian filmmakers.

Derivatives of Godzilla flourished in Japan in the 1960s. As the domestic motion picture industry began its descent into creative and financial bankruptcy, Japanese studios cast about desperately for any cinematic sure things to buoy their bottom lines. In the early and mid-1960s, at least, the Tōhō Godzilla franchise, though rapidly declining in quality and box-office draw itself, seemed to have a winning formula and was copied brazenly by rival moviemakers. Most of the major studios entered the *kaijū eiga* fray, at least briefly, and offered giant reptile features made using the cost-effective and time-honored methods of suitmation. For Tōhō competitors Daiei, Nikkatsu, and Shōchiku, Godzilla rip-offs were a way station on a downward economic spiral, an ultimately futile strategy to be pursued prior to the production of soft-core *roman poruno,* the conversion of theaters into bowling alleys and grocery stores, the transformation of back lots into theme parks, the fire sale of all assets and, for most, the eventual humiliation of going belly up.

Daiei was the most successful with monster movies, creating the giant turtle Gamera, an unlikely leading man who nonetheless became a fan favorite and long challenged Godzilla for the hearts and minds of Japanese grade-school moviegoers. Gamera was a peculiar invention: huge, green, and generally bipedal, with flame-thrower breath and massive, superfluous tusks, the overgrown terrapin had the peculiar ability to fly through the air, almost Frisbee-like, using fiery jets from under its shell. Debuting in the 1965 black-and-white film *Daikaijū Gamera* (subsequently released in America as *Gammera the Invincible*), the world's most irascible airborne turtle went on to headline a film a year until 1971, when Daiei slipped temporarily into receivership. Produced by consummate industry insider Nagata Masaichi (who had worked closely with the eminent directors Mizoguchi Kenji before the war and Kurosawa Akira after it) and directed primarily by Yuasa Noriaki, the first Gamera series ran the gamut from relatively big-budget films with reasonable production values to cheap-and-nasty cheese fests built largely around stock footage and inexpensive child actors. The creature was reborn for 1980's *Space Monster Gamera,* an embarrassing effort even by Daiei standards, only to be immediately killed off. In the late 1990s, the big turtle was revived in a critically acclaimed and unexpectedly polished trilogy of films masterminded by Kaneko Shūsuke, the *kaijū eiga* visionary who would go on to make *Godzilla, Mothra, and King Ghidorah.*

From the very start, Gamera was conceived as a bald-faced copy of the king of the monsters. Even the official story of Gamera's genesis was a complete rip-off, unsubtly cribbed from the legend of Tanaka Tomoyuki's creation of Godzilla: according to the Daiei mythology, Gamera was the brainchild of producer Nagata, who, agonizing over the

Oh, the humanity! The world's biggest, meanest turtle makes like Godzilla in the flaming wreckage of Tokyo. Photograph © 1965 Kadokawa Pictures.

unexpected cancellation of a blockbuster giant rat picture (reportedly undone by a nasty infestation of fleas), supposedly hit upon the idea of a flying turtle while looking out the window of a jetliner. The further parallels between the two film series are almost too numerous to mention: Gamera, like the other huge, amphibious reptile of Japan's silver screen, ravaged Tokyo in its first picture, Osaka (with the city's castle much in evidence) in the second; the turtle, like the lizard, premiered in a somber, reflective film as a ticked-off, homicidal badass but was quickly repositioned as a friendly, obliging defender of Japanese society; both fought a procession of ludicrous ten-story-tall adversaries, often with confusingly similar names and appearances (Did Daiei think audiences might confuse Barugon with Godzilla's Baragon? Oh, surely not!). What's more, *Gammera the Invincible,* in the spirit of *Godzilla, King of the Monsters* a decade before, featured a bevy of wooden American actors, all doing their best Raymond Burr imitations for the benefit of overseas audiences. And the mimicry didn't end with Godzilla: the original Gamera feature contained many memorable moments first seen in *The Beast from 20,000 Fathoms,* from the monster's initial defrosting in the wake of an arctic A-bomb explosion to a dramatic nighttime attack on a lighthouse.

But for all the creative poaching, the Gamera franchise did prove original and imaginative, developing in distinctive ways from the Godzilla series and other *kaijū eiga* properties. Gamera, more so even than the anthropomorphized Godzilla of the early 1970s, is consistently portrayed as having an inexplicable weakness for youngsters: in Gamera's 1965 debut film, the monster goes out of its way to rescue Toshio, a pudgy little turtle lover with a knack for getting into trouble; in *Attack of the Monsters* (1969), a couple of annoyingly precocious eleven-year-olds are rescued from interplanetary cannibals and ferried back to Earth by the agreeable king of the tortoises; and, as a scheming baddie in one of the movies declares, "Gamera has formidable destructive power, but there is a weak point, and that is his unusual and overpowering kindness to children." Despite the proliferation of adorable pint-size characters and heroic interventions, the Gamera offerings are also consistently more graphic in their depiction of violence than any other films in the Japanese sci-fi oeuvre. Unlike Tōhō creatures, Gamera's adversaries regularly find themselves decapitated, forcibly separated from a limb, or otherwise physically maimed, all portrayed in vivid detail; human characters viciously attack each other with ray guns, explosives, flammable liquids, poisonous insects, or any other lethal weapons at hand; monster wrestling is not an antiseptic affair, but flows invariably with gallons of reptilian blood, as even Gamera spurts a grayish-blue liquid from his frequent wounds. Such carnage contributed to the turtle's popularity—the movies' kiddie audiences were said to have relished the gruesome spectacles—and Godzilla's creators were forced to inject more explicit violence into the late Shōwa films to keep up with the competition.

None of the Gamera features had the sobering subtext of the original *Gojira* and, as pure escapist money spinners aimed at a youth market, few in the series even tried to develop a message or engage with larger social and political issues. Gamera himself was not radioactive—the monster was thawed by an atomic warhead but apparently not mutated by it—and the films are surprisingly matter-of-fact about doomsday weaponry: in *Gammera the Invincible*, the authorities are ready to unleash a volley of American atomic missiles until it is decided they will be ineffective against the fire-eating tortoise. Gamera's first outing does offer a neat kind of narrative closure, much more redolent of Hollywood science fiction that the *kaijū eiga* genre, as the monster is sealed in a space capsule and blasted toward Mars, allowing the triumphant powers-that-be to revel in the reassuring might of international cooperation and modern technology. The last film in the early string of sequels, *Gamera vs. Zigra* (1971), which appeared just a few months before the similarly themed *Godzilla vs. the Smog Monster,* also aspired to a serious message, superficially exploring the pressing ecological issues of the day. Most of the movies, however, end simply with sappy moralizing—"Why must man be so greedy?" one character laments in *Gamera vs. Barugon*—or with childish hopes for a world of utopian peace, safety, and prosperity. In short, the Gamera films were certainly no more (and were often considerably less) profound than the Godzilla offerings simultaneously being made, amidst the same constraints of low budgets and low aspirations, across Tokyo at Tōhō.

If the Gamera series—very much the Avis, Pepsi, or Burger King of *kaijū eiga*—could boast anything, it was monstrous adversaries, movie plots, and special effects yet sillier, more outlandish, and more hilariously cheesy than even the cinematic fluff being offered up in flicks like *Godzilla vs. Megalon.* Gamera's opponents were a motley troop of science-defying, rubber-suited misfits, more likely to split your sides with humor than evince even the slightest tinge of terror. Gyaos was a kind of Rodan manqué, a flying reptile with a flatiron head and a savage laser ray; Guillon, the beastly guard dog of the shapely brain-eating aliens Flovera and Barbella, was a machete-headed quadruped, armed with *shaken* throwing stars that would spring off his temples and slice into his enemies; Barugon was a Freudian nightmare, a huge unicorn lizard with plenty of suggestive glowing horns, a rainbow beam that flashes out of his back ("It's a Skittles commercial!" the *Mystery Science Theater* crew enthused) and a long, rigid tongue that shoots a white freezing spray from the end. Story lines were comparably ludicrous. In *Gamera vs. Monster X* (1970), as much a promotional film for Expo '70 in Osaka as a creature feature, the spiny dinosaur Jiger implants eggs in Gamera through its tail (don't even think about the physiology here) and our favorite turtle is rescued only when a couple of intrepid preteens pilot a minisub into the monster's lungs, kill the fetal Jigers, and make the discovery that saves the world. Not exactly what one would call a credible narrative, but darned good, laugh-out-loud fun all the same, especially if you can thoroughly suspend disbelief and imagine yourself a geewhiz, daydreaming fifth-grader all over again.

After Gamera's cinematic swan song in 1980, the franchise lay dormant for almost fifteen years. In the mid-1990s, however, the eighty-meter-tall flying tortoise was resurrected, like the Heisei Godzilla, by a group of creative professionals who had grown up with *kaijū eiga* and yearned to see giant reptiles stomping through Japan once again. The crew that brought Gamera back to life was young and imaginative, and included many individuals with backgrounds in anime and video games, most prominently the screenwriter Ito Kazunori, who had scripted the animated classic *Ghost in the Shell*. Dedicated to preserving the spirit of Gamera while infusing a more serious tone, a hipper sensibility and greater technical proficiency, director Kaneko's three efforts—*Gamera, Guardian of the Universe* (1995), *Gamera 2, Attack of Legion* (1996) and *Gamera 3, Revenge of Iris* (1999)—set a new standard for *kaijū eiga*. As one critic has noted, "With the Gamera movies widely regarded as inferior and absurd, Daiei had no image to maintain, no legacy to preserve; they could recreate Gamera from scratch without restraint."[4] As a result, the new Gamera films have been more imaginative than most of the Heisei and Shinsei Godzilla offerings, have garnered remarkably good reviews in Japan and the United States, and have appealed strongly to women (even if viewers cannot immediately recognize that Gyaos in *Gamera, Guardian of the Universe* was played by a woman, the first female suitmation actor). *Gamera 3* has been hailed by many, including a number of diehard Godzilla fans, as one of the greatest Japanese monster movies ever, combining a substantive plot with thrilling special effects and an unforgettable climactic battle inside the new Kyoto railway station (which, in good Gamera tradition, involves severed claws and lots of satisfying gore). The latest Gamera films are not quite perfect—like the 1990s Godzillas, they rely too heavily on revenge themes, weepy motherless-child motifs, uninspired adversaries, and a psychic who channels the monster (here portrayed by the ingenuous Fujitani Ayako, the real-life daughter of Steven Seagal)—yet they demonstrate that there's still plenty of vigor left in the *kaijū eiga* formula and that Godzilla, although the prototype and the enduring box-office champion, ain't the only monster act in town.

Daiei was also responsible for the only Japanese movie creature other than Godzilla, Gamera, and (belatedly) Mothra to have a series of his own. The three Daimajin features, all released in 1966, were outliers in the world of *kaijū eiga,* idiosyncratic fusions of monster movie conventions and *jidaigeki,* Japanese period-piece dramas featuring samurai warriors (a specialty of the Daiei studio, not coincidentally). Daimajin himself is a huge stone god, inspired both by *haniwa,* Japan's ancient terracotta tomb sculptures, and by the old Jewish legend of the Golem. A humorless stickler for truth and justice, Daimajin stirs whenever he senses oppression or wrongdoing, wreaking his vengeance on the evil and redeeming the pure hearted. Slow and methodical in his destruction, this statuesque champion of justice is not a particularly large monster; at twenty feet tall or so, Daimajin looks like Buffy lugging around Mrs. Beasley when he's got a victim in his arms. Daimajin has attitude, however: the green-complexioned deity's face was said to be modeled on Kirk Douglas (chin cleft and all!) and glares with the intense eyes of the suitmation actor inside, the former Mainichi Orions

The passion of the Gamera. Iris sticks one to the king of the turtles in Gamera 3. *Photograph © 1999 Kadokawa Pictures/TNHN.*

baseball player Hashimoto Riki (who would later appear with Bruce Lee in *Fist of Fury*). The sixteenth-century setting does not make for particularly interesting battle scenes; without chemical plants, high-tension wires and fighter jets, the pyrotechnics are quite limited, and spears, catapults, and swords deflecting off a huge stone idol just don't add up to much cinematic flash. The production values and special effects of the series are very high, including strong scores by Ifukube Akira, but the prohibitive cost of the films and their limited overseas appeal doomed any additional sequels. Kevin Costner was said to have optioned the property in the 1980s, but—thankfully—we have not been subjected to *Dances with Daimajin. Waterworld* was scary enough.[5]

Nikkatsu's sole entry in the *kaijū eiga* derby was the charming 1967 cheese puff *Gappa the Triphibian Monster* (also released in America under the misleading and much less cool title *Monster from a Prehistoric Planet*). The film was heavily subsidized by the Japanese government as a means of helping the ailing motion picture industry and generating much-needed foreign currency; as one of the film's screenwriters explained it, "The only kind of movie we could export internationally was something like *Godzilla.*"[6] With a plot based closely on the British *Gorgo* (of which more below), *Gappa* was also a thinly veiled takeoff on *King Kong vs. Godzilla,* complete with the South Seas islanders, blimp airlifts of monsters, gentle critiques of commercialism gone awry, and a sometimes none-too-subtle parodic edge. The creatures themselves—Gappas? Gappae?—are rather cute winged lizards who look like mutant mongrels of Godzilla, Rodan, and giant chickens. The plot revolves around a heartwarming family drama: Japanese theme park developers steal a baby Gappa (as well as an aggravating little native boy in blackface) from a tropical island; this sets off an amber alert, as an enraged mother and father Gappa follow junior to Japan, exhibiting their triphibian nature by swimming, flying, and walking en route; most of the country's tourist sites and military hardware ends up being trashed before the family of prehistoric survivors is finally reunited on the tarmac at Haneda airport; this final scene of monstrous domestic bliss is so touching that the film's stereotypical career woman with a heart of ice decides to chuck the rat race, get married, and settle down to birth some creatures of her own. "The Gappa made me realize there's more to life than ambition," she concludes contentedly. The theme of giant murderous reptile as gentle-hearted, misunderstood, anthropomorphized family man was a popular one at the time, as *Gappa* appeared in the same year as the syrupy *Son of Godzilla*. Nikkatsu was not committed to the *kaijū eiga* genre, however, so audiences never had the chance to revel in wholesome, fun-for-the-whole-family sequels like *Gappa Goes to Summer Camp* or *Co-ed from a Prehistoric Planet*.

Shōchiku also made a single creature feature, *The X from Outer Space* (1967), a swanky, hip space opera whose utter obscurity is the only thing that keeps it from being an all-time camp classic. As one online reviewer described it, "Imagine *Godzilla* with a severe dose of *Our Man Flint*. . . . Imagine Gerry Anderson's *UFO* meets Japanese *kaijū eiga*. Imagine flying to the moon where men in silver space suits recline in bean bags, sip martinis, and cut the rug with their female counterparts, who have taken the time to switch out of their shiny space suits and into orange cocktail dresses. Then throw a giant monster smashing up Japan into the works, and you will just barely begin to fathom how insanely cool this movie is."[7] A retro hoot, *The X from Outer Space* is light on plot and heavy on cheese (the astronauts appear to be flying to Mars on barber's chairs) and features a goofy, rubbery monster (Godzilla with antennae and a face lift) who eventually is done in by a coating of radioactive shaving cream. The beast also packs a strained message of sorts: a buxom American astrobabe forsakes her interracial love for the short, dark, and handsome Captain Sano in the finale, declaring: "All things should remain where they belong. . . . That's the lesson the monster taught me." What would we do without Dear Abby, Dr. Phil, and helpful alien marauders?

Godzilla's descendants also found a welcoming home on the small screen in Japan. In 1966, *Ultra Q,* a kind of monster-of-the-week show produced by Tsuburaya Eiji, the special effects mastermind of *Gojira,* premiered on the TBS network; not long thereafter, Ultraman made his debut and created an entirely new genre of television entertainment for kids in Japan. The convoluted world of Ultraman is about as incomprehensible as the rules of cricket: in a nutshell, Ultraman is a kind of cosmic cop, a red and silver giant alien from Nebula M–78 ("You're from Nebula M–78 too? Do you know my friend Gigan?"), who comes to defend Earth from a ceaseless stream of gargantuan monsters and intergalactic invaders. In each week's episode, Ultraman would take on another gruesome reptilian creature from Tsuburaya's imagination, several of them just recycled Godzilla costumes with the new frill here, a fresh spot of paint there. Fun, colorful, and untaxing intellectually or morally (good Ultraman always beats bad creature), the series was an immediate hit with the kiddie crowd and spawned an entire entertainment empire. Over the decades, Ultraman has starred in numerous television series (produced in Australia and America, as well as Japan), inspired feature films, comic books, and anime, headlined a theme park in Kyushu, and sold almost as many toys and collectibles as the king of the monsters himself. Ultraman's imitators became a virtual industry unto themselves, from Tōhō's *Zone Fighter* series to *Johnny Sokko and His Flying Robot* and Tōei Studios' *Five Rangers,* the basis for the hugely successful Mighty Morphin Power Rangers. Thus latex suitmation creatures and teams of superhero defenders became the stock-in-trade of Japanese children's television, contributing—ironically enough—

to the downfall of the Godzilla film series that had sired them. By the 1970s, most Japanese kids were understandably unwilling to part with good money to see cheesy monsters wrestling on the big screen if they could get the same thing for free on TV every single day.

Watching all the clones, heirs and forgeries of Godzilla that appeared in Japan from the 1960s on, one can't help but be struck by the energy and imaginativeness that have gone into the business of making monsters. The joie de vivre, spunky good humor, and sheer creativity that shine through Gamera, Gappa, Ultraman, and the others, despite the common constraints of low budgets, low technology, and low average viewer age, are quite remarkable. Though the Godzilla franchise was, and remains, constrained by a successful formula, a venerable history, and the sense that the king of the monsters is too valuable a property to change significantly, Godzilla's imitators have been less conservative, less bound by tradition, and, consequently, a little more free-wheeling, off-the-wall, and just plain wacky. And for that—the unlikely alignment of the stars that gave us a giant fanged turtle, a score-settling statue, and a nuclear family of prehistoric poultry—we should be forever thankful.

The prototypical giant monster movie may well be the American *King Kong,* and the genre may only have reached its fullest flowering in postwar Japan, yet Europe has a history of cinematic invasion by giant lizards as well. In fact, in the first ever "monster on the loose" picture, Willis O'Brien's 1925 silent classic *The Lost World,* a Brontosaurus runs amuck in London, horrifying some clubby aristocrats, caving in a building or two, and crushing London Bridge before swimming off to freedom. In *The Giant*

Behemoth (1959), directed by Eugene Lourie of *The Beast from 20,000 Fathoms* fame, a radioactive Paleosaurus (more or less a quadrupedal, stop-motion Godzilla) also victimizes the British capital, spreading radiation burns and general destruction until a well-placed torpedo saves the world.

The greatest English contribution to *kaijū eiga*, however, is undoubtedly the 1960 technicolor extravaganza *Gorgo*. Also the creation of Lourie (who, like Honda Ishirō, had the rap of working well with monsters), *Gorgo* was a sober, cautionary tale about the consequences of upsetting the natural order of things. Originally planned as a Japanese coproduction called "Kuru Island" and set in the South Pacific and Tokyo, *Gorgo* was reworked as the story of prehistoric survivors off the coast of Ireland who, awakened by seismic activity, eventually find their way to the streets of London. With quality personnel both in front of and behind the camera, Lourie's film is a polished job, and the special effects, especially mother Gorgo's rampage through the city to rescue her baby from a circus freak show, are almost as good as what Tōhō could muster at the time. The attack sequences have some memorable moments: dozens of people crushed by a falling masonry wall, the fatal folly of trying to hide in a Tube station, the sandwich-board man screaming "Repent, the end is near!" who is unceremoniously trampled to death by a swell of fleeing Londoners. Like *Gojira*, *Gorgo* consciously evokes memories of wartime bombings—an announcer specifically compares the destruction to the Blitz, just so viewers are sure to get it—and other nods to Godzilla are numerous, from a silhouette of mama Gorgo against the burning skyline to the use of the futile old high-tension-wire defense strategy. And the creatures themselves, upright lizards with flapping Prince Charles ears, bear a striking resemblance to the king of the monsters and were, unlike the stars of *The Beast from 20,000 Fathoms* and *The Giant Be-*

hemoth, played by stuntmen in rubber suits. And lest one think that such similarities to *kaijū eiga* were just coincidental, it is worth noting that *Gorgo* was not premiered in New York or Hollywood, or even in London, the city where it was made and set, but in Tokyo, the world's undisputed capital of suitmation and giant reptiles.

If *Gorgo* made Europe's reputation as a source of decent monster movies, then *Reptilicus* (1962) promptly demolished it. The lavish Danish production—directed by American sci-fi schlock-master Sid Pink, featuring some of the finest actors Denmark could offer, and made with the full cooperation of the nation's army and navy—has gone down as one of the worst films in creature feature history (and that, of course, is really saying something). One recent reviewer, echoing the general critical opinion, wrote that "*Reptilicus* is a dreary little fart of a movie with lousy puppet monster effects and cardboard miniatures, zombie acting by a plank-faced cast of Danes, and an idiot script shoveled through the sausage conveyor of fast-forward production by sci-fi vandal Sid Pink. It is, you might say, a *bad* film."[8] No argument there. *Reptilicus* follows the standard "monster on the loose" formula: a bit of dinosaur tail is found in Lapland and eventually grows into a giant beast, looking more like a dragon from a Chinese restaurant place mat than a Scandinavian native, with tiny little wings, great long fangs and a big forked tongue. Reptilicus proceeds to wander around the countryside, nibbling on livestock and sending everyone into a tizzy, before turning on Copenhagen. The authorities are powerless, not least because of the monster's secret weapon, "acid slime," a bright green vomit that Reptilicus generously spews on anyone and anything in its way. The death-puking threat to humanity is finally put away by a bazooka shell full of tranquilizer, right in the mouth (and you thought a little syringe full of Novocain at the dentist's was bad!). Audiences end up feeling relieved and thankful not so much because the monster is killed and Denmark saved (would we have noticed its obliteration anyway?) but because the movie is over and no sequels have ever been made.

Other *kaijū eiga* oddities seem to lurk in Europe's cinematic history. In 1977, Luigi Cozzi (apparently an Italian version of Sid Pink) made a "colorized" and heavily reedited version of *Godzilla, King of the Monsters.* Now a mercifully obscure work, the Italian reimagining of *Gojira*—affectionately nicknamed "Cozzilla" by some fans—was a psychedelic hodgepodge of wartime newsreel footage, antinuclear invective, and classic Godzilla sequences.[9] Other indignities were inflicted upon the Japanese giant over the years, most notably the curious renaming of many of his movies for release in European markets. Though Godzilla quickly became a catchword in the United States and Britain, Continental audiences appeared less receptive to the odd-sounding Japanese name. Thus in Germany, at least five of the Tōhō films were released under the banner of the favored local monster Frankenstein, including *Frankensteins Höllenbrut* (Frankenstein's Progeny of Hell, aka *Godzilla vs. Gigan*) and *Frankensteins Kampf gegen die Teufelsmonster* (Frankenstein's War against the Devil Monster, aka *Godzilla vs. the Smog Monster*). Such confusion appears to have been widespread: in at least three European countries, Godzilla was rechristened Gorgo. In Italy, *Destroy All Monsters* was re-released as *Il Retorno di Gorgo;* in Greece, *Son of Godzilla* became *Gorgo, Monster of Amazonia;* and, oddest of all, *Godzilla vs. Mechagodzilla* was transformed into *Gorgo y Superman se Citan en Tokio* (Gorgo and Superman Fight in Tokyo) for Spanish moviegoers. In the fluid linguistic soup of European monsterdom, Gamera was sometimes called Godzilla, the king of the monsters was referred to as King Kong, and odd new coinages (Galien the Galaxy Monster? *Satans Creatuur?*) sprouted from Holland to Turkey. Is it any wonder that we admire the Old World for its castles, chocolates, and wine rather than for its monster movies?

Asian moviemakers outside of Japan have tried their hands at *kaijū eiga* several times over the past half century. Few of these films are well known in the West and, in virtually every case, this obscurity seems to be well deserved. The prolific studios of Hong Kong have produced thinly veiled knockoffs of Ultraman (would you buy a used car from a guy named Inframan?), and, in the late 1970s, the Shaw Brothers came out with a Chinese version of *King Kong,* known variously as *The Mighty Peking Man* and *Goliathon,* which drew upon the special effects talents of Godzilla veterans Arikawa Teisho and Kawakita Kōichi. Thailand does not seem to have contributed to the world's library of original creature features, but the rumor is that the king of the monsters actually *sings* in one of the Tōhō films edited and dubbed for Bangkok audiences. One can only imagine what "It's Not Easy Being Green" sounds like in Thai, and in Godzilla's resonant baritone.

If any country other than Japan has taken up the giant monster genre with real gusto, it certainly is Korea. The fiercely proud residents of the peninsula, never wanting to be second-best in anything to their wealthier neighbors (and former colonial masters), the Japanese, have struggled long and hard to establish themselves as credible players in the *kaijū eiga* game. Success has been elusive, however, and embarrassing efforts like *A*P*E,* a 1976 Joanna Kerns vehicle too painful even to be funny, have given South Korean sci-fi an enduring black eye, even among the many international admirers of B-movie campiness. But Korean filmmakers, even if not terribly talented in the dark arts of suitmation, are a tenacious and focused lot, and they continue to produce big-lizard stinkers for the cheese lovers of the world.

South Korea has a long history in the cinematic monster business. In the late 1960s, at about the same time that pseudo-Godzillas like Gamera and Gappa were pouring out of Japanese studios, Korean filmmakers produced two *kaijū eiga* offerings of their own. One, the now-legendary *Wangmagwi,* nicknamed the "lost creature feature" by some Western fans, is said to have been a lightweight tale of alien invasion featuring a Kong-like monster and the destruction of a miniature Seoul. Although once enshrined in the *Guinness Book of World Records* as the film made with the most extras (only to be topped in 1982 by *Gandhi*—Darn those non-violent visionaries!), *Wangmagwi* has never been released outside Korea. The same cannot be said of *Yongary, Monster of the Deep* (1967), an amusing little groaner of a film well known to American audiences as a longtime staple of late, late shows and "Million Dollar Movies" everywhere. *Yongary* has all the components of a *kaijū eiga* classic: a big rubbery monster (think Godzilla with a nose horn and tiny tusks) released from his primordial slumber by a rogue Chinese nuclear test; scientists, generals, and astronauts coming out the wazoo (including a slack-jawed Korean "war cabinet" that I wouldn't trust to clean out my gutters, let alone defend a country); and a pesky little eight-year-old whose grating high jinks make you wish Yongary's rampages had claimed just one additional victim. The special effects, despite technical assistance from Japan's Tōei Studios, are often charmingly primitive. Unusual moments abound in the film: at one point, the monster, awakened from a coma by the aforementioned brat, boogies down to a surf-music version of the Korean folk song "Arirang"; in trashing downtown Seoul, Yongary carefully obliterates lingering symbols of Japanese colonialism (like the old capitol building) while sparing Korean historical sites; and, in the finale, as Yongary is undone by a dusting of ammonia powder, twitching and bleeding in the remarkably realistic throes of reptilian death, whole families of Koreans buzz by in helicopters, incongruously laughing and cracking bad jokes. Lactose-intolerant viewers should take care when watching *Yongary, Monster of the Deep:* this film comes with a triple helping of cheese.

Amazingly enough, more than thirty years after Yongary's debut, a sequel of sorts was made. Titled *Yonggary* in Korea and released straight-to-DVD as *Reptilian* in America, this big-budget, high-profile production was intended to capitalize on the buzz from the TriStar Godzilla and the Jurassic Park series. Screened first in 1999, and then distributed again in 2001 after substantial remedial work on special effects, *Yonggary* was the baby of producer Shim Hyoung-Rae (Ray Shim), a Korean comic known for his slapstick portrayals of a retarded boy, who indulged his love of science fiction in a series of undistinguished monster film parodies in the 1990s (*Young-Goo and Dinosaur Zuzu, Tirano's Claw,* etc.). *Yonggary* was intended as a serious blockbuster, however, and Shim spent (according to some reports) more than $13.5 million on the picture, a fortune by Korean movie standards, much of it raised from the industrial giant Hyundai and from government subsidies. Shim's movie, even in the "improved" state, is an overblown, computer-generated bore, a pale shadow of the 1998 *Godzilla* without even the high-tech flash to recommend it. Made in English with a cast of no-name American and British actors, *Yonggary* is a virtual instructional video on bad acting and lame screenwriting. An insipid cast of animated monsters—the beast of the title is a panther-like T-Rex, his nemesis Cyker is a lizardy scorpion—and a ridiculous alien invasion story line (Is that C–3PO trying to take over the Earth?) don't help out at all. A few memorable lines are all that keep *Yonggary* from being a total loss. Facing a clash of creatures in downtown Los Angeles, a stolid Army ranger declares, "This place is turning into a freaking prehistoric petting zoo!" And when confronting all five hundred feet of digital Yonggary, the same wooden captain roars, "Compared to this guy, Godzilla is a pussy!" Yeah, right.

This brings us unavoidably to what is, without question, the oddest incarnation of Godzilla ever to make it to the silver screen, the incredible North Korean morality play *Pulgasari* (1985). Conceived by pompadoured dictator, playboy, and film buff Kim Jong-Il, *Pulgasari* looks like an ill-fated attempt by the Great Leader to feed his starving people with a rich diet of cinematic cheese. This unique take on *kaijū eiga* traditions was made by famed South Korean director Shin Sang-Ok—kidnapped in 1978 by Kim to revitalize the North's moribund film industry—and showcased the work of Nakano Teruyoshi, then the master of Godzilla's special effects.[10] Kim also imported suitmation pro Satsuma Kenpachirō to play the monster Pulgasari, an iron-eating, despot-crushing deity who looks like a cross between Godzilla and a Texas longhorn. The resulting movie is a long martial-arts, period-piece epic with violence aplenty, a cast of thousands, echoes of *Daimajin*, and a message at once heavy handed and fundamentally incomprehensible. The irony of *Pulgasari*'s story—which tells of repressed, hungry peasants rising up against a distant, brutal tyrant—was apparently lost on Kim Jong-Il, who is said to have hailed the movie as a masterpiece. Few other viewers would likely share this evaluation, but *Pulgasari* does show flashes of real imagination and has an undeniable appeal, an "Axis of Evil" sensibility and an old Iron Curtain kind of earnestness that are bizarrely enchanting. Who would have thought that Godzilla, that poster boy of global commercialism, could be morphed into a proletarian liberator, a North Korean *Braveheart,* and a tool of Communist propaganda? But then again, who could have imagined that Hollywood would screw up the king of the monsters as royally as it did in 1998?

Fortunately, I didn't have the kind of mother who admonished, "If you can't say something nice, then don't say anything at all." If I had, I wouldn't be able to write even a single sentence about the TriStar *Godzilla* without getting a maternal box around the ears. The Tinseltown sequel was an overblown flop, a profound disappointment to Godzilla fans the world over, and (not to put too fine a point on it) a disgrace to the heritage, character, and spirit of the king of the monsters. Perhaps I should take the high road and leave the obvious deficiencies of *Godzilla* unspoken, but honesty— even more so than size—does matter. And so, to be perfectly honest, that 1998 lizard-on-the-loose flick was bad, really bad, beyond *Reptilicus* bad, a hollow dud of a film that makes even the weakest of the Tōhō offerings (Remember *Terror of Mechagodzilla,* anyone?) look like masterpieces of world cinema.

Licensing an American version of Godzilla, a project which promised a huge windfall of free-flowing Hollywood cash, was long a twinkle in Tōhō's corporate eyes. Even *Gojira*'s original creators publicly yearned to see what a major U.S. studio (and above all its special-effects talent) could do with the tried-and-true king of the monsters. Over the decades, a variety of American interests pitched ideas, including the very unlikely notion of a Godzilla musical, to the Tōhō top brass in Tokyo, but consistently without success. Finally, in 1992, impresario Henry Saperstein (who often referred to Godzilla as his "golden goose") brokered a deal between Tōhō and TriStar Pictures to develop a big-budget, big-talent, big-profits, made-in-America Godzilla movie. In

1993, the screenwriting team of Terry Rossio and Ted Elliott, fresh off work on Disney's cartoon feature *Aladdin,* signed on to the project; a year later, after striking out with most of the leading action film directors in the business, TriStar convinced Jan DeBont, a very hot property after his megahit first film *Speed,* to try his luck with a giant monster movie. By the end of 2004, however, DeBont and TriStar had parted ways over the issue of money (the director demanding $120 million for the project), and the American Godzilla slipped into limbo. Only in May of 1996 did Roland Emmerich and Dean Devlin, the creative team behind the hyperprofitable disaster film *Independence Day,* take up the baton, co-writing a new screenplay, completely redesigning the monster, and attempting to breathe life into what they clearly considered a moribund franchise. Both Emmerich and Devlin professed to being dyed-in-the-wool Godzilla fans, though few would consider their film an homage or tribute; indeed, not many viewers familiar with the Tōhō series would consider their 1998 effort a Godzilla movie at all.[11]

The Hollywood *Godzilla* is, as one would expect, a technological tour de force, a computer-generated simulacrum of *kaijū eiga* with all the flashy bells and whistles any gum-popping Memorial Day moviegoer in middle America could ask for. If the quality and quantity of special effects tricks is the yardstick, then Godzilla measures up reasonably well: the top blows off of the Chrysler Building as convincingly as I can imagine, Madison Square Garden is realistically vaporized, and a credibly huge, leggy lizard scurries around midtown before being fatally entangled in the Brooklyn Bridge. Overshadowed perhaps by the spectacle of digital destruction, the script, story, and overall tone of the movie are weak, uneven, and frequently downright embarrassing. A kind of watered-down rehash of *The Beast from 20,000 Fathoms,* the TriStar *Godzilla* has only the flimsiest of plots holding together its chase scenes and special-effects sequences. The film wavers uncomfortably (throughout its interminable two hours, nineteen minutes of running time) between the poles of serious action film and parodic send-up. Emmerich and Devlin obviously aimed for a contrived campiness but, without suitmation and the cheesy goodness of low-tech effects, their attempts at tongue-in-cheek humor generally fall flat. Cartoonish characters, strained one-liners, and disengaged acting (Matthew Broderick, presumably the biggest star who could be afforded once the SFX bills had been paid, obviously approached the film with Ferris Bueller–like detachment) combine to make *Godzilla* more forced than funny, a failure both as a lighthearted parody and a rock-'em-sock-'em thriller.

More than anything else, it was the design and behavior of the monster that made the Hollywood Godzilla such a letdown to so many *kaijū eiga* aficionados. Fans have coined a number of colorful nicknames for the TriStar creature: Newzilla, Fraudzilla, Crapzilla, Deanzilla (after Dean Devlin) and, best of all, GINO, an acronym for *Godzilla In Name Only*. Gripes about the look of the new monster are too plentiful to catalogue here: described by one critic as "an anorexic, unisex, runaway model of Godzilla," GINO was more *Jurassic Park* than Tōhō, a fleet-footed velociraptor with the head of an iguana and a chin (believe it or not) based on that of the tiger Sher Khan in Disney's *The Jungle Book*.[12] A few vestigial dorsal fins suggested some genetic relationship to the original king of the monsters, but the Manhattan upstart lacked one of Godzilla's trademark features, the signature radioactive ray that can level cities and incinerate opponents; in its place, GINO could muster only a sort of combustible belch, a rapid exhalation of digestive gas that would send cars flying and spark at an open flame. Many fans complained that the American Godzilla, so unlike the Japanese prototype, appeared scared—running rather than fighting when the Blackhawks swarm—and weak, succumbing to just a handful of run-of-the-mill Air Force missiles. Only the slaughter of its hatching brood makes GINO conspicuously angry and destructive, and even then, the Army's friendly fire does more damage to the Gotham infrastructure than does good old-fashioned stomping and thrashing.

Indeed, the so-called Godzilla of the TriStar feature does not even seem to be a monster, not a godlike being of legend, not a score-settling, conscience-rattling phantom of the imagination. Fraudzilla is just a huge, overgrown animal, a pumped-up reptile that, for reasons never fully articulated, believes New York City is a great place to raise a family. Thus, despite the cynical nuclear theme, *Godzilla* is not a cautionary tale, not a musing on science, nature, human arrogance or the mysteries of creation. The monster is not a message or a symbol, but simply a pest, an unwanted, annoying intruder that needs to be exterminated like a termite in the foundation or a cockroach in the cupboard. This is not an epic battle, this is the Orkin man, here wearing the drab fatigues of the U.S. Army, struggling to dislodge a particularly large and nasty nest of vermin from some prime real estate in the heart of Manhattan. And the creature itself is not a saurian superhero in anything but sheer bulk: a reclusive and ever-hungry breeding machine (the American Godzillas are "born pregnant"—Eeewww!), GINO runs through the sewers and subway tunnels of the Big Apple like an outsize rat, an aesthetic aggravation rather than a threat to humanity.

One could fill a whole book with gripes about the Hollywood Godzilla, and many *kaijū eiga* fans have just about done that. The chronicle of failings starts at the scapegoating of France: the reallocation of the blame for creating the monster from American H-bombs (in the Japanese original) to French nuclear testing (in the TriStar incarnation) shows just plain cowardice on the part of Emmerich and Devlin. The stupid Siskel and Ebert parody that runs through the film (supposedly inserted because the critics had roundly panned *Independence Day*) is petty and juvenile, even in a work whose "primary target" was boys ages four to eleven. The fact that Godzilla dies—and really without much of a fight—in the Tinseltown movie was profoundly disturbing to many fans. Monster master Kaneko Shūsuke could only ascribe this to weaknesses in the American national character: "It is interesting the U.S. version runs about trying to escape missiles," the director told one Japanese magazine. "Americans seem unable to accept a creature that cannot be put down by their arms."[13]

Godzilla ended up being a bloodless, soulless film, an empty vehicle inflated with a $50 million publicity campaign and enough promotional tie-ins—Taco Bell, Hershey, Duracell—to make a NASCAR driver envious. The critics rightly panned it. Roger Ebert hit the nail on the head by calling *Godzilla* "a cold-hearted, mechanistic vision, so starved for emotion or wit." Another damned it as "a film which is all shallows and no depth, all show and no subtext" that is "ultimately about nothing."[14] The American Godzilla has technology but not spirit, flash but not substance. The monster lacks personality, the film lacks a core, and everything we've come to expect from Godzilla movies—from a man in a rubber suit, to a campy chuckle, to an earnest stab at relevance—is missing from this perfunctory effort. Sure, size does matter, but so does heart, and the TriStar feature can't make up in big-budget polish what is so obviously missing in fundamental character. *Godzilla* was a certified Hollywood blockbuster, but the king of the monsters it ain't.

Over the years, Godzilla has been imitated (and even officially licensed), but the big reptilian original has never been duplicated, equaled, or bettered. Some of the knockoffs have shown a certain flair, a creative élan, and even, in the case of Gamera, a remarkable longevity in the public eye. Others have run the gamut from the derivative and obscure, to the odd and hilarious, to the insipid but pretentious. And ersatz Godzillas have blossomed in all corners of the globe, leaving big footprints, mangled miniature cities, and loads of cinematic cheese on virtually every continent. The basic formula of the Tōhō series—suitmation, the bipedal lizard, etc.—has been widely appropriated, but the things that make Godzilla great—the look and personality of the monster, the good-natured innocence, the big-time wrestling, the reveries of destruction, the music, the roar, that campy genius—have proven far more elusive for the world's filmmakers to replicate. Godzilla, for all the global exposure and all the pretenders, is unique, peerless and thoroughly Japanese. Really, now, who could ask for anything more?

GODZILLA FOREVER

OVER THE YEARS, I HAVE GIVEN MANY A TALK on Godzilla in school classrooms. Last May, in the final days before summer break, I presented my standard forty-minute lecture, complete with video clips and Japanese snacks, to a raucous group of fifth-graders in the small town of Carbondale, Kansas. As a veteran of middle-school crowds, I usually know what to expect: nonexistent discipline, projectiles if I turn my back, an intense desire to see Godzilla wrestling other monsters, a litany of familiar questions about the creature's size, weight, toughness, prospects against various adversaries (Sylvester Stallone, The Rock, Pokemon), and so forth. But I wasn't prepared for what happened that warm afternoon in Carbondale.

Near the end of my talk, a quiet boy with glasses raised his hand. Among his screaming and jeering classmates, many of whom were attempting to replicate the tangle between

Godzilla and King Ghidorah which we'd just watched on the VCR, the eleven-year-old shyly posed a single question. Not how high Godzilla could jump, not whether the monster ate spinach, not why bazookas can't penetrate giant reptile skin. "When watching the old Godzilla movies," he innocently asked, "did Americans enjoy seeing all those Japanese people die?" I was taken aback and was, for one of the few times in my life, completely speechless. Not once had that thought ever crossed my mind, no matter how obvious, how plausible—and how chilling—it may indeed be. I managed to stammer out some answer but, ever since that day, I have been haunted by the boy's question and ashamed of my blissful ignorance, never having considered Godzilla's global popularity in such a disturbing light. Sometimes from the mouths of babes. . . .

The lesson I take from this little story is that Godzilla is not simple, not irrelevant, not just campy, kiddie pap good for a giggle, a wink and a turn on *Mystery Science Theater 3000*. Figuring out why we love Godzilla and why the king of the monsters has enjoyed such enduring appeal in America means asking some unexpectedly tough questions and, when all is said and done, it means understanding ourselves. And that, needless to say, can be challenging, uncomfortable, and, so much of the time, virtually impossible. The story also should remind us that for all the goofy WWF moments, silly plot twists, and anthropomorphic clowning that came to characterize the Godzilla series, the monster began his career fifty years ago as a sober cinematic warning, a harbinger of nuclear annihilation, and a haunting specter of total war. To understand the king of the monsters we must appreciate the complexity, ambiguity, and fluidity, not just of the fictional creature and the films in which he starred, but of our reactions, our assumptions, and the meanings we have invested in Godzilla the international cultural icon. Godzilla, it turns out, is one complicated guy.

Godzilla, according to sci-fi critic John Pierce, is "a monster for all seasons": "Given the host of weapons used against him, it is evident that Godzilla has infinite powers of regeneration. But that regeneration can also be considered a metaphor: Godzilla lives on and on because he can always be reborn in whatever guise works best for the time, and can be invested with whatever greater significance suits our psychological needs."[1] The king of the monsters, another scholar has observed, "is at once a product of the Other and a projection of the national self, the destroyer (tragically) foredoomed to be grandly (or pathetically) destroyed, the tainted one and the one who purifies, perpetrator and—somehow—victim." Godzilla thus turns out to be "the perfect floating, empty metaphor."[2]

What makes Godzilla such a malleable monster, an interpretive chameleon, a ready vehicle for others' hopes, agendas, and fantasies, is by no means obvious. Curiously, one reason why Godzilla has proven such an accessible and multipurpose symbol may well be the monster's mysterious and stubbornly unknowable nature. Although we have observed the saurian giant's behavior in twenty-seven feature films, he remains a self-contained, private, and almost cryptic character, a cipher to whom many motivations and meanings may be credibly ascribed, a figure who is (if one can still use such a term in this day and age) thoroughly inscrutable.

Godzilla, of course, is silent, and save for that trademark roar, he never utters a word on screen or off. As Vincent Canby has noted, "Godzilla is to Japan what Clark Kent is to the United States—an inarticulate savior."[3] Godzilla never eats, unlike the TriStar Fraudzilla who scarfs down fish with rare gusto. Godzilla seldom bleeds, though Gigan's abdominal buzzsaw does draw a drop or two of precious bodily fluids. We certainly never see Godzilla defecating, and even imagining monster spoor is not a pretty thought. Godzilla is sexless, recognizable as neither male nor female, with no apparent carnal drives or instinctual urges to mate. And perhaps this is fortunate, because Godzilla seems to be alone in his species, with no family, no mother or father, virtually no history, and no personal entanglements—other than the occasional monstrous battle to the death, and the curious foster parent arrangements with Minilla and Baby—to speak of. Godzilla is unaging and, indeed, virtually unchanging physically over the decades. Godzilla is like a celebrity who died young— Marilyn Monroe, James Dean—remaining forever frozen in the collective imagination, never succumbing (like Elvis, Jerry Lewis, and Jackie O) to the ravages of time in the public eye. And, events in 1954 and 1995 notwithstanding, Godzilla is eternal, never dying or, at the very least, rebounding from death with uncommon speed, certainty, and vigor.

As a being with minimal needs, dormant instincts, a shadowy past, no personal life, an air of permanence, and a resolute reticence, Godzilla can be (and long has been) invested with a far wider range of implications and connotations than most run-of-the-mill pop culture idols. The king of the monsters can be imagined male or female, ultimate tough guy or sensitive mentor, defender or renegade; his heroism is never undermined by off-screen scandals, his stature never diminished by a bulging waistline or varicose veins; he can be the object of affection, empathy, pity, fear, revulsion, or respect, all depending on how we the viewers wish to see him. As times change, so does Godzilla; across cultures and continents, generations and genders, the creature remains ever available as a metaphor, ever compliant to interpretation and appropriation. Godzilla is the icon we all can make our own.

Perhaps the most important reason why we find it so easy to relate to Godzilla, and why we are so eager to attribute to him our own individual messages and meanings, is the fact that Godzilla is a monster with personality. In contrast to the soulless, inhuman creatures beloved of Hollywood filmmakers (think Ridley Scott's *Alien*) or the animalistic, instinctual dinosaur that TriStar tried to pawn off as the king of the monsters, Godzilla has always seemed to have character, a combination of heart and mind that sets him apart from the average mutant radioactive reptile on the silver screen. Some of this air of humanity comes, no doubt, from the very process of suitmation, a low-tech, low-budget technique that maintains the connection between man and monster in a way that the cool, high-tech precision of computer-generated imagery never can. And while the spectacle of Godzilla doing a victory jig or playing boulder volleyball with an opponent may make many a fan wince in embarrassment, the anthropomorphized monster—ridiculous Muppet head and all—is undeniably charming, likeable and unique. That Tōhō endowed its *kaijū eiga* headliners with names and identities—the gentle Mothra, the brutal Ghidorah, the cowardly Minilla—further highlights the divide between Godzilla and the faceless, passionless, nameless nightmares (think *Them!, The Beast from 20,000 Fathoms, Attack of the Crab Monsters,* etc.) mass produced in Tinseltown back lots.

As a recurring character, Godzilla has become a monster we've gotten to know like an old friend. One Japanese fan suggested that "Godzilla's personality is sort of like the neighborhood *oyaji* (middle-aged man), who's friendly and grumpy at the same time. Godzilla kicks down Tokyo over and over again in the same way that an *oyaji* kicks over a piece of furniture if he's in a bad mood."[4] Many of the

American Godzilla admirers who wrote me expressed similar sentiments, describing the king of the monsters as though he were a longtime buddy or family member, praising him for his tenderness, his courage, his resourcefulness, and a hundred other virtues. One correspondent stated, "I think that Godzilla is an enduring pop culture icon because he does what young people are often told to do: Be a leader, not a follower. Don't care what other people think. Do the best you can. Be brave. I think that Godzilla shows very human characteristics that people can connect with." Of course, like anyone, Godzilla has his foibles (that insatiable desire to destroy Japanese cities, for example), his strengths and weaknesses, and his unpredictable moments. But that's what makes him *real* (at least as real as a fictional fifty-foot lizard can be) and gives him *heart,* a kind of depth that I would argue no other movie monster has ever attained. Godzilla is larger than life—literally as well as figuratively—and yet is always down to earth and, on some level at least, just one of the guys. There is a hokey moment at the end of *Godzilla 2000* where one of the characters, musing about why the monster continues to defend Japan, suggests, "Godzilla is inside each one of us." And, one might well add, there's a little bit of each of us in Godzilla.

When I watch a Godzilla movie, I don't just see a man in a rubber suit dragging his feet through cities and executing perfect hammerlocks on monstrous opponents. I also see my youth, I see days gone by, I see a world that was small and simple and no scarier that the average creature feature on late-night television. Many Godzilla fans, and certainly a great many of the baby boomers who grew up with plentiful drive-in and UHF fixes of *kaijū eiga,* would seem to feel the same way. To us, the king of the monsters is not just a motion picture superstar, not just a reliable old friend, but is also a cherished keepsake of a personal past, an evocative memento of childhood, a powerful emblem of nostalgia for an age now lost.

Susan Napier has written that the elegiac mode—"a mood of mournfulness and melancholy, perhaps mixed with nostalgia"—has a long history in Japanese cultural expression and is an important theme in contemporary anime.[5] The original *Gojira* was an excellent example of this aesthetic as well, an elegy for lost prenuclear innocence, for a time before the ever-present threat of annihilation and the opening of a Pandora's box of technological marvels. The later Godzilla films were not made as elegiac lamentations but can easily become poignant vehicles for nostalgia—for those halcyon days when we first watched monster movies, for carefree youth, for a time when we could embrace Godzilla without cynicism, irony, or sophisticated disdain—as we slip them into the DVD player and let them carry us back through the decades. The literary critic Susan Stewart, among others, has observed that the souvenir serves as a nostalgic symbol of a purer time, emblematic of our alienation and frustrated desire for wholeness and coherence in modern society.[6] If so, then Godzilla is a souvenir of our collective childhoods, an expression of an unrealizable desire to return to a simpler, gentler, less demanding era, to the sheltered security of youth. The world into which Godzilla allows us temporary and therapeutic escape may just be a fantasy, a phantom of our wishful yearnings, but it is comfortable and welcoming and satisfying nevertheless. None of us can be children again, we can't turn back the clock on history, maturity, and change, but perhaps, just for a few minutes, Godzilla can make us feel like we're eight-year-olds once more, wrapped in our parents' arms, in front of the old Zenith, waiting for Tokyo to be destroyed, and on top of the world.

Godzilla gives us so much, and yet asks for so little in return. For the price of a movie admission, a video rental or a monthly cable bill, we get a rich symbol to warp, construe or manipulate, a faithful cinematic friend to call our own, and a restorative, nostalgic vehicle for our spiritual cravings. What's more, and perhaps most important of all, the king of the monsters affords us the all-too-rare opportunity to imagine, to suspend disbelief, and to lose ourselves in the ultimate freedom of our own dreams.

Hollywood movies—of which the 1998 TriStar *Godzilla* is a sterling example—have come to embrace a kind of extreme and literal visual realism, a commitment to hyperverisimilitude in every death, explosion, or monstrous footfall. Thanks to the wonders of American special-effects technology, perhaps the ultimate weapon in the global struggle for pop culture dominance, the image of a giant velociraptor scampering through the skyscraper canyons of Manhattan can appear startlingly lifelike (not, of course, that anyone has actually seen such an event ever take place). Although this digital bravado is undoubtedly very, very cool, it is also extremely limiting: in a U.S. blockbuster, the moviegoer becomes a passive consumer of spectacle, an unthinking voyeur whose every perception is channeled and controlled by a seamless feed of computer-generated fabrications. The Japanese Godzilla—the only true Godzilla—does not offer viewers such an easy way out. With primitive special effects, that are realistic to (at best) a four-year-old, the classic Godzilla films challenge you to imagine and to dream, to shed your jaded, media-savvy cynicism and return to the gee-whiz, gosh-darn ingenuousness of youth, to take disbelief and throw it out the window. Reveling in one of the great Godzilla movies can liberate your creativity and set your inner child—and your deepest fantasies—free.

The imaginative release afforded by a *kaijū eiga* feature is also reflected in the character and behavior of the king of the monsters himself. Who can't feel a childish exhilaration at seeing a footloose and fancy-free Godzilla, not constrained by social convention, not tied down by cell phones, family obligations, or the niceties of adult decorum, letting it all hang out as he trashes cities, mops the floor with alien invaders, and vaporizes chemical plants at will? Godzilla is the ultimate free spirit, born to be wild and not shy about showing his true feelings, even if that might involve some urban redevelopment and industrial demolition. A Freudian critic would spoil this joy with solemn theorizing about the id, repression, and problems sexual; all that may indeed be mixed up somehow in Godzilla's charm, but overanalyzing and overintellectualizing can rob the monster of the unbridled exuberance, the devil-may-care abandon that is his greatest appeal. Don't worry, be stompy. Godzilla, when all is said and done, is about letting go and having fun.

Although rooted in a specific history and place—that flash of light at Bikini Atoll, the postwar context of U.S.-Japanese relations, the age of the movie palaces and exploitation pictures—Godzilla is a timeless and eternal icon. The monster lives on, not just in the movies still being churned out by Tōhō, but on video and DVD, in fan-made models, costumes, and poems, in song lyrics, movie tributes, and throughout the intricate and sprawling mosaic of international pop culture. But most important, Godzilla lives on in the hearts and minds of those who grew up with him, those who can never forget his haunting roar and resounding footsteps, those who love him. Even if no other Godzilla films are ever made—and that, of course, is *very* unlikely— Godzilla will remain real and alive within each of us. Because Godzilla's not just a man in a latex costume, not just a cheesy B-movie hero, not just a misty memory from a Saturday afternoon double-bill. Godzilla is a state of mind.

NOTES

INTRODUCTION

1. Janne Nolan, "When Three Heads Are Better Than . . . Three Heads," *Bulletin of the Atomic Scientists* 56:4 (July/August 2000): 11.

CHAPTER I

1. I have followed the customary practice of rendering Japanese names in the traditional Japanese style, with the family name preceding the personal name. Japanese authors of English-language works and Japanese natives who are celebrities in the West (such as Ichirō Suzuki) have been cited with the personal name first. Macrons in Japanese place names have been omitted for well-known locales (Tōkyō, Ōsaka, Kyōto, Kōbe, Hokkaidō, etc.).

2. Tanaka Tomoyuki quoted in John Burgess, "Godzilla Rises Again," *Washington Post,* December 19, 1984. Two excellent sources on the origins of the Godzilla series are David Kalat, *A Critical History and Filmography of Tōhō's Godzilla Series* (Jefferson, NC: McFarland, 1997), pp. 13ff, and Steve Ryfle, *Japan's Favorite Mon-Star: The Unauthorized Biography of "The Big G"* (Toronto: ECW Press, 1998), pp. 19ff.

3. Terence Barrow, "Ghosts, Ghost-Gods and Demons of Japan," in Nikolas Kiej'e, *Japanese Grotesqueries* (Rutland, VT: Charles E. Tuttle, 1973), p. 7.

4. Carmen Blacker, "The Snake Woman in Japanese Myth and Legend," in J. R. Porter and W.M.S. Russell, *Animals in Folklore* (Ipswich: D.S. Brewer, 1978), p. 114. An exceptional source of the relationship of Godzilla to Japanese folklore is Gray Ginther, *Godzilla: The Assault of Modernism and the Counterattack of Tradition* (unpublished M.A. thesis, University of Kansas, 1999).
5. J. D. Lees and Marc Cerasini, *The Official Godzilla Compendium* (New York: Random House, 1998), p. 17.
6. Tanaka Tomoyuki quoted in Ryfle, *Japan's Favorite Mon-Star,* p. 20.
7. On the *Lucky Dragon* incident, see Ralph Lapp, *The Voyage of the Lucky Dragon* (New York: Harper and Brothers, 1958).
8. Honda Ishirō quoted in Stuart Galbraith IV, *Monsters are Attacking Tokyo: The Incredible World of Japanese Fantasy Films* (Venice, CA: Feral House, 1998), p. 22.
9. Donald Richie, *Japanese Cinema: An Introduction* (New York: Oxford University Press, 1990), p. 80.
10. Galbraith, *Monsters,* p. 19.
11. Kalat, *Critical History,* p. 3.
12. This anecdote is recounted in numerous sources, including Ryfle, *Japan's Favorite Mon-Star,* p. 29.
13. Steven Spielberg quoted in Kalat, *Critical History,* p. 50. Nice descriptions of *Gojira*'s special effects are presented in Ryfle, *Japan's Favorite Mon-Star,* pp. 26–30 and in Kalat, *Critical History,* pp. 16–17. Remarkable behind-the-scenes photographs of the making of *Gojira* are compiled in Kishikawa Osamu, *Godzilla First, 1954–1955* (Tokyo: Dai-Nihon Kaiga, 1994).
14. Ryfle, *Japan's Favorite Mon-Star,* p. 32.
15. Details on Ifukube and Godzilla's sound effects can be found in Ryfle, *Japan's Favorite Mon-Star,* pp. 32–33, 48–50; Kalat, *Critical History,* pp. 20–22; and Guy Mariner Tucker, *Age of the Gods: A History of the Japanese Fantasy Film* (Brooklyn, NY: Daikaiju Publishing, 1996), p. 36.
16. Ryfle, *Japan's Favorite Mon-Star,* p. 23.
17. Galbraith, *Monsters,* p. 24.
18. Donald Richie, "Gojilla Wreaks Havoc on Miniature Tokyo," *Japan Times,* November 4, 1954.

19. Joseph Anderson and Donald Richie, *The Japanese Film: Art and Industry,* expanded edition (Princeton, NJ: Princeton University Press, 1982), p. 262; "Kikaku dake no omoshirosa: Gojira," *Asahi Shinbun,* November 3, 1954; Ryfle, *Japan's Favorite Mon-Star,* p. 37.

20. Richie, "Gojilla Wreaks Havoc."

21. Honda Ishirō quoted in Galbraith, *Monsters,* p. 23.

22. Kim Newman, *Apocalypse Movies: End of the World Cinema* (New York: St. Martin's Griffin, 2000), p. 87.

23. Honda Ishirō quoted in Galbraith, *Monsters,* p. 49.

24. Bill Warren, *Keep Watching the Skies! American Science Fiction Movies of the Fifties, Volume 1, 1950–1957* (Jefferson, NC: McFarland, 1982), p. xiii.

25. Jonathan Lake Crane, *Terror and Everyday Life* (Thousand Oaks, CA: Sage, 1994), p. 102.

26. Susan Napier, "Panic Sites: The Japanese Imagination of Disaster from *Godzilla* to *Akira,*" *Journal of Japanese Studies* 19:2 (summer 1993): 331.

27. Anderson and Richie, *The Japanese Film,* p. 263.

28. Napier, "Panic Sites," p. 331.

29. Tucker, *Age of the Gods,* p. 42.

30. Ifukube Akira quoted in Yoshikuni Igarashi, *Bodies of Memory: Narrative of War in Postwar Japanese Culture, 1945–1970* (Princeton NJ: Princeton University Press, 2000), p. 116. See also Jim Bailey, "Your City Could Be Next: Godzilla Takes on the World," *Asiaweek* (December 21–28, 1994), pp. 38ff.

31. Kalat, *Critical History,* p. 26.

32. Donald Richie, *A Hundred Years of Japanese Film* (Tokyo: Kodansha International, 2001), p. 267.

33. *Variety,* April 28, 1956; *New York Times,* April 28, 1956.

CHAPTER 2

1. Douglas Slaymaker, "Popular Culture in Japan: An Introduction," in Douglas Slaymaker, *A Century of Popular Culture in Japan* (Lewiston, NY: Edwin Mellen Press, 2000), p. 80.

2. Stuart Galbraith IV, *Monsters are Attacking Tokyo: The Incredible World of Japanese Fantasy Films* (Venice, CA: Feral House, 1998), p. 169.

3. Honda Ishirō quoted in Steve Ryfle, *Japan's Favorite Mon-Star: The Unauthorized Biography of "The Big G"* (Toronto: ECW Press, 1998), p. 82.
4. Joseph Anderson and Donald Richie, *The Japanese Film: Art and Industry,* expanded edition (Princeton, NJ: Princeton University Press, 1982), pp. 412, 456.
5. Ibid., p. 345.
6. David Kalat, *A Critical History and Filmography of Tōhō's Godzilla Series* (Jefferson, NC: McFarland, 1997), p. 129.
7. Ryfle, *Japan's Favorite Mon-Star,* p. 161.
8. Anderson and Ritchie, *The Japanese Film,* p. 456.
9. Galbraith, *Monsters,* p. 115.
10. Donald Richie, *A Hundred Years of Japanese Film* (Tokyo: Kodansha International, 2001), p. 210.
11. On wrestling in postwar Japan and the fascinating case of Rikidōzan, see Yoshikuni Igarashi, *Bodies of Memory: Narrative of War in Postwar Japanese Culture, 1945–1970* (Princeton: Princeton University Press, 2000), pp. 122–129. "Spectacle of excess" is Roland Barthes's term.
12. J. D. Lees and Marc Cerasini, *The Official Godzilla Compendium* (New York: Random House, 1998), p. 98.
13. A nice survey of changes in the Godzilla suits over time is Robert Biondi, "The Evolution of Godzilla," *G-Fan* 16 (July/August 1995), pp. 24–33.
14. Ryfle, *Japan's Favorite Mon-Star,* p. 124.
15. Ibid., p. 77.
16. Ibid., p. 135.
17. A useful source is Keith Sewell and Lenell Bridges, "Johnny Sokko and His Flying Robot," *G-Fan* 52 (August-October, 2001), pp. 30–39.
18. Ryfle, *Japan's Favorite Mon-Star,* p. 165.
19. *People* magazine, January 14, 1985 as quoted in Ryfle, *Japan's Favorite Mon-Star,* p. 213; see also Kalat, *Critical History,* p. 161.
20. Quoted in Kalat, *Critical History,* p. 162.
21. Ryfle, *Japan's Favorite Mon-Star,* p. 261.
22. Mark Shilling, *The Encyclopedia of Japanese Pop Culture* (New York: Weatherhill, 1997), p. 61.
23. Guy Mariner Tucker, *Age of the Gods: A History of the Japanese Fantasy Film* (Brooklyn, NY: Daikaiju Publishing, 1996), p. 249.

24. Karl Schoenberger, "Japanese Film: The Sinking Sun," *Los Angeles Times,* April 4, 1990.
25. Mark Shilling, *Contemporary Japanese Film* (New York: Weatherhill, 1999), p. 14.
26. "Godzilla's Godfather: A G-Fan Interview with Koichi Kawakita," *G-Fan* 59 (November/December 2002), p. 13.
27. Satsuma Kenpachirō quoted in Ryfle, *Japan's Favorite Mon-Star,* p. 264.
28. Tanaka Tomoyuki quoted in Kalat, *Critical History,* p. 162.

CHAPTER 3

1. David Milner, staff writer for *Cult Movies* magazine, quoted in Steve Ryfle, *Japan's Favorite Mon-Star: The Unauthorized Biography of "The Big G"* (Toronto: ECW Press, 1998), p. 159.
2. Godzilla's greatest hits of the 1970s are brought together on a 2001 Vap CD *Gojira Songubukku* (Godzilla Songbook).
3. Susan Napier, "Panic Sites: The Japanese Imagination of Disaster from *Godzilla* to *Akira,*" *Journal of Japanese Studies* 19:2 (summer 1993): 349.
4. Nakano Teruyoshi quoted in Ryfle, *Japan's Favorite Mon-Star,* p. 169.
5. Yoshikuni Igarashi, *Bodies of Memory: Narrative of War in Postwar Japanese Culture, 1945–1970* (Princeton: Princeton University Press, 2000), p. 121.
6. Tanaka Tomoyuki quoted in David Kalat, *A Critical History and Filmography of Tōhō's Godzilla Series* (Jefferson, NC: McFarland, 1997), p. 162.
7. Honda Ishirō quoted in Guy Mariner Tucker, *Age of the Gods: A History of the Japanese Fantasy Film* (Brooklyn, NY: Daikaiju Publishing, 1996), p. 127.
8. Takarada Akira quoted in Stuart Galbraith IV, *Monsters are Attacking Tokyo: The Incredible World of Japanese Fantasy Films* (Venice, CA: Feral House, 1998), p. 50.
9. Ono Kōichirō, Iwabana Hisaaki and Akaboshi Masanao, eds., *Gojira daizenshū* (Tokyo: Kodansha, 1994), p. 5.
10. Susan Sontag, "The Imagination of Disaster" (1965) in *Hibakusha Cinema: Hiroshima, Nagasaki and the Nuclear Image in Japanese Film,* ed. Mick Broderick (London: Kegan Paul International, 1996), p. 50.

11. Joseph Anderson and Donald Richie, *The Japanese Film: Art and Industry,* expanded edition (Princeton, NJ: Princeton University Press, 1982), p. 269.
12. Igarashi, *Bodies of Memory,* p. 115.
13. Kobayashi Toyomasa, *Gojira no ronri: A Study of the Godzilla Era* (Tokyo: Chūkyō shuppan, 1992), p. 23.
14. Arikawa Teisho quoted in Jim Bailey, "Your City Could Be Next: Godzilla Takes on the World," *Asiaweek* (December 21–28, 1994).
15. "Godzilla's Serious Side," *G-Fan* 32 (March/April 1998), p. 19.
16. See Igarashi, *Bodies of Memory,* p. 121.
17. Ryfle, *Japan's Favorite Mon-Star,* p. 268.
18. Japanese commentators have also long linked Godzilla with Saigō Takamori, a nineteenth-century samurai warrior who led an ultimately futile revolt in 1876–1877 against a modernizing, Westernizing national regime. Saigō, beloved in Japan as a principled and sincere rebel in the mold of Robert E. Lee, was the model for the character Katsumoto in the 2003 Hollywood epic *The Last Samurai.* Some suggest that Godzilla, like Saigō, turned his wrath on Tokyo as a protest against slavish Westernization and the dilution of Japan's national spirit. *Godzilla, Mothra, and King Ghidorah* repeatedly invokes the Saigō connection: Mothra first appears in a lake associated with Saigō and the midget submarine that Admiral Tachibana pilots in the decisive battle against Godzilla is named the *Satsuma,* after the home province of Saigō in southwestern Japan.
19. Bosley Crowther, "Monsters Again," *New York Times,* May 6, 1956.
20. See, for example, Tom Miller, "Struggling with Godzilla: Unraveling the Symbolism in Toho's Sci/Fi Films," *Kaiju-Fan* 10 (winter 1999).
21. Charles Derry, *Dark Dreams: A Psychological History of the Modern Horror Film* (South Brunswick, NJ: A.S. Barnes and Company, 1977), p. 74.
22. Chon Noriega, "Godzilla and the Japanese Nightmare: When *Them!* Is U.S." (1987), in *Hibakusha Cinema: Hiroshima, Nagasaki and the Nuclear Image in Japanese Film,* ed. Mick Broderick (London: Kegan Paul International, 1996), p. 54.
23. Ibid., p. 61.

24. Brian Murphy, "Monster Movies: They Came from Beneath the Fifties," *Journal of Popular Film* 1:1 (winter 1972): 38.

25. Andrew Tudor, *Monsters and Mad Scientists: A Cultural History of the Horror Movie* (Oxford: Blackwell, 1989), p. 215.

26. Napier, "Panic Sites," p. 332.

27. Sontag, "The Imagination of Disaster," pp. 41, 42–43, 52.

28. Noel Carroll, "Nightmare and the Horror Film: The Symbolic Biology of Fantastic Beings," *Film Quarterly* 34:3 (spring 1981): 17.

29. Margaret Tarratt, "Monsters from the Id" (1970), in *Film Genre Reader,* ed. Barry Keith Grant (Austin: University of Texas Press, 1986), p. 259.

30. Noriega, "Godzilla and the Japanese Nightmare," pp. 73–74.

31. Tarratt, "Monsters from the Id," p. 273; Carroll, "Nightmare and the Horror Film," p. 22.

32. See, for example, David J. Skal, *Screams of Reason: Mad Science and Modern Culture* (New York: W.W. Norton, 1998), pp. 191–194.

33. Jeffrey Jerome Cohen, "Preface: In a Time of Monsters," in *Monster Theory,* ed. Jeffrey Jerome Cohen (Minneapolis: University of Minnesota Press, 1996), p. ix. See also Jeffrey Jerome Cohen, "Monster Culture (Seven Theses)," in *Monster Theory;* James Sheehan and Morton Sosna, eds., *The Boundaries of Humanity: Humans, Animals, Machines* (Berkeley: University of California Press, 1991).

34. David D. Gilmore, *Monsters: Evil Beings, Mythical Beasts, and All Manner of Imaginary Terrors* (Philadelphia: University of Pennsylvania Press, 2002), p. 14.

35. See Gerald Figal, *Civilization and Monsters: Spirits of Modernity in Meiji Japan* (Durham, NC: Duke University Press, 1999).

36. James B. Twitchell, *Dreadful Pleasures: An Anatomy of Modern Horror* (New York: Oxford University Press, 1985), p. 259; Frank Hauser, "Science Fiction Films" in *International Film Annual,* ed. William Whitebait (New York: Doubleday, 1958), p. 89.

CHAPTER 4

1. Thomas Doherty, *Teenagers and Teenpics: The Juvenilization of American Movies in the 1950s* (Boston: Unwin Hyman, 1988), p. 18.

2.   Ibid., pp. 160, 170.
3.   Vincent Canby, "Presley Shares Billing," *New York Times,* December 16, 1965.
4.   Randall Clark, *At a Theater or Drive-In near You: The History, Culture and Politics of the American Exploitation Film* (New York: Garland, 1995), p. 45.
5.   Robin Cross, *The Big Book of B Movies, or How Low Was My Budget* (London: Frederick Muller, 1981), pp. 24–25.
6.   David Kalat, *A Critical History and Filmography of Tōhō's Godzilla Series* (Jefferson, NC: McFarland, 1997), p. 71; Steve Ryfle, *Japan's Favorite Mon-Star: The Unauthorized Biography of "The Big G"* (Toronto: ECW Press, 1998), p. 163.
7.   James Sterngold, "Does Japan Still Need Its Scary Monster?" *New York Times,* July 23, 1995.
8.   An excellent treatment of the business of dubbing is presented by Ryfle, *Japan's Favorite Mon-Star,* pp. 149–153.
9.   Stuart Galbraith IV, *Monsters are Attacking Tokyo: The Incredible World of Japanese Fantasy Films* (Venice, CA: Feral House, 1998), p. 102.
10. Ryfle, *Japan's Favorite Mon-Star,* p. 241.
11. "Topics: A Clash of Monsters," *New York Times,* August 24, 1964.
12. Dan O'Neill, "Tiger's Aura Rapidly Fading," MSNBC News, June, 15, 2003; Garth Woolsey, "Godzilla Becks," *Toronto Star,* June 19, 2003.
13. Nigel Andrews, "Political Muscle," *Financial Times,* July 11, 2003; M. Tye Wolfe, "Big Time Politics," *Ithaca Times,* June 18, 2003; Kim Levin, "A Foreign Affair," *Village Voice,* July 28, 2003; Thomas Friedman, "A Theory of Everything," *New York Times,* June 1, 2003; Riad Tabbarah, "Why We Hate the United States, and Why We Need It," *Daily Star* (Beirut), July 30, 2003.
14. Kenichi Ohmae, "The Godzilla Companies of the New Economy," *Strategy and Business* (first quarter, 2000), available online at www.strategy-business.com.
15. See www.glennbeck.com/archives/04-29-03.shtml and www.sarsart.org.
16. See slate.msn.com/Features/GodzillaSUV/page2.asp.
17. Mark Price, "Hey, What's That? Kudzilla!" *Charlotte Observer,* September 10, 2002.
18. Images of Godzilla and Minilla sharing some quality time can be found at www.fatherhood.org/psa_tv.htm.

19. Jay Snodgrass, *Monster Zero* (Minneapolis: Elixir Press, 2002).

20. Ohashi Yasuhiko, *Godzilla*, trans. M. Cody Poulton (Winnipeg, Manitoba: Scirocco Drama, 2002), p. 20.

21. Mark Jacobson, *Gojiro* (New York: Bantam Books, 1991), p. 28.

22. Carl Matheson, "*The Simpsons*, Hyper-Irony and the Meaning of Life," in *The Simpsons and Philosophy: The D'oh! of Homer*, ed. William Irwin, Mark Conard, and Aeon Skoble (Chicago: Open Court, 2001), pp. 108–125.

23. Nice overviews of the American comic book series are Patrick Green, "Godzilla Invades the Marvel Universe," *G-Fan* 24 (January/February 2002), pp. 25–30, and Danny DeAngelo, "Godzilla and Gamera in Comics: The Dark Horse Years," *G-Fan* 60 (January/February 2003), pp. 42–53.

CHAPTER 5

1. John Tulloch and Henry Jenkins, *Science Fiction Audiences: Watching* Doctor Who *and* Star Trek (London: Routledge, 1995), p. 4.

2. "Readers Poll Results," *G-Fan* 11 (September/October 1994), pp. 26–31.

3. Steve Ryfle, *Japan's Favorite Mon-Star: The Unauthorized Biography of "The Big G"* (Toronto: ECW Press, 1998), p. 245.

4. James Sterngold, "Does Japan Still Need Its Scary Monster?" *New York Times*, July 23, 1995; Jim Bailey, "Your City Could Be Next: Godzilla Takes on the World," *Asiaweek* (December 21–28, 1994).

5. Among the excellent treatments of Godzilla "stuff" are Sean Linkenback, *An Unauthorized Guide to Godzilla Collectibles* (Atglen, PA: Schiffer, 1998); Dana Cain, *Collecting Japanese Movie Monsters* (Norfolk, VA: Antique Trader Books, 1998); Kuraji Takashi, ed., *Gojira TOY hakubutsukan* (Tokyo: Bandai, 1992); Sanada Kuniko, "Why Are These Figurines So Popular?" *Nipponia* 16 (2001): 24–27. A charming picture book on toys based on Japanese live-action sci-fi television (such as Ultraman) is Jimbo Matison, *So Crazy Japanese Toys!* (San Francisco: Chronicle Books, 2003). An accessible introduction to the postwar Japanese toy industry

and exports to the United States is Ron Tanner, "Mr. Atomic, Mr. Mercury, and Chime Trooper: Japan's Answer to the American Dream" in *Asian Popular Culture,* ed. John A. Lent (Boulder, CO: Westview, 1995), pp. 79–102.

6. "Readers Poll Results," p. 30.

7. The weird world of Kaiju Big Battel is online at kaiju.com; see also hustlerofculture.typepad.com and Tanya Edwards, "Kaiju Big Battel Mixes Movie Monsters and Wrestling to Conquer Universe" at www.vh1.com.

8. Henry Jenkins, *Textual Poachers: Television Fans and Participatory Culture* (New York: Routledge, 1992), p. 46.

9. G-Fan once organized a "Super Monster Contest" that asked readers under fourteen to draw and describe a new *kaijū eiga* superhero. Among the marvelous entries were beasts like Incineraptor and Spikezilla (who boasted "head in stomach so Godzilla can't knock it off") and the tongue-in-cheek Cammera, depicted as Godzilla with a Nikon around his neck and powers listed as "bright flash, radioactive lens, and paper cuts from photos." *G-Fan* 56 (May/June 2000), pp. 22–24.

10. See Surfrider 21, *Gojira kenkyū josetsu* (Tokyo: PHP kenkyūjo, 1998).

11. Kenneth Carpenter, "A Dinosaur Paleontologist's View of Godzilla," in J. D. Lees and Marc Cerasini, *The Official Godzilla Compendium* (New York: Random House, 1998), pp. 102–106.

12. While the vast majority of responses I received were supportive, enthusiastic, and helpful, a few were slightly odd (like a card stuffed with apparently unrelated newspaper clippings on Pakistan, the Nobel Prizes, and parking meter politics in New England), and a couple were downright hostile. One writer chided me for wasting taxpayer money on "some idiotic, moronic, sophomoric personnal [sic] project" and advised me to "Get lost you clown." The other, echoing William Shatner's famous admonition to *Star Trek* fans to "get a life," suggested none too politely that I "GET A REAL JOB." Ah, the crosses one must bear for loving the king of the monsters . . .

13. "Godzilla Widows Revisited," *G-Fan* 16 (July/August 1995), p. 41. Of the personal communications I received, about one-third of those for which I could identify the sex of the writer came from women.

14. Randall Osborne, "Godzilla as a Parenting Tool" in J. D. Lees and Marc Cerasini, *The Official Godzilla Compendium* (New York: Random House, 1998), pp. 107–109; Randall Osborne, "Why We Love Godzilla: A Psychologist's Perspective," *G-Fan* 35 (September/October 1998), pp. 36–39.

15. James Babbo, "Monster Memories of Godzilla," *G-Fan* 51 (May/June 2001), p. 46.

16. "G-Mail," *G-Fan* 37 (January/February 1999), p. 33.

17. "Interview with TriStar Godzilla Extra Diva Velez," *Kaiju Fan* 8 (spring 1998), p. 16.

18. Howard Thompson, "Screen: Happy Horrors for Children," *New York Times,* December 14, 1970.

19. "G-Mail," *G-Fan* 21 (May/June 1996), p. 13.

20. Henry Saperstein quoted in Stuart Galbraith IV, *Monsters are Attacking Tokyo: The Incredible World of Japanese Fantasy Films* (Venice, CA: Feral House, 1998), p. 119.

21. "G-Mail," *G-Fan* 29 (September/October 1997), p. 12; "Godzilla Monster Memories," *Scary Monsters Magazine, 1996 Yearbook,* p. 50.

22. On America's love of dinosaurs, see W. J. T. Mitchell, *The Last Dinosaur Book: The Life and Times of a Cultural Icon* (Chicago: University of Chicago Press, 1998); and John O'Neill, "Dinosaurs-R-Us: The (Un)Natural History of *Jurassic Park*," in *Monster Theory,* ed. Jeffrey Jerome Cohen (Minneapolis: University of Minnesota Press, 1996), pp. 292–308.

23. This confirms the findings of Susan Napier's study of anime fans in the United States. See Susan J. Napier, *Anime from* Akira *to* Princess Mononoke: *Experiencing Contemporary Japanese Animation* (New York: Palgrave, 2001), pp. 253–255. Remarkably, in the 1994 survey of *G-Fan* readers, almost 70 percent of respondents indicated that they would like to see more Japanese language instruction in the magazine. *G-Fan* subsequently published a series of lucid "how to" articles by a Godzilla devotee fluent in Japanese and resident in Japan; not many Japanese language textbooks include "monster," "war," "battle," "giant," and "cell" in the vocabulary lists of their first lessons, as this series did!

24. "G-Mail," *G-Fan* 53 (November/December 2001), p. 56.

25. Armand Vaquer, "King Kong vs. Godzilla in L.A.," *G-Fan* 45 (May/June 2000), p. 29.
26. Vincent Canby, "Stop Kidding Around!" *New York Times,* July 23, 1972. See also www.geocities.com/WestHollywood/ 2680 and pages.nyu.edu/~scs7891/megalon.html.
27. Constance Penley, *NASA/TREK: Popular Science and Sex in America* (London: Verso, 1997), p. 2; Jay Snodgrass, *Monster Zero* (Minneapolis: Elixir Press, 2002), pp. 13–14.
28. See, for example, www.christianity.com and www.hollywood-jesus.com/godzilla.htm.
29. Candy Hatcher, "Evergreen Journal: Welcome to the Church of God-Zillah," *Seattle Post-Intelligencer,* January 25, 2001.
30. J. J. Martin, "The Thunder Lizard Speaks!" *Cineaste* 23:3 (1998): p. 24.
31. J. D. Lees, "Dear G-friends," *G-Fan* 53 (November/December 2001), p. 18.
32. "G-Mail," *G-Fan* 53 (November/December 2001), p. 18.
33. Mike Bogue, "Terrorism and Godzilla's Future," *G-Fan* 53 (November/December 2001), pp. 16–17; "G-Mail," *G-Fan* 54 (January/February 2002), p. 14.
34. "G-Mail," *G-Fan* 54 (January/February 2002), p. 15.
35. David Rennie, "Plot to Destroy Brooklyn Bridge," *Daily Telegraph,* June 20, 2003.

CHAPTER 6

1. Mark Shilling, *Contemporary Japanese Film* (New York: Weatherhill, 1999), p. 189.
2. Ann Billson, "Monster Movie," *The New Statesman* 11:513 (17 July 1998): 39.
3. Ibid., p. 40.
4. David Kalat, *A Critical History and Filmography of Tōhō's Godzilla Series* (Jefferson, NC: McFarland, 1997), p. 232.
5. Patrick Macias, *Tokyo Scope: The Japanese Cult Film Companion* (San Francisco: Cadence Books, 2001), p. 30.
6. Stuart Galbraith IV, *Monsters are Attacking Tokyo: The Incredible World of Japanese Fantasy Films* (Venice, CA: Feral House, 1998), p. 110.
7. www.teleport-city.com/movies/reviews/w-z/x_from_outer_space.html.

8. David Schow, foreword to Kim Newman, *Apocalypse Movies: End of the World Cinema* (New York: St. Martin's Griffin, 2000), pp. 13–14. A nice treatment of Reptilicus is Jack Stevenson, "It Came from beyond Belief—The Incredible B-Movies of Sidney Pink in Denmark," available at hjem.get2net.dk/jack_stevenson/pink.htm.

9. Steve Ryfle, *Japan's Favorite Mon-Star: The Unauthorized Biography of "The Big G"* (Toronto: ECW Press, 1998), pp.207–208.

10. John Gorenfeld, "The Dictator Who Snagged Me," www.salon.com.

11. On the origins of the TriStar *Godzilla*, see Ryfle, *Japan's Favorite Mon-Star,* pp. 321–341.

12. Brant Elliott, "*Godzilla* is not Godzilla," *G-Fan* 33 (May/June 1998), p. 10; Ryfle, *Japan's Favorite Mon-Star,* p. 335.

13. Ryfle, *Japan's Favorite Mon-Star,* p. 346.

14. Ibid., p. 344; Billson, "Monster Movie," pp. 39–40.

CONCLUSION

1. John J. Pierce, "Godzilla Beyond the Atomic Age" in J. D. Lees and Marc Cerasini, *The Official Godzilla Compendium* (New York: Random House, 1998), p. 17.

2. Comments by Peter B. High at pears.lib.ohio-state.edu/Markus/kjthreads/godzilla.html.

3. Vincent Canby, "A Midsummer Night's Screams," *New York Times,* June 24, 1979.

4. "Godzilla 2000," *G-Fan* 46 (July/August 2000), p. 17.

5. Susan Napier, *Anime from* Akira *to* Princess Mononoke: *Experiencing Contemporary Japanese Animation* (New York: Palgrave, 2001), p. 31.

6. Susan Stewart, *On Longing: Narratives of the Miniature, the Gigantic, the Souvenir, the Collection* (Durham, NC: Duke University Press, 1993).

INDEX